MW01118646

Hard Rain

Common Questions About The End Times

Willy Minnix

Water Moccasin Press

ISBN-10: 1482039567
ISBN-13: 978-1482039566

For Trevor,
I wouldn't have been able to write this book without you. You have been my best friend though so many difficult times, and have helped me to keep clinging to Christ through it all. Your faithfulness to research and Bible study has enabled me to write this book. I love you.

Scripture quotations marked KJV are from the King James Version of the Bible

"He that answereth a matter before he hears it, it is folly and shame…" - Proverbs 18:13

"A good decision is based on knowledge and not on numbers." - Plato

CONTENTS

Quick List of Some Signs We Should Be Looking For

Biblical Signs

Wars & Rumors of War
Plague
Pestilence
Mass Death of Animals in the Sea
Mass Death of Animals on Land
Mass Death of People
Famine & Food Shortage
Earth Quakes
Signs in the Heavens
Apostasy and Rebellion
A Great Deception
Revival
7th Empire Resurrected as 8th Empire
Trumpets/Seals/Bowls
Dead Animals
Massive Extinction and Death
Wormwood/Fiery Mountain
Scorching Heat
Corruption
2 Prophets/Witnesses
False Prophet/Beast
Antichrist/Man of Lawlessness Revealed
Destruction of Damascus
Temple Rebuilt
One World Global Economy
One World Global Government
Mark of the Beast
World Wide Persecution of Saints
Shaking of Church

Non-Biblical Prophecies that may or may not have anything to do with what will really happen

What Muslims Are Looking For…
Death of King Abdulla of Saudi Arabia
Rise of Chaos All Over The World
Mahdi on a White Horse

What Catholics Are Looking For…
Last Pope – Petrus Romanus
Time of Great Trial for Catholic Church
Destruction of the City of 7 Hills By Fire (Rome)

What Jews Are Looking For…
Rebuilding of the Temple
Kabbalist Jews looking for return of Messiah between 2012 and 2016 according to the Zohar

What Occultists are Looking For…
Pyramid Prophecy - 5776 Jewish Calendar, or 2016 AD Rosh Hashanah
7 Years between 2009 and 2016 are significant in their prophecy
The Return of "Lucifer the Light Bringer"
Albert Pike's 3rd of 3 World Wars – Which will bring the end of Christianity
Return of the Gods to Earth
Dawning of a New Age

Quick Guide to Debunking Pre-Trib Doctrine

Pre Trib Teachers Teach…	**But The Bible Says**
Rapture before Antichrist is Revealed	Rapture after AC revealed *2 Thessalonians 2*
Antichrist rules for 7 years	Antichrist rules for 3.5 years *Daniel 9:27, Daniel 11:12, Rev. 11:2*
Rapture & 2nd Coming Separate Events	Rapture is part of 2nd Coming *1 Thess. 4:15-17, 2 Thess. 1:7-10, 1 Cor. 15:20-23*
Holy Spirit Removed for Tribulation	H. S. Active through Tribulation *Joel 2:28-29*
God removes from Tribulation	God guides through Tribulation *John 17:11-15*
There are 2 "Last Trumps"	There is only 1 "Last Trump" *1 Cor. 15:51-53, Matt. 24: 29-31, John 6:39, 40, 44 and 54*
Church is immune to Apostasy	Church is in danger of Apostasy *2 Thess. 2, Matthew 24:10*
Rapture will be Secret	Rapture will be Visible *Joel, Amos, Matthew 24, Rev.* 16
Christ Could Return Any Time	Prophesies Fulfilled First *Matthew 24*
Church Raptured Before Signs	Signs Will Point to Rapture *Matthew 24*
Tribulation is God's Wrath	Tribulation is Satan's Wrath *Luke 21:36, Joel 2:31*
Tribulation So Bad No One Will Live	Survivors from Tribulation *Matthew 24:30*
Tribulation is only for Jews	Tribulation is for Saints *Rev. 7:1-10, Romans 1 and 2*
Church Needs No Purification	Church Needs Purification *James 1:1-9*

8 Steps to Good Exegesis

1. Pray For Guidance

2. What is the text telling me?

3. How does this passage fit in with all I know about Context? Use cross references to provide further insight.

4. Is there something I am missing from the original language?

5. Is there something about the history surrounding this text that will help me understand it better?

6. Are there any theological implications about this passage that need to be weighed in light of basic doctrine, or is there something that strengthens or weakens certain doctrines.

7. Logically consider what you have learned & Pray again for more Guidance. Be willing to admit and accept it if you just don't have an answer.

8. Does it fit in with the simplicity test based off of Proverbs 15:19 and Isaiah 35:8?

Our ultimate goal, if we believe the Bible is God's inspired word, is to harmonize the passages so that they make sense.

We go to the Bible to find truth, not support a man made idea or theory.

Steps to Good Exegesis Continued – 12 Contextual Questions That Will Help You With Step Number 3 Mentioned Above

1. What is the preliminary idea the Bible is teaching me?

2. What is the verse saying?

3. How does this verse fit in with the context of the passage it's found in?

4. How does the passage fit in with the chapter it is in?

5. How does this chapter fit in with the overall section that it's in?

6. How does the section fit in with the book that it's in?

7. How does the book fit in with other books/passages that are from similar categories or genres?

8. How does the genre and category, and all of the preceding information fit in with the Bible as a whole?

9. How does this teaching fit in with the story of Salvation?

10. How does this teaching fit in with what we know about God's nature and principles?

11. Is this teaching logical in what we know about the rest of our knowledge of the truth?

12. The Simplicity test – Does my information adhere to the simplicity test of Proverbs 15:19 and Isaiah 35:8?

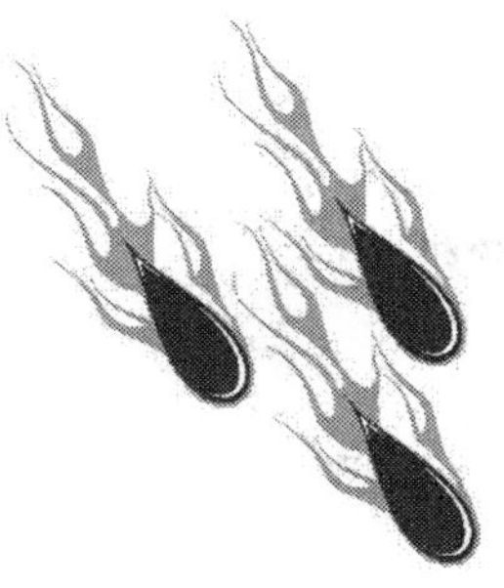

Introduction

Many people are convinced that they will be "raptured out of here" when the horrible things that are mentioned in the Book of Revelation come to pass on this earth. But is that point of view really Biblical?

For almost 2,000 years the church was divided between two points of view. The first, and most common was that at the end of time there would be a Great Tribulation, and the church would have to endure it, and after that there would be a 1,000 year reign of Christ physically on the earth. The second, and only slightly less popular was that the church age after the close of the first century had entered into the millennium, a figurative 1,000 year reign of Christ spiritually, and His return would be the complete end of time, and conclude the final portion of testing for the saints known as the Great Tribulation.

In the early 1800's, people began to question these historical views of eschatology (the study of the End Times), and began to explore other ideas. One of the most popular was set forth by John Nelson Darby, an Anglo-Irish theologian, who believed that the church would not have to endure the Tribulation, based upon a vision received by a Scottish woman named Margaret MacDonald. Taking off from where traditional Post-Trib thinkers stopped, Darby developed the doctrine of different dispensations, giving rise to the term Dispensationalism.

His view was that there were different time periods in God's calendar, and each one had various events that marked the episodes. Modern Post-Trib, Mid-Trib and Pre-Trib people all seem to be in some form or another influenced by Darby as regards the dispensations of time.

There is also a newer point of view related to the Post-Trib doctrine, called by many Pre-Wrath. This view is gaining ground in some circles recently, as well as a rebirth of Amillennialism called today Partial-Preterism which teaches that most of the events of prophecy were fulfilled in the first century of the church. Yet the most popular by far has been the Pre-Trib doctrine, focusing on the Pre-Tribulational Rapture of the Church into heaven to be with Jesus.

Instead of dealing with the harsh realities of the Tribulation, in Darby's opinion, followers of Christ will enjoy instead seven fun filled years of bliss with Jesus, or as one church I visited recently put it, "A big party with Jesus." Pre-Tribbers debate on just how much time Christians will spend in Heaven; some suggest that the

Tribulation is a seven year period, while some point to Daniel and say that the actual Tribulation is only three and a half years.

The three and a half year Pre-Trib position is historically more closely associated with Mid Trib position, but currently there is also a form of the Pre-Wrath position very similar to Mid-Trib. For the layman it can all be a bit confusing and overwhelming, but in the end it all boils down to three basic ideas which encompass both dispensationalists and amillennialists ideology: either Jesus comes back before the Tribulation, sometime in the middle, or at the end of it.

I think it is very important to point out from the outset that both Amillennialists and Post Tribulation Theologians were technically Post Tribulational. The difference being that Post Trib people saw the Tribulation as a short period of intense suffering, whereas Amillennialists saw all of history after the Ascension as both the reign of Christ and the Tribulation of the Church. It is also important to point out that Jesus coined the phrase "Post Tribulation" in Matthew 24.

In Tim Warner's very insightful work found at www.answersinrevelation.org, under an article entitled "Introduction," which can be downloaded for free, under the heading of "Pre-tribulation or Post-tribulation Rapture," we find this fact about Matthew 24:

"The post-tribulation view was actually named by Jesus in the above passage. The words, 'after the tribulation'

(verse 29) in the Latin Bible are literally rendered, 'post tribulationem.'" (Warner, Introduction, pg 2)

The subtitle of this book is "Common Questions About the End Times," but there is a very important question that is rarely ever asked: *If Jesus was Post Trib, so much that he actually coined the term, then how in the world did a Pre-Trib doctrine ever take hold in the church?*

It might surprise you to learn that the rise of the Pre-Trib doctrine is actually a rather short history. The main reason Pre-Trib doctrine took hold in America is because it was spread by the popularity of the Scofield Bible, named after C.I. Scofield, a popular preacher who wrote the best selling commentary Bible that was first published in 1909. One of Scofield's areas of commentary dealt with the Pre-Trib rapture of the church, and many theologians who followed in Scofield's footsteps were greatly influenced towards a Pre-Trib ideology. And since most of the mission work of the 19th, 20th and 21st centuries originated out of America, the unsound doctrines of Scofield spread like a plague throughout Christendom.

Many people in the church today do not want to argue over the end times, as in the past these discussions have led to church splits, denominational splits, and anger and hurt feelings on many sides of the discussion. However, I believe we may already be living in what many would describe as the End Times, and the popularity of this doctrine has produced some very unfortunate fruit in the church today. These issues need to be addressed in a serious study of the Biblical facts.

I have found that many people who cling to a Pre-Trib view feel they do not need to be concerned with the evils in this world, that are steadily encroaching upon us, because they will not be around to see the culmination of the mechanizations of Satan.

Chances are, if you are a Christian in the United States, you have been taught this teaching because it has been popularized by Christian films, books and preachers. If you are a member of certain denominations you may be totally indoctrinated into this teaching, since some denominations require their pastors to agree with this doctrine to obtain ordination.

I am not convinced that the Pre-Trib doctrine is Biblical, and in fact would go so far as to claim that it should be considered false teaching, as it is not based on Biblical fact, but rather on subjective sources. Furthermore, should this doctrine continue to hold sway in the Church until the time when she will have to endure the Tribulation, I am convinced this doctrine will lead to unnecessary deaths from the catastrophes that are going to happen during that time.

And though I would like to have fellowship with those who hold to these doctrines, as a pastor it is my duty to carefully study and give the most educated and prayerful teaching I can on the doctrines I preach. I would not be a faithful teacher of the Word by not calling this doctrine false teaching.

I hope that you do not shut the book at this point and dismiss what I have to say. Please continue on and see if I am right. Do not take what I have to say as truth, until you have tested it in light of the scriptures yourself. And if you are convinced that the Pre-Trib doctrine is truth, then you have nothing to fear from my conclusions on the matter. Please read on and prove me wrong. However, I believe that if you approach this topic with an open mind, and open Bible, you will find that I have thoroughly debunked many of the Pre-Trib building blocks, and even some that support the Amillennial stance.

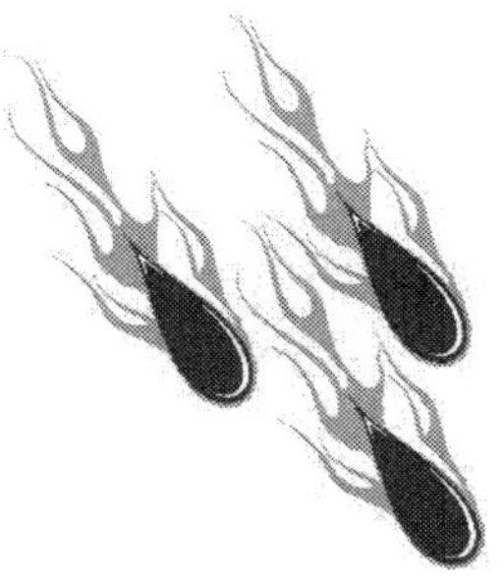

Rapture

Will the church be raptured before the Great Tribulation?

There is not one single verse anywhere in the Bible that teaches that the church will be raptured before the Tribulation. Pre-Trib teachers use many verses out of context as a proof of a Pre-Trib rapture of the church, but when read *in context*, none of the verses they use prove that there will be a Pre-Trib rapture of the church. On the contrary, there are many verses that emphatically prove that the Rapture will occur *after* the Tribulation. We will explore many of them in the next question.

One of the big problems that the church faces when studying this subject, is that many of the verses and passages used to defend the Pre-Trib Rapture view are subject to incredibly bad exegesis of the text in question.

Incorrect methods that are commonly employed in explaining so-called "Pre-Trib Proofs" include:

1. *Passages out of context* – Many of the Pre-Trib proof texts are taken completely out of context. When the texts are examined in their proper context, one can quickly see that the passage is not talking about a Pre-Trib Rapture.

2. *Combination of Out of Context passages* – The second method often used by Pre-Trib teachers is to apply several passages that are taken out of context in an attempt to overwhelm the End Times student with the volume of "proof texts." But the mere fact that there is a volume of badly treated texts, does not prove anything other than the complete inability of the Pre-Trib teacher to read the Bible in context.

3. *Misuse of the Greek or Hebrew* – Often Pre-Trib teachers will point to a Greek or Hebrew meaning of a word to lend support to their argument, when in fact the Greek or Hebrew word often does not mean what they say it means. Another related incorrect technique they use is to not give the full possible meanings of a Greek or Hebrew word, instead giving only one possible translation of a word that supports their argument without also giving the additional meaning(s) that would defeat their argument entirely. An example is the common misuse of the Greek word "ek" by Pre-Trib teachers, to mean "from" where it often is translated "through."

4. *Reliance on obscure or unclear passages to lend support to their argument* – After taking several passages out of context, good Bible students often point to the rest of the verses that are being taken out of context by the Pre-Trib teacher, and so the Pre-Trib teacher falls back onto passages that often have nothing to do with eschatology or if they do are obscure and are not clear enough for us to bolster any argument, let alone a Pre-Trib argument. An example of this technique is the false pairing of 1 Thessalonians 4:16 where we are told Jesus descends with a shout to Revelation 19:11-21 where it doesn't mention a shout. These passages are often used incorrectly by most Pre-Trib teachers. They simply obscure the facts, and then present a text that does not provide conclusive evidence as if it were some sort of proof for their false position.

5. *Reliance on "traditional" interpretations or commentaries to bolster their opinion* – I personally believe this has become a big problem in Bible study in general. Now a days the proliferation of Bible study tools make it possible for someone to study many different authors without the benefit of knowing the particular theological stance of the authors. Without knowing the theological background of the author, readers are often subject to heretical doctrines that they otherwise would avoid or reject. Many times people will turn to the

"experts" without praying about it first. When they do point to so called "experts," they give their opinions more weight than they deserve, without examining the author's historical background. Because of this tactic many people think that the Pre-Trib doctrine is a very old and ancient concept, when in fact it's only been around for less than two hundred years.

6. *Tradition over Truth* – This is similar to the last point, many people are reluctant to study the Bible on their own, because they fear they cannot truly understand it. So they put their confidence on the traditions that came before them without examining what the Bible actually says.

7. *Taking Scholars out of Context* – Another travesty of the Pre-Trib movement is to take Biblical scholars out of context. It's bad enough to take the Bible out of context, but to quote biblical scholars regardless of their stance out of context is adding insult to injury.

8. *Propagation of fear* – Pre-Trib teachers often use fear tactics to get people to accept their doctrine rather than teaching people to be strong in preparation for persecution. These teachers will also often accuse other eschatological opinions as "fear mongering" when they try to warn people to repent and prepare for the end. I can see no greater example of fear mongering than the horrible exegesis found in films such as

the films from the 70's by Don Thompson, such as "A Thief in the Night," and the most recent "Left Behind" series by Tim LaHaye. A similar thing happened to Jeremiah the prophet in the Bible, so it is nothing new, just the same old tactic being brought into modern times.

9. *Using Text to Prove a Point, Not Using Text to Find Truth* – One of the worst things I have found, not only in the Pre-Trib movement but also in many areas of research, is that people often use the text to prove their point, rather than going to the text to find truth. As Christians we should always be of the mindset that we are in a search for Truth, because God is the Truth. We are diligent seekers of Him, and therefore we are diligent seekers of the Truth. As Richard Wurmbrand once said, the Bible is the truth about the Truth. So we must approach the Bible with a humble attitude. "What does the Bible teach me about this topic?" Not "This is my opinion on the topic, or this is what I've been taught, now where can I find that in the Bible to prove it?" If we follow the latter approach we will always be able to find passages that prove our point, but we will be in danger of abusing the text by ripping passages out of context.

The entire history of the Pre-Trib movement is based on faulty methods of study, fear mongering and out right lies. But proper Bible study, sound exegesis and careful connection of prophetic passages leads to strength to endure persecution and an understanding of the glory that lies beyond the momentary afflictions that this world has to offer.

What does the Bible Teach Us About the Rapture and the Tribulation?

A lot of people are concerned about the return of Jesus Christ and the event that all Christians look forward too, commonly known as the Rapture. Most Christians have been taught the basics of the rapture, that there will be a trumpet, the dead in Christ will rise first and then those who are still alive when Jesus returns will be caught up in the air to meet Him.

Many people who are not Christians probably think we are crazy for waiting for Jesus to return. But we have a great deal of Biblical teaching that has always been a key doctrine of Christianity that separates our religion from all the other religions of the world.

The rapture notion isn't isolated to Christianity, however, as the first recorded place in the Bible that sets up the concept of a rapture event is in Genesis. So the concept of a Rapture, or an event where God takes someone out of the earth to be with Him is Jewish in origin. The first place where we see this is with Enoch.

Enoch was a righteous man who lived before Noah's flood. The Bible records very little about Enoch other than he was close to God and at some point he vanished because God took him. We don't know why God took Enoch away, and we don't know if He ever sent him back at some point, or will in the future. What we do know is that Enoch obviously pleased God and so God took him away to be with Him sometime before the flood.

Another Old Testament friend of God who was taken away was Elijah. Elijah was a prophet who performed a great deal of mighty acts to testify to the Lord's power and greatness. On one occasion Elijah had an epic duel with the prophets of Baal, where Elijah prayed and fire came down from heaven to consume a sacrifice and prove that Jehovah was more powerful than Baal. In the end Elijah slew a great number of the evil prophets, and really ticked off the queen Jezebel who decided to kill him.

So while hiding in a cave, God sent more information for Elijah, telling him what to do next. Elijah then found his protégé Elisha and continued to prophesy for a while longer, until the day when Elijah and Elisha were walking, and God took Elijah away into Heaven. This is the second "rapture-style" event in the Bible.

In the New Testament, we see a rapture-style event again, when Jesus Christ, after His resurrection from the dead, was taken up into heaven on a cloud. We see this recorded by both Matthew and Luke. And after Jesus had ascended into Heaven, an angel standing near the disciples, asked them why they were still looking on, and informed them that in like manner, Jesus would return to the earth. This information was a reference to Daniel's vision in chapter 7 that the Messiah would be seen coming in the clouds.

So Christians have been awaiting the return of Jesus for almost two thousand years, because we believe that Jesus will return to the earth to establish His reign that was prophesied all those years ago by the Old Testament prophets.

Many people think that most of our teaching on the Rapture comes from the Book of Revelation, but surprisingly, the Book of Revelation has very little to say about the actual event itself. The bulk of our theology about the Rapture comes from St. Paul's writings which are found in First and Second Thessalonians, and First Corinthians.

In Chapters four and five of First Thessalonians Paul gives us the gist of what will happen at Jesus' Second Coming.

1 Thessalonians 4:13-5:11 (NLT)

And now, dear brothers and sisters, we want you to know what will happen to the believers who have died so you will not grieve like people who have no hope. For since we believe that Jesus died and was raised to life again, we also believe that when Jesus returns, God will bring back with him the believers who have died.

We tell you this directly from the Lord: We who are still living when the Lord returns will not meet him ahead of those who have died. For the Lord himself will come down from heaven with a commanding shout, with the voice of the archangel, and with the trumpet call of God. First, the Christians who have died will rise from their graves. Then, together with them, we who are still alive and remain on the earth will be caught up in the clouds to meet the Lord in the air. Then we will be with the Lord forever. So encourage each other with these words.

Now concerning how and when all this will happen, dear brothers and sisters, we don't really need to write you. For you know quite well that the day of the Lord's return will come unexpectedly, like a thief in the night. When people are saying, "Everything is peaceful and secure," then disaster will fall on them as suddenly as a pregnant woman's labor pains begin. And there will be no escape.

But you aren't in the dark about these things, dear brothers and sisters, and you won't be surprised when the day of the Lord comes like a thief. For you are all children of the light and of the day; we don't belong to darkness and night. So be on your guard, not asleep like the others. Stay alert and be clearheaded. Night is the time when people sleep and drinkers get drunk. But let us who live in the light be clearheaded, protected by the armor of faith and love, and wearing as our helmet the confidence of our salvation.

For God chose to save us through our Lord Jesus Christ, not to pour out his anger on us. Christ died for us so that, whether we are dead or alive when he returns, we can live with him forever. So encourage each other and build each other up, just as you are already doing.

But what many Pre-Trib preachers overlook, either on purpose because it destroys the Pre-Trib doctrine, or perhaps because they have just not studied it enough, is that in the second chapter of Second Thessalonians, Paul expands on the teaching that he laid down in chapter five of First Thessalonians. In this passage Paul expressly tells the reader *that the Rapture will not happen until after the Antichrist has been revealed.*

2 Thessalonians 2:1-12 (NLT)

Now, dear brothers and sisters, let us clarify some things about the coming of our Lord Jesus Christ and how we will be gathered to meet him. Don't be so easily shaken or alarmed by those who say that the day of the Lord has already begun. Don't believe them, even if they claim to have had a spiritual vision, a revelation, or a letter supposedly from us. Don't be fooled by what they say. ***For that day will not come until there is a great rebellion against God and the man of lawlessness is revealed****—the one who brings destruction. He will exalt himself and defy everything that people call god and every object of worship. He will even sit in the temple of God, claiming that he himself is God.*

Don't you remember that I told you about all this when I was with you? And you know what is holding him back, for he can be revealed only when his time comes. For this lawlessness is already at work secretly, and it will remain secret until the one who is holding it back steps out of the way. Then the man of lawlessness will be revealed, but the Lord Jesus will kill him with the breath of his mouth and destroy him by the splendor of his coming.

This man will come to do the work of Satan with counterfeit power and signs and miracles. He will use every kind of evil deception to fool those on their way to destruction, because they refuse to love and accept the truth that would save them. So God will cause them to be greatly deceived, and they will believe these lies. Then they will be condemned for enjoying evil rather than believing the truth.

Paul even refers back to his first letter, and tells the believers not to be swayed into believing that Jesus has returned because it will be an unmistakable event, implying that the whole world will see it, and we as believers will be ready because certain events will happen that will clue us in to the actual "imminence" of the Second Coming.

I think it is very important to point out that Paul warns his readers not to be shaken by a supposed vision telling the believers something other than what he teaches, because as we shall see later on, the entire Pre-Trib doctrine is based on a vision by a Scottish woman named Margaret MacDonald in 1830. Before that time, there was no Pre-Trib doctrine ever taught by anyone in the history of the Christian faith.

In the following pages, we are going to cover some of the basic questions that people have about the Rapture, the Tribulation, the Millennium and current events that relate to Biblical Prophecy.

With regard to the Tribulation, there are many passages which teach that we *need to go through tribulations.*

Acts 4:22 (KJV)

Confirming the souls of the disciples, and exhorting them to continue in the faith, and that we must ***through much tribulation enter into the kingdom of God****.*

2 Thessalonians 1:4-9 (KJV)

So that we ourselves glory in you in the churches of God for your ***patience and faith in all your persecutions and tribulations that ye endure****: Which is a manifest token of the righteous judgment of God, that ye may be counted worthy of the kingdom of God, for which ye also suffer: Seeing it is a righteous thing with God to recompense tribulation to them that trouble you; And to you who are troubled rest with us, when the Lord Jesus shall be revealed from heaven with his mighty angels, In flaming fire taking vengeance on them that know not God, and that obey not the gospel of our Lord Jesus Christ: Who shall be punished with everlasting destruction from the presence of the Lord, and from the glory of his power.*

This passage teaches us that while we will endure many tribulations for following Christ, there will come a day, when Christ returns, that Tribulation will be poured out on the unbelievers. But this does not explain how long the time period is that God's persecution on the unbelievers will last. It also says that the tribulation we endure is a purifying process that shows that we are worthy of the Kingdom of God.

Another key passage that teaches this truth is 1 Peter 1:6-7.

1 Peter 1:6-7 (KJV)

Wherein ye greatly rejoice, though now for a season, if need be, ye are in heaviness through manifold temptations: That the trial of your faith, being much more precious than of gold that perisheth, though it be tried with fire, might be found unto praise and honour and glory at the appearing of Jesus Christ…

Here again, Peter teaches us that persecution and tribulation will actually be honorable and glorious when the Lord returns.

But does the Bible teach that we are to go through the Great Tribulation? Let's find out. The rest of this book is made up of frequently asked questions about the Rapture, the Tribulation and the End Times in general.

Where did the idea of a Pre-Trib Rapture come from, and isn't it the historical doctrine of the church?

Actually, no, the Pre-Trib Rapture theory is not an historical doctrine of the church. Though there were some writers throughout the history of the church who espoused theories that have been claimed by Pre-Trib teachers to be the modern Pre-Trib doctrine, these writers were in reality vastly different in their theories than modern Pre-Trib theologians, and were often considered false teachers during their time periods.

The most recent document that is being touted by the Pre-Trib movement as a teaching of a Pre-Trib rapture is a passage taken out of context of a document called Pseudo-Ephrem. Ephrem (Or Ephraem as the name is sometimes spelled) was a deacon at the church in Syria during the mid 300's AD, though the document itself is said to date anywhere between the late 300's to the late 600's AD. His writings are clearly speaking of the gathering of the church for murder at the rise of the Antichrist, and how most (possibly all) of the church will be destroyed during what he calls the "eleventh hour." Using this document as a proof text for Pre-Trib rapture theory is not doing justice to the actual text. This is a subject that could be discussed at great length, but suffice it to say, the use of this sermon as a Pre-Trib proof is very controversial, and not at all as clear a case for Pre-Tribulationalism as pretribulationists would have you believe.

There were other people that are often pointed to as Pre-Trib theologians prior to 1830, but each one of them is equally dismissible.

The Pre-Trib doctrine as we know it, was developed primarily by two men, John Nelson Darby, writer of the Darby Bible, and Edward Irving, founder of the sect the Irvingites.

Both of these men based their teachings on the vision of a young woman named Margaret MacDonald, from Scotland. Miss MacDonald had a vision of the Lord's Return, and she believed that God was telling her that there would be a *secret Rapture* before the Lord actually returned.

The full details of her vision can be found in Dave MacPherson's book "The Incredible Cover-Up." MacPherson traces the origins of the Pre-Trib rapture backwards from groups like Dallas Theological Seminary, to the Scofield Bible, to Irving and Darby and finally back to Margaret MacDonald. He also gives a full copy of MacDonald's vision. MacPherson comes to a conclusion that MacDonald believed in a Pre-Trib interpretation of her vision, but after reading the vision for myself, I see that her vision could just as easily be interpreted as more of Pre-Wrath vision. What she describes in her vision is merely a Rapture event that happens before God pours out His wrath on evil doers, which is essentially what the Post Tribulation Rapture theory claims.

The problem that I find with MacDonald's vision has nothing to do with the details of her vision. It has more to do with interpretation. Paul said that we were not to believe anyone or anything, including a vision supposedly from God, if it contradicts anything that he taught to the church. A Pre-Trib secret rapture is in total direct contradiction to what he teaches in 2 Thessalonians 2:1. Some teachers have tried to explain away 2 Thessalonians, by saying that 1 and 2 Thessalonians are written out of order, but that theory doesn't matter. Even if 1 and 2 Thessalonians are out of order, Paul gives very specific details to look for that will help us recognize when the Rapture will happen, and one of them *is the revealing of the Antichrist*, which as far as I am concerned is the nail in the coffin for the Pre-Trib Rapture theory. However, in order to fully convince you, we will continue on to cover many other details that defeat this false doctrine.

What does "Rapture" really mean?

The word that we use for rapture is taken from 1 Thessalonians 4:17 and comes from the Greek word "harpazo," which literally means "to snatch away," or "to Catch Up." This word was used on many tomb stones of the ancient times meaning that the people died young, or as we might say, "before their time." In other words, they were "snatched away" from life.

But the use here doesn't mean that we are going to die in the Rapture. It just means that we will be brought up into the air to meet with Jesus when He comes.

In ancient times when a visiting dignitary came to a town, it was a common practice to send out a delegation of the town officials. They would meet the dignitary, and then usher him back into town, where they would usually hold a celebration in honor of their guest.

We can see from Revelation 14 -19 that this is essentially what happens. In Revelation 14 the believers are gathered by the angels. They meet with Jesus while hardship is poured out onto the evil doers. Then Jesus appears in splendor and glory for all to see. He descends and then sets up His kingdom.

Is the Rapture Christ's Second Coming?

1 Thessalonians 4:15-17, 2 Thessalonians 1:7-10 and 1 Cor. 15:20-23 specifically say that the Rapture is at Christ's second coming. The Rapture is an event that happens when Jesus returns. It is not the same as Jesus' Second Coming, but it is an event that happens on the same day, and is a result of His return.

Furthermore, 2 Thessalonians 2 specifically states that the early church will be raptured at the Second Coming. Matthew 24:29-31 (as well as Mark 13:24-27) specifically says that the Second Coming happens after the Tribulation. If Pre-Trib and Mid-Trib teachers were right, the early church would not be raptured at the Second Coming. They would have been raptured 7 or 3.5 years beforehand. Therefore, the Rapture cannot occur Pre-Trib.

If there was a Pre-Trib Rapture of the Church, one would expect to see Paul, Peter, John and James, etc. included in the number who were accompanying Jesus at His return. Because they would have been raptured 7 years prior to the Return. But we do not see this mentioned in the Bible. In fact, what we do see is Paul telling us that he will be with those who are raptured at Jesus' Return. Paul states in verse 51 that "we will all be changed" when the Rapture happens. He includes himself in the number who are caught up at the Return, by using the word "we." This means that he was not part of a group that went up 7 or 3.5 years before the Return. In verse 23 Paul explains when this will happen, at the Second

Coming. *"...after that those who are Christ's at His coming..."* This really debunks both a Pre-Trib and a Mid-Trib Rapture. There can be no rapture before we are raptured! And Paul explains that the Resurrection of the Dead (which the Bible calls what we commonly refer to as "the Rapture") will happen when Jesus Returns.

True, there are some Pre-Trib theologians who try to explain that the Rapture and the Second Coming are two different events, but the clear Biblical verses above, taken on their own and without all the theological gymnastics, make it clear that they are the exact same event.

Some like to explain I Cor. 15:23 as different stages. Christ, The First Fruits, Those who are Christ's at His coming, and then the End. But this is not true. Paul is clearly saying that Jesus is the "First Fruits." So really it should be The First Fruits (Which is Christ) and then Those Who are Christ's at His Return. Two different groups, not three different groups. But immediately before this verse, Paul explained that he understood that Jesus was the first fruits of God's good work. In verse 20 he explains that Jesus is who he considered the "first fruits."

The fact that the Second Coming and the Rapture are simultaneous events (or at least causal events, i.e. one event causes the other) is also a strong point of attack against Preterism, as well. Preterism teaches that since Jesus said in the above passage that "this generation would not pass away..." then all of the prophesies had to have been completed some time before the generation that was listening to Jesus give that speech.

However, this is not true to the context of the passage. The passage is referring to the time when people see these things come to pass. The generation that sees these things will not pass away. When you start to see these things that Jesus described being fulfilled, then *that* generation will not pass away.

Some might point to this passage and say that Jesus commanded us to pray that we would escape these things, so we must be raptured before hand. However, this is not the case either. If I were to ask anyone who escaped from hurricane Katrina, "were you miraculously raptured out of New Orleans?"

The person would rightly look at me as if I were insane, and say, "No, I barely escaped with my life." Escaping from a situation is not the same as being completely removed from the situation before hand.

In light of all of the other passages about the Rapture, End Times and the Day of the Lord, I believe it makes far more sense to interpret this passage as meaning that we are to pray that we will be able to escape from the tribulations that are coming, so that we can still be alive to see Jesus when He returns.

It is important also to notice that Jesus commands us *to watch*. Some Christians would rather not watch, and just be blissfully ignorant and pretend that His coming is generations away. Maybe it is. Maybe I'm wrong, but if that's so, why are there so many things that were foretold in the Bible happening right now?

We're living in a time when we are seeing these things come to pass. Many of the prophecies are being fulfilled right before our eyes. The specific armies mentioned in the passages about End Times wars, which we'll get into soon and which have never marched on Israel in the particular alliances mentioned in Biblical prophecy, are gathering today, even as I write this book.

I truly believe we are living in the last generation. We are living either on the cusp of the Tribulation, or perhaps by the time you are reading this book, we may have passed into the time period known as the Tribulation.

This is good news! Jesus is coming soon! Get ready, repent. Throw away your evil deeds. Don't be lukewarm. Get on fire for Jesus! He's coming soon, and we want to be found working. Do something for Him. Repent first, pray, turn from evil, embrace Jesus and ask Him what He has for you to do. He will tell you. Get on fire for Him. As Paul said to the church in Ephesus, "you were created for good works in Christ…" You will have resistance from the enemy, but keep going, and you will see victory. You will see Jesus' face, and hear those coveted words, "Well done my good and faithful servant!"

Will the Rapture Be Visible or Secret?

It will be visible.

According to the book of Revelation, Joel, Isaiah, Amos, Matthew 24, 1 and 2 Thessalonians and several other sources, the rapture is accompanied with many *visible signs, earthquakes, hail, lightening, the sun going dark, the moon turning blood red, etc.* How can it be some secret event? Also, the purpose of the rapture, as we mentioned in the previous section is to meet Jesus in the air, as a selected delegation, to welcome His return. The entire world sees this and trembles in fear and anger. See Revelation 16, which describes the fact that the entire world has seen His return. As the evil doers are brought to Armageddon, they curse God. It appears that their anger stems from the thwarting of their plans by Jesus' second coming.

It appears that the events of Revelation after chapter 14 happening in a quick succession. I think many of the mistakes previously made by Pre-Trib theologians and others, is to see these events as slowly being poured out on earth. They are not. All of these events have to happen quickly and in a *short time span*.

Some of these events, such as the turning of drinkable water to blood, found in Revelation 16:3, give us a fairly accurate time frame. A human can only go from one to two weeks without drinking water under normal circumstances. We're told in this passage that the very next plague was a scorching blast from the sun, causing a heat unlike anything that had ever been felt on the earth before. This event would lower the time frame considerably. I would say these events have to be less than one week long in order for people to exist until the end as is described by Revelation and Joel.

After each bowl is poured out, the people curse God who has control of these plagues. So it is obvious that they recognize where the plagues are coming from. They didn't miss the rapture accidentally. They did not fail to recognize when it happened. They will know very well that they've entered the time they probably had laughed about before hand, thinking Christians were just foolish.

Aside from the plagues that are being poured out, the absence of Christians will most certainly tip them off. It will not be secret.

Furthermore, Daniel 7:13-14 says that Daniel saw the coming of the Son of Man on the clouds, and that the Ancient of Days gave Him authority over every person on earth. Matthew 24:30 tells us that this is a *sign*, and all the people of the earth will see the Son of Man in the clouds.

Paul tells us in I Thessalonians 4:16 that a *loud trumpet call and shout* will accompany the Lord's return. So the idea that the rapture is some secret event is just plain false.

Finally, I must point out that several Pre-Trib teachers accept this truth, and have switched their view to the Rapture being a visible event. Hopefully, they will fully embrace the truth and accept that the Rapture will happen after the Tribulation like the Bible says as well.

Why does the Bible teach that Jesus' Second Coming Will Come Like A Thief in the Night If We Aren't Going To Be Secretly Raptured?

"Thief In The Night" is not associated with the Pre-Trib doctrine. It is a direct warning to the Church and is one of the strongest supports to the Post-Trib Rapture viewpoint. 1 Thess. 4 and 5 associates the phrase "Thief in the Night" with the "Day of the Lord."

The "thief in the Night" expression is also used in Jesus' warnings to the 7 churches at the opening of Revelation. Though, I believe that here He might be using the phrase as a way of saying that discipline is coming to the churches quickly, and it may or may not be directly related to the Second Coming. I cover this more in the "I am coming soon..." section. Jesus uses this phrase to warn them that they should be prepared.

Regardless of the use in Revelation, there is no evidence anywhere in Scripture of two "Thief in the Night" rapture experiences, both taking people by surprise. But if the Pre-Trib argument is true, there would have to be two "Thief in the Night" experiences. One happening at a Pre-Trib rapture and the other happening after a 7 year tribulation. Logically, there can't be two of these experiences. If the first "Thief in the Night" experience happened, causing millions of people to suddenly disappear as the Left Behind books would have us believe, then it would alert every single person on earth of the second "Thief in the Night" experience, which they could time to happen in exactly seven years, or three and a half years for the Mid-Tribbers.

People all over the world, would see all of the Christians gone, and would start digging into the Scripture seeking an explanation. "Faith comes from hearing the Word of God," so all of those people would spark a world wide revival, and the Second Coming would be further delayed, defeating the prophecy of a seven or three and a half year tribulation period.

It is bad exegesis to teach that a Pre-Trib Second Coming would be a "Thief in the Night" experience. The Pre-Tribber's teach that the rapture will come unexpectedly even for Christians, but the whole point of this passage is to let the believers know that THEY will not be taken by surprise, only the world will be taken by surprise. In Daniel 12:20 we are told that none of the wicked will understand, but those who have insight will understand. If the Rapture was Pre-Trib then Daniel would be wrong. The entire plot of the "Left Behind" series (and even the "Thief in the Night" movies of the 70's) is that the wicked *will* understand later and repent during the Tribulation. But this contradicts what we learn from Daniel and later the Apostle Paul in the Bible.

In Matt 24 this reference is linked to a Post Trib Rapture. Paul tells us in the Thessalonians passages that we are not to be taken by surprise. In other words, we'd better not be taken by surprise, or we haven't been paying attention. We have been warned in several places to be "watching" and "alert."

Is it because of the Rapture that the church is not mentioned after Rev. 4:1?

This is really a ridiculous argument, one cannot argue something's absence simply because one word that describes it isn't used. For instance, if I wanted to write a poem about the church, I could use various words such as the assembly, the congregation, the gathering, the elect, the saints, the people of God, the lovers of God, the worshipers, etc. There are many words that clearly describe the church without actually using the word church.

One such word is found quite a bit in the book of Revelation. The church is made up of "saints," which as I just mentioned is another term synonymous with the church throughout the entire NT. We see the word "saints" quite frequently after 4:1. (See: Rev. 13:7, 13:10, 14:9-12, Mt 24:15-25 and Dan. 7:25.) So this is no real sign that the church is not mentioned in Revelation after 4:1.

Some theorize that this could simply mean that under the authority of the Antichrist, assembling for worship, the main identifying mark of the "church," has become outlawed. Which makes sense, when you see that if one does not receive his "mark" the penalty is execution.

In Revelation we see different groups of saints, all of whom are part of the larger church. Not using the word "ecclesia" does not mean that the church was raptured. This is a real stretch of all that is credible. Jumping to this conclusion without any solid scriptural support is performing incredibly bad exegesis of the text, and reading into it something that cannot under any circumstance be proven to be there.

Since God told John to "come up" in Rev 4:1 and 18:4, we must be raptured "out from" the tribulation, right?

This argument often precedes or follows the previous point in some type of attempt to bolster the Pre-Trib argument. This too is really a great stretch, because the voice John hears is speaking only to John in the context of this passage. If we follow the rules that our preachers tell us to follow about every other part of Scripture, i.e. reading the passage in the context it is found in, then it is easy to see that God is referring to John and not the church.

Revelation 4:1 (KJV)

After this I looked, and, behold, a door was opened in heaven: and the first voice which I heard was as it were of a trumpet talking ***with me****; which said, Come up hither, and I will shew* ***thee*** *things which must be hereafter.*

Notice the singular nature of the words "me" and "thee." Here we clearly see that John is relating that he was about to receive a vision.

This shows that John is being brought up to receive a message for the 7 churches who are not with him at the time, since he is stranded on the Isle of Patmos, and they are elsewhere. For those who are not familiar with the details, John was tortured for his faith, boiled in hot oil and then exiled to the Isle of Patmos for a certain amount of time before receiving this vision while there.

Afterwards, John was sent back to Ephesus, where we can assume God made it possible for him to share the vision that God gave, though some scholars believe that John may have been able to smuggle out letters from prison, which could explain some of the obscurity of the Book of Revelation. These scholars claim that John's writings would look like the writings of a mad man if the Roman guards happened to discover them on the visitors that may have visited John on Patmos, but the leaders of the 7 churches would have understood John's references even though some of them seem to be lost to the average layman today.

Regardless of whether John could smuggle out letters or not, it is John, not the churches, who is receiving this vision. Furthermore, it is John who is commanded to record the vision so it can be delivered it to the churches. This is in contradiction to what Pre-Tribbers claim "to come up" means. *This passage is not and cannot possibly be referring to the church at all, but only John.*

If it were referring to the church as a whole, it would show that more than just John had been brought into heaven at this point. There are several other places in the book of Revelation where we see other believers in heaven, mostly those who have been martyred for the Gospel, but who are in heaven observing the goings on of the earth. If this was the case, why not show the other Raptured Christians at this point too? But the Bible doesn't show anyone other than John.

Many pastors are happy to use this passage to teach that we will be raptured at this event, but when you read the very next verse this idea is clearly debunked.

Revelation 4:2 (KJV)

And immediately ***I was in the spirit:*** *and, behold, a throne was set in heaven, and one sat on the throne.*

There is a problem here for Pre-Trib people, because immediately after being told to come up, John is "in the spirit." Now, we know from I Thessalonians 4 that when the Rapture happens, the Resurrection happens, and any Pre-Tribber will tell you that when they are raptured they will receive their *"resurrection bodies."* But if this verse is referring to the Rapture, they will not receive their resurrection bodies, but will be in the spirit. Because as we are told in 2 Corinthians 5:8 that when we are absent from the body we are present with God.

So if John was in the spirit, and this represents the Rapture, then all of those Pre-Trib rapture cars will not be un-manned in the event of the Rapture, but will be filled with the un-souled bodies of the Christians who are "in the spirit" with God. In other words, instead of being Raptured, as is commonly portrayed, this scenario shows that there would be a mass extermination of Christians.

This version is clearly not true, because when the Rapture does happen, we will be given resurrection bodies and will reign with Jesus.

Isn't the rapture the "Blessed Hope of the Church?"

But speak thou the things which become sound doctrine: *That the aged men be sober, grave, temperate, sound in faith, in charity, in patience. The aged women likewise, that they be in behavior as becometh holiness, not false accusers, not given to much wine, teachers of good things; that they may teach the young women to be sober, to love their husbands, to love their children, to be discreet, chaste, keepers at home, good, obedient to their own husbands, that the word of God be not blasphemed. Young men likewise exhort to be sober minded.*

In all things shewing thyself a pattern of good works: ***in doctrine shewing uncorruptness,*** *gravity, sincerity, sound speech, that cannot be condemned; that he that is of the contrary part may be ashamed, having no evil thing to say of you. Exhort servants to be obedient unto their own masters, and to please them well in all things; not answering again; not purloining, but shewing all good fidelity; that they may adorn the doctrine of God our Saviour in all things. For the grace of God that bringeth salvation hath appeared to all men, teaching us that, denying ungodliness and worldly lusts, we should live soberly, righteously, and godly, in this present world;* ***looking for that blessed hope, and the glorious appearing of the great God and our Saviour Jesus Christ;*** *who gave himself for us, that he might redeem us from all iniquity, and purify unto himself a peculiar people, zealous of good works. These things speak, and* *exhort, and rebuke with all authority. Let no man despise thee. (Titus 2, KJV)*

Yes, Titus 2:13 tells us that Jesus' appearing is our blessed hope, but Titus never said WHEN that blessed hope would happen. He also said it was the "glorious appearing" that is our blessed hope, as you can see from the entire passage. The idea that some "secret rapture" would deliver us away from the Tribulation is just not in this passage. This passage has been twisted and taken out of context to prove something which it isn't talking about.

In fact, this passage makes just the opposite argument, because it is an *appearing*. If Jesus appears to the world, then it is not secret at all, but a *global world wide event* that everyone *will see*.

I have also bold faced a couple spots which warn that we must have sound doctrine. God is expecting us to have sound doctrine, and it is not a trivial matter to God to propagate false teaching.

The Bible says that we're raptured because the time is cut short or else even the very elect wouldn't be able to endure, so doesn't that prove that we will be raptured out before the Tribulation starts?

No, it doesn't. The Bible says that the *time* will be cut short, not the experience itself. The length of time that the Tribulation could have happened might have been as full as 7 years, but instead of giving the Antichrist full reign over everything, he has 3 ½ years to establish his empire, and 3 ½ years to rule. Some point to Daniel 2 to explain that his empire will be one of Iron and Clay. While I am not entirely sure Daniel 2 relates here, it is conceivable that some parts of his empire will be strong, and some parts weak.

This is possibly why we will be able to flee from one town to another, or to endure in spite of persecution. The Antichrist will never have complete control over the entire earth. Because "the earth is the Lord's and everything in it," it is only on loan to the Antichrist for the duration that God appoints. Nebuchadnezzar's dream of the statue with feet of iron and clay, the vision of the woman being chased by the dragon in Revelation, and Jesus' warning to flee into the mountains, are all examples of how the Antichrist empire will not be all-powerful and entirely consuming.

Satan tried a similar thing with the Tower of Babel, an attempt to establish a one world government. But God intervened and stopped him, and will do so again with Christ's second coming during the reign of the Antichrist.

The Church will experience the Tribulation, and this passage is only making a point about God's love for the church. Because God cares about the church He has shortened the days. There are other places in the Bible where prophecy is given, and God either withdraws His punishment, or lessens it a bit. We can see this principle in the healing of King Hezekiah in 2 Kings 20. God was going to cut short his life span, but he prayed and God relented. We can see this is the story of Sodom and Gomorrah. God was going to wipe the town out, but He was willing to make a deal with Abraham to spare the city if 10 righteous people were there. Unfortunately for those towns, Lot was the only righteous person.

It seems that God at some point when He ordained the Tribulation decreed that the initial amount of time was too great. So He *shortened the days*. It says that He did this or otherwise there would be no flesh left alive. *(Matthew 24:22)*

If the transhumanists are any part of the Tribulation, it is possible we might just see another fulfillment of this phrase, in that they would like to "enhance" us with animal DNA, producing some kind of strange hybrid. Some have gone so far as to suggest that there is already talk in the Pentagon and by DARPA about creating super soldiers. God, who knows everything in His wisdom, perhaps saw this happening, and the strange dreams of the leaders of the Transhumanist movement could come true if not for Divine intervention.

But the bottom line about this verse, is that the Tribulation time period has been limited by God, but not the fact that we will experience the Tribulation. There is no evidence, as I hope you can see by now, that we will be delivered from that time. And this verse does not mean that because the time period will be so devastating no Christian would be able to hold up under it. The fact is, Christians hold up under persecution and minor tribulation all the time, as well as holding up under demonic attack. We have the God of the universe living inside of us, so nothing short of death will ever stop us from completing the mission God has for us.

It appears that Satan would like to stamp out our mission. There are really only two things that could destroy our mission: the death of all humans (because as long as there are humans, there will be God working to bring them to salvation), or as mentioned before, the actual complete corruption of human DNA so that we are no longer human. But these two things will not happen. God has promised that the days will be shortened so that the very elect will remain.

One thing that I have often wondered about pertains to the matter of election. We have seen that there are differing levels of reward in heaven. The parable of the talents makes this point, as does the fact that some will sit on thrones, etc. I wonder if there is a level of election as well. Perhaps when Jesus used this phrase in this context, He was referring to the fact that the people who have to endure through the Tribulation were chosen especially by God to endure that time period.

So in a way, it would be like the Green Berets or the Navy Seals are the "very elect" of our nation's armed forces, and in a similar way, those who survive the Tribulation are the "very elect," as opposed to just the "elect." I do not know if this is the case, but it is food for thought.

Is the Harvest mentioned in Matthew 13:39 the Same As The Rapture?

“The harvest is the end of the world…” Yes it is. We see this harvest theme repeated also in Revelation 14. The harvest also refers to the last of the 7 Jewish/Biblical feasts.

In the parable of the wheat and the tares in Matthew 13, we also see Jesus equating the harvest with His second coming. We see that there is a gathering of the saints, to be with Jesus (or in His barn as the parable goes), and there is also a gathering of the evil doers to the fire (many scholars believe this is a reference to Armageddon, rather than hell). Actually, this parable shows that the tares are gathered first to the fire, and then the wheat is gathered.

We are also told throughout the New Testament that we are to bear fruit for the Lord. There will be a day to come when Jesus will come back to harvest the fruit that we produce for Him, and the rapture will happen at that time.

If We're Going To Be Raptured Out Before The Tribulation, Why Do We Have So Many Details About It In The Bible?

Good question. Why does Jesus give this vision to John if we're not going to be around for the Tribulation? Why is Satan allowed to rule the earth for 7 years if there are no Christians to persecute? There's no point in it. Why does the rhetoric from the Radical Islamists such as Ahmadinejad claim that the 12th Imam, or who we would call the Anti-Christ, involve stamping out Christianity and Judaism?

If we're going to be raptured out of it, there's no need to stamp it out. It will not exist when we are gone. Satan must know if we were going to be raptured out, and his plan would be to destroy us before we get raptured. It doesn't seem consistent with Satan's character for him to make the destruction of Christians and the victory over Christianity part of his follower's end times belief system, if they wouldn't get a chance to actually kill a bunch of Christians. And since this is a major part of the doctrine that currently is fueling the Islamic attacks on Christians around the world, it seems more likely that we Christians in American will experience persecution as well, rather than we will escape any persecution. If we consider that we might just in fact be around for persecution perhaps the warning would allow us to prepare somewhat, if not physically, then at least mentally and spiritually. John was given a vision, the only book that gives the student a blessing, to warn us. *Why would God want to warn us about a bunch of things we won't be around for?* There would be no point.

Everywhere else in Scripture where God gave warnings, it was ultimately for the benefit of the people, so that they would be safe or protected from coming trials. What point is there to the book of Revelation, if there is a lot of detail about the coming Tribulation that Christians would not have to endure? The amillennialists have a much more sound argument that Revelation was a warning to the early church to watch out for Nero and Vespasian. But they fall short by not realizing that Nero's wrath was not a global wrath as described by the prophesies of the end times in all of the Bible. Mark 13:19 teaches that there will be tribulation such as has not occurred since the beginning of creation, and there will never be such tribulation again. Now we must consider that Jesus tells us this with an understanding that Noah's flood happened after creation, yet still He tells us that this tribulation will be worse. Surely, Jesus would recognize a global tribulation of such magnitude and wouldn't confuse it with a local phenomenon?

It is important to know that there were absolutely no Pre-Trib teachers before Scofield and Darby. In addition to creating his own Bible, which is tainted by his personal opinion throughout rather than scholarly research, Darby based the majority of his eschatological doctrine on a vision received by a young woman in Scotland named Margaret MacDonald. Miss MacDonald was from a sect of the Catholic Apostolic Church, called the Irvingites (not to be confused with the Roman Catholic Church). David MacPherson, in his book *The Incredible Cover-Up: The True Story of the Pre-Trib Rapture,* lays out a strong well researched argument that prior to 1830 there was no Pre-Trib doctrine.

And yet despite the fact that the Pre-Trib theory is not an historical biblical doctrine based on Scripture, but instead based on the fantasies of a young woman, their doctrine has been perpetuated by many groups including Dallas Theological Seminary. The *absolute verifiable fact* is before DTS, Tim LaHaye, Hal Lindsey, Scofield and

Darby, Christians were traditionally either amillennialists or post trib.

An aside note, it seems strange that Dallas Theological Seminary, arguably one of the largest seminaries against the charismatic gifts practiced by many groups that were derived from the same charismatic movement that spawned the Irvingites, and whose affiliated churches are by and large against the ordination of women, have based their eschatological theology on the charismatic "vision" of a woman. Most people that I have met from DTS would argue against any such vision today, yet they openly embrace one from 1830.

There are some who try to explain that we didn't have the full understanding of the scripture, and Daniel said his vision was to be locked up until the end times, and so now we who are in the End Times are now seeing these truths come to life. But if that were true we'd have to reject everything written by any Christian theologian prior to Scofield and Darby, as false teaching. And furthermore we'd have to reject the parts in the New Testament which teach that all times since Jesus left are technically the End Times.

The bible makes it clear that *a false teacher is one who teaches falsehood.* It should be very obvious, in comparison to the simplicity of the Gospel message, or the simplicity of any of our other doctrines, that someone is teaching falsehood when it comes to the complication of the End Times message.

So if someone is teaching falsehood, then either the ones teaching us falsehood prior to Scofield and Darby are the ones in the wrong, *OR* Scofield, Darby, and those who came after are the false teachers, by perverting the Biblical, historical Christian doctrine of what would happen in the End Times. Doesn't it make more sense to reject Scofield, Darby, LaHaye and Hal Lindsey's teaching and keep the previous 1800 years of Christendom's teachings that were actually rooted and grounded in the Bible, not on someone's interpretation of Margaret MacDonald's vision?

And just to put a fine point on it, I am not claiming that Ms. MacDonald did not indeed have a vision from God. I believe, contrary to DTS, that the charismatic gifts were never taken away from the church, and that visions have been something many people throughout church history have seen. So, perhaps she did have a vision, but from what I read in her account of it, she clearly did not go back to the Scriptures to determine whether her interpretation of her vision fit with what Jesus and the Apostles taught about the End Times scenario.

What does "the End of the Age" mean, and does it give us a clue as to when we will be raptured?

In Matthew 28:20 we have the last part of what we commonly refer to as "The Great Commission." Jesus concludes the Great Commission with this statement:

"Teach these new disciples to obey all the commands I have given you. And be sure of this: I am with you always, even to the end of the age." (Matthew 28:20, NLT)

The King James translates it as "end of the world." The literal Greek uses the phrase συντελείας τοῦ αἰῶνος. Literally, this means "the conclusion of the eon." The word, "συντελείας," transliterated as "sunteleias," is a word that means the conclusion, or end, or finish, whereas αἰῶνος, "aionos" literally means eon, or a long time period, or age.

Dispensationalists, such as Darby, have come up with many distinctions between various biblical time periods such as the Old Testament period, the time period when Jesus was on earth, the "Apostolic Age" when the disciples lived, the "Church Age" that we are currently in, the Tribulation period, and the Millennium. While I also agree that there is a distinction between some of these time periods, I do not agree with many of the other dispensational periods that theologians like Darby invented.

Jesus' words in this passage clearly show that there is only one long time period between the Resurrection and the Return. Jesus is telling His disciples that He will be with them always until the end of the age, i.e. the age or eon that they are currently in, one He instated at the event of His resurrection.

Now if the Apostolic Age is different from the Church Age, and the Church Age is different from the Tribulation period, then that would mean Jesus was only with the disciples spiritually until the "very end of the age" that those disciples lived in. If this is true, then it would mean that Jesus' Spirit left the world at the end of the first century with the death of John the apostle. This is clearly not true, because without the Holy Spirit we cannot evangelize, grow in the Lord, understand the Word of

God, commune with God or partake of any of the many other blessings that the Holy Spirit gives us.

So since the Holy Spirit is obviously still here, and since His presence is the verification that Jesus is still with us "until the very end of the age," then the only alternative is that Jesus is still with us until the very end of *this* age.

This means that we are *still* in the same age as the Apostles, and therefore there is no specific distinction between the Apostolic Age, the Church Age and the Tribulational Period. As far as I am concerned, the divisions of dispensational ages are a good way to categorize the events of prophecy and history for study purposes, but they are not characterized by things such as the cessation of gifts, or a different outpouring of the Spirit, or a rapture that divides the church age from the Tribulation.

There really are only four dispensations: the time period before the fall of man, the Old Testament Period (which begins with God's prophesy to Adam about the coming of the Messiah until the Death of Jesus where that prophesy is fulfilled), the period after Jesus' resurrection until His 2nd Coming, and the Millennium. One could also argue that the time period after the Millennium when God recreates everything, could be classified as a 5th age or dispensation.

There is no change in time period between the early church and the church now. Paul shows us that there isn't when he explains that he intends to be included in the Resurrection when Jesus returns. We also see in Revelation that the Tribulation Martyrs are included in that number as well. We will discuss this in greater detail later.

Furthermore, Jesus said He would be with us until the "very end" of this age, the eon that we entered after His resurrection. If He will be with us until the "very end" then this again shows that we will go through the Tribulation which He said would be at the very end of *this* age. So we should ask ourselves: How is He with us now? He is with us through His Holy Spirit which indwells us and allows us to commune with Him. So He will continue to be with us in the same capacity until He physically returns.

Some might argue that there is a difference between the end of the age, or eon, and the Tribulation period. However, Jesus uses this same phrase "συντελείας τοῦ αἰῶνος" in Matthew 24 to describe the time period when the events of the Tribulation unfold.

So if Jesus in Matthew 28 uses this phrase to describe the duration of time that He will spiritually be with us, and in Matthew 24 He uses the same phrase to describe the Tribulation, it is obvious that He meant that He would be with us *even through the Tribulation* at the very end of the age.

This gives us a clue as to when we will be raptured. *Jesus is going to be with us spiritually until He returns physically.* He says that He will be with us spiritually until the very end of the age, and when He returns He will be with us physically. He also tells us that the very end of the age is the time period that He labeled the Great Tribulation. So we must endure through the Tribulation before we can be raptured to meet Him at His physical return.

Another important passage worth considering is John 6:44, *"No one comes to me unless the Father who sent me draws him, and I will raise him up at the Last Day."* When will Jesus raise him up? The last day, not the day 7 years or 3.5 years before the Last Day, but the Last Day. What else do we call the process of being raised up? The Rapture. So when is the Rapture? The Last Day.

What will physically happen to believers when we are raptured?

As I write this, sitting beside me is a cherry pit left over from some cherries that my family and I had after supper tonight. I have been looking at the cherry pit and pondering it's potential.

A cherry pit is the seed of a cherry fruit that when planted produces a cherry tree. It begins by being a flower on a cherry tree, that flower slowly transforms into a cherry which I was fortunate enough to eat. Somehow inside of the wet mushy flesh of a cherry this pit formed, and after it dries out, then I can plant it in another wet mushy environment (the moist soil). Once in the moist soil, it will split open, sprout roots and send up the very first shoot that will eventually become the trunk of a tree that will in turn produce more cherries.

It is amazing to me as I look at this cherry pit that something so small could one day become something that my children (or more likely my grandchildren) would enjoy climbing. It is so small and it fits so nicely into the palm of my hand. I can actually balance it on the tip of my finger and it feels almost weightless. How can all of this be possible?

And yet it is. In a similar way, we are like that cherry pit. We are given these bodies that deteriorate, break down and die, and are eventually planted in the ground. But one day they will be transformed and become something other than what they are now. Apparently they will be recognizable, but different, because the Apostle Paul tells us that we will be known as we are known. The best passages on this are in 1 Thessalonians 4 and 5, and also 1 Corinthians 15. Paul describes in vivid detail what will happen when we are resurrected.

Our bodies that were once broken down and defective will raise to be something better than what they were. We will be "glorified," which apparently means we will be like Jesus was when He came back to life.

After He rose from the dead, He did several things that we might be able to do as well. He apparently either walked through a wall, or teleported into the midst of the disciples when they were in the upper room. His physical appearance was different enough that on the Road to Emmaus the disciples that He met there didn't recognize Him at first. And He ascended into heaven. Perhaps we will be able to levitate? Who knows?

Now imagine that you had never seen a cherry. You had never seen a cherry tree, and in fact, you had never even seen a seed before. And someone handed you a cherry pit. You might think that it was a little pebble, or something. But would you ever be able to imagine that a whole tree complete with edible fruit could spring from such a little "stone?"

Now, just as it is impossible to look at a cherry pit and imagine what the tree would look like. It's virtually impossible to imagine what we will look like and be like as well, but the God who designed a system that can make a cherry pit turn into a cherry tree and produce cherries, certainly has a much better design in mind for our broken down old bodies as well!

Tribulation

Jesus promised to "keep us from the hour of trial, so why would we go through the tribulation?

Many Pre-Trib theologians refer to the use of the Greek word "ek" in this passage from Revelation 3:10 translated here as "from." But the word "ek" can also be translated several different ways depending on the context of the passage. From the Strong's Concordance, the word Ek and also Ex, is a preposition and can also be used to denote "through." So it can also be read "Because thou hast kept the word of my patience, I also will keep thee *through* the hour of temptation, which shall come upon all the world, to try them that dwell upon the earth."

First of all, this passage that is being referred to is specifically referring only to the church of Philadelphia. We know this because Jesus specifically told John to pass this message onto Philadelphia, as opposed to asking John to record it for the other churches. Furthermore, other translations render this as, "I will protect you from," "I will deliver you through," etc. Amillennialists argue that this is referring only to the persecution of the early church by the Romans. But if that were so, why does it refer to the time of testing for the *whole world*?

It is interesting to note that of the seven churches that are listed in Revelation, the church of Philadelphia still had a minority Christian presence in the present day city of Alashehir, Turkey up until modern times. And according to a New York Times article from May 4, 2011 entitled, "Turkey Cultivates Sites of Its Christian Heritage," by Susanne Güsten, we find out that many of the sites of the seven churches are now open to pilgrims, with over 1,000 pilgrims a day coming to see some of the sites. According to Ms. Güsten's article, Turkey has even allowed annual services to be held there.

Could we see a revival of the seven churches in the Last Days? I don't know, but it is very interesting to see such developments. Perhaps, Jesus foresaw such an event, and is saying to this church that when the End Times do come, He will protect them. More likely, He was referring to the persecution that was coming because His Spirit was bringing it to *discipline the churches.* You can read more about this idea in the section in this book about the churches and Jesus' use of the phrase, "Coming Soon," below. But it is a great stretch to use this verse to say that the entire church is going to be raptured out of the Tribulation, based on what Jesus said to this one particular church.

Furthermore, even if this was meant for the entire church, this does not necessarily mean a literal taking away from the earth. It could go along with Rev. 12:13 where it says there will be a safe place in the desert to be safe through the Tribulation.

In John 17:11 and 15, this same word "*ek*" is translated as "*keep you through*," in most translations.

We should ask ourselves which doctrine is the more Biblical, being *kept through trials*, or being *removed from problems*?

Being kept through trials is a common biblical doctrine that is often neglected by pastors who are steeped in Pre-Trib doctrine. We can see this by the abundance of false teachers on television preaching that God wants all of His children to be rich, healthy and happy at all times. This is the exact opposite of what the Bible teaches, which is when trials come, God will keep us through them and help us overcome them.

Daniel in the lion's den, Shadrach, Meshach, and Abednego, Noah and Lot are all examples of being "kept through" their trials. Psalm 23 shows this as well: "Yea, though I walk *through* the valley of the shadow of death..." David was kept through a great deal of trials following him most of his life. And yet through the trials came, David clung to his faith in God and was brought through each and every one.

In fact, one could argue that all of the heroes of the Bible had to go *through* hardship. Gideon still had to go through the battle, but God promised never to leave him. Nehemiah had to stand strong against opposition, but in the end he went through the trials and the wall was built. Isaiah went through a great deal of opposition to bring us his prophecy, and in the end he was martyred, but afterwards we can be assured he received a greater glory from His father who brought Isaiah through it all the way until the very end.

The Israelites were taken through the desert, and through the Red Sea. In fact, every example in the Bible was of someone who came through some trail.

But it seems Christians today are afraid of discomfort. They don't want to go though any kind of trouble. So many today preach that we can have whatever we want and God will be our great big Santa Claus, but God is not Santa Claus. When you turn on Christian TV you can find any number of preachers teaching you that you can have your best life now, if you give money to their ministry you will be rewarded a hundred fold.

Anyone who preaches this type of lie is a false teacher and should be shunned by Christians. Preachers need to stand up, and stop excusing this type of teaching with phrases like "we shouldn't judge." This isn't true. Paul teaches us in I Corinthians 5:12 and 6:2 that we are to judge those in the church. These false teachers are rampant on "Christian" TV, and we need to be stronger and louder about denouncing them as the false teachers that they are.

Being brought through trials is God's modus operandi.

A secondary comment about this passage that many Amillennial theologians point to is that when combined with the Greek word "*mello*" it implies imminence, which means that this trial Jesus was speaking of was coming in the immediate future.

I agree that this implies imminence, but this is not conclusive proof that 70 AD was the year of the Great Tribulation, especially since Jesus did not return in 70 AD. The fact that this passage states that it will cover "all the world," dismisses the idea that the immediacy is related to our time line, but could very well belong to the "thousand years is a day," category of time that God uses throughout the Scripture. It could simply mean that Jesus' Spirit was going to allow the hardship to come to the churches in the very near, i.e. imminent, future.

There is also the fact that sometimes in prophecy we see multiple events being referred to in a single sentence. This can be very confusing. We see this a lot in the Old Testament where some events refer to the immediate destruction of Israel, and also to events that will happen when the Messiah comes, both the first time and the second time. Most Biblical scholars will agree to this fact. It is plausible to believe the phrasing of this passage could be referring to both the immediate threat of the first century persecution of the church, as well as the farther advanced Great Tribulation that would be at the end of the AD timeline.

Jesus told us to "Pray that you will be kept from God's wrath," so doesn't that mean we'll miss the Tribulation?

When Jesus commanded the church to pray to escape from God's wrath, He was not referring to the Tribulation. The Tribulation is a time of *trial* upon the whole earth, when some will follow Satan, and some will follow God. Praying is something that we as Christians do as part of being in a relationship with God. It is the relationship with God that will allow us to escape God's judgment and wrath. All Christians agree on this. *But the Tribulation is not God's wrath. The Tribulation is Satan's wrath against the Church.* As we see in the book of Joel, "The Day of the Lord" is God's wrath. We will talk more about the Day of the Lord soon, but for the purpose of this discussion, it is important to realize that there is a distinction between God's wrath and Satan's wrath.

Just to clarify, Jesus never said that the Tribulation that He described in Matthew 24 was God's wrath.

We see many places in Scripture that Satan is given permission by God to do certain things. In Job, he had to get permission to persecute Job. In the Gospels, Jesus tells Peter that Satan asked to sift him. We even see where Satan tempts Jesus, and we must assume that he had to have God the Father's permission to do so.

The Tribulation is a time when Satan will finally be allowed to rule on the earth for a short time, though as we see in another section, he will never completely rule everything. He will embody the man of lawlessness, the Antichrist, and will wage war against the saints.

Now if we were to escape this time by being raptured out, then it would mean that the Rapture precedes the Day of the Lord. However, according to 1 Thess. 5:2 we see that the Rapture is actually one of the events of the "Day of the Lord." We also see in Joel that there are several things that evil people do, such as warring against God's people, marching against the Messiah when He returns, etc., that agree with everything that happens at the end of the Tribulation as described in the NT. So we can clearly see that the time period called the Tribulation is not God's wrath. It is a time of *testing for the church,* to be sure, but not His wrath against His people.

The seven bowls of wrath mentioned in Revelation are God's wrath upon the people of the earth who are unrepentant. But the time period known as the Tribulation, will be a time of global catastrophe followed by the Antichrist's reign. The time of the Antichrist's reign is Satan's wrath on the earth. *Saints will escape God's wrath but only because they endured through Satan's wrath*, which as you can now see is the Tribulation.

Even in Margaret MacDonald's vision, what she claimed to have seen was a rapture that occurred just prior to what she termed the "Day of Vengence," which is another way of saying the "Day of the Lord," as shown in Isaiah, Amos, Joel, etc. So what she really saw was a pre-wrath rapture and not a Pre-Trib rapture, though she obviously interpreted her vision incorrectly, as her interpretation does not line up with the Bible.

Dave MacPherson, in his book "The Incredible Cover-Up" gives a very good explanation of the difference between God's wrath and Satan's wrath. *"The opposite of salvation is not merely a time of tribulational testing, but the eternal wrath of God." (MacPherson, 111)*

MacPherson points out that many Pre-Trib theologians point to passages such as John 5:24, Romans 5:9 and 8:1 and I Thessalonians 1:10 and 5:9 to show that we will not endure God's wrath, but as we have just seen, the Tribulation is in no way God's wrath upon the church, or even upon the world. The Tribulation is a time of wrath from Satan on the church. In fact it is Satan's very last time that he can attack the church, so from his perspective it had better be his very best attack, because it's the last chance he's going to get. We must keep in mind 1 Peter 4:17-18 that judgment begins with the church.

My pastor said that since Lot was taken out of Sodom and Noah was taken out of the Flood we won't endure the Tribulation, isn't this true? (See Luke 17:26-30)

First of all, Noah was NOT taken out of the Flood. This is really a total misunderstanding of what is described by

Noah's flood, and very bad exegesis of the passage on the flood. Imagine if you will the minutes following God's closing of the Ark door. Perhaps it started with the onlookers laughing at Noah. Soon the rain began and people perhaps began to see their dire situation, but maybe didn't realize the gravity of the situation, until the really heavy rain began. At this point they probably began pounding on the ark, screaming to be let on board. Now we can understand why God closed the door instead of Noah. Only a few inches or at the most a few feet of wood separated Noah from the people he preached to during his time building the Ark. Soon enough those screams and banging began to die out as the Ark was lifted up on the flood waters, and the rest of the reprobate people were swept away by the flood. The text shows that everything on the earth died. Can't you imagine that Noah had to hear some people screaming as the flood took them away? And I am sure that even though they were safe in the Ark, Noah and his family knew many of the people who had been killed in the flood, and some that begging him to be let in, could have been friends or neighbors. But as the text shows, God shut the door, so Noah had no way of letting them in even if he had wanted to.

Noah *endured* through the Flood. He was saved because of God's direct intervention (i.e. God explained to him how to build the Ark.); likewise with Lot. Lot was in the general vicinity of the destruction of Sodom. He barely escaped with his life, and his wife did not escape with her life. He was not on some other planet, some other dimension or even somewhere far away on the other side of the world. He was right there in the immediate area where the destruction fell.

Now let's consider the Luke passage, as well as the parallel passage in Matthew 24.

Luke 17:26-30 (NLT)

"When the Son of Man returns, it will be like it was in Noah's day. In those days, the people enjoyed banquets and parties and weddings right up to the time Noah entered his boat and the flood came and destroyed them all.

"And the world will be as it was in the days of Lot. People went about their daily business—eating and drinking, buying and selling, farming and building— until the morning Lot left Sodom. Then fire and burning sulfur rained down from heaven and destroyed them all. Yes, it will be 'business as usual' right up to the day when the Son of Man is revealed.

Matthew 24:37-44 (NLT)

"When the Son of Man returns, it will be like it was in Noah's day. In those days before the flood, the people were enjoying banquets and parties and weddings right up to the time Noah entered his boat. People didn't realize what was going to happen until the flood came and swept them all away. That is the way it will be when the Son of Man comes.

"Two men will be working together in the field; one will be taken, the other left. Two women will be grinding flour at the mill; one will be taken, the other left.

"So you, too, must keep watch! For you don't know what day your Lord is coming. Understand this: If a homeowner knew exactly when a burglar was coming, he would keep watch and not permit his house to be broken into. You also must be ready all the time, for the Son of Man will come when least expected.

In the Luke passage mentioned above, the disciples asked where the people would be taken and Jesus told them to look among the dead bodies and where the vultures gather. That doesn't sound like being raptured away from the trouble to me. True, this could be referring to the evil people, if compared with Matthew 24:37-44. However, it could also show that there will be many martyrs before His return, as demonstrated by Revelation 20, 12 and 7. In the context of the passage, the disciples are showing obvious concern. If they were asking about the evil people, why would they be concerned? They were concerned I believe, because they understood Jesus' statement as being about His followers, and they were concerned because they wanted to know where the followers would be taken. Jesus said the other people would be *left behind*, and so the disciples would have no reason for concern about them, only those who were taken.

Remember we get most of our rapture doctrine from the Apostle Paul, who wrote after Jesus made this statement. So in the context of the sermon Jesus was delivering, the disciples would not immediately think of being "raptured." They would think of their own context that of seeing Roman soldiers drag people off on a daily basis. So to their minds, Jesus was referring to an unfortunately common event that they were afraid of, that of being arrested and killed by the Roman authorities. When Jesus said to look for them where the vultures feed, they knew that there was always a possibility that the Romans could come in and destroy them.

In fact, this same scenario did happen about forty years later when the Romans destroyed Jerusalem in 70 AD. Because of this event, many Amillennialists preach that the Great Tribulation has already happened. However, in several passages such as Matthew chapter 24, Mark 13, and Revelation 3:10, and also based on the events recorded in the book of Revelation, such as in chapter 8 where a third of all trees on earth are burned, we see that the Great Tribulation will be a *global* event. And though the Romans controlled most of the known world at the time, there is more recent evidence outside of the Bible that shows that the ancients were not unaware of the rest of the world.

The existence of artifacts such as the Red Bird Petroglyph in Kentucky, the findings of ancient Hebrew and Phoenician coins in the Ohio River Basin, and the Los Lunas, the so called "New Mexico 10 Commandments" and many other artifacts from the Ancient World found in the New World, suggests that the ancients were aware of the existence of the entire world.

So they most likely wouldn't have described a local event as a global event. (*If you would like to investigate these strange "Out Of Place Artifacts" from a Christian perspective check out www.s8int.com.)*

Also, the fact that Jesus who gave the Revelation to John and who gave His disciples this warning, certainly as God of the cosmos, knew of the existence of the rest of the world. We know from Matthew 4:8, that if Jesus in His humanity might not have been aware of the rest of the world, Satan took Him up on a mountain and showed Him "all the kingdoms of the world." So Jesus obviously was aware of the global scope of things. So this begs the question why would He describe something as a global event, if it was only going to be a localized event?

We know that at the time of the Romans, the Indian and the Chinese civilizations were in full swing, and God certainly was aware of these cultures. Alexander the Great made it all the way to India before his army was turned back. The Romans certainly knew about this, Jesus should have too. In fact, most historians agree that Thomas made it to India and died there for preaching the gospel. And based on the command that Jesus gave us at the end of Matthew that most of us refer to as the Great Commission, and the word that Jesus gave in 24:14 that after the Gospel is preached in all the world, the end would come. So if the Great Tribulation was not a world wide event, why would God mislead us, lie to us and confuse us by telling us that something localized was global? He certainly wouldn't do such a thing, because He is God, and He is omniscient, and knows everything.

Some will argue that the global language here is similar to what Luke used in the Christmas narrative when he says "…all the world should be taxed..." However, there is a difference of perspective between these two passages. In Luke's Christmas narrative, found in Luke chapter 2, the perspective is from Caesar who was taxing "all the world," that was under his authority. And if we look at the historical accounts, Rome's goal was global domination, and so it is not a stretch to believe that from his perspective he had the authority to tax the entire world. It was not uncommon for Roman emperor's to levy taxes against provinces that were not Roman, but were under Roman protection. And it was also not uncommon for the emperor to believe he was a god and entitled to rule the entire world.

However, this is in direct opposition to God who does have the authority to rule the entire world, and who does know everything that is going on in it. The Roman emperor was not omniscient, and did not have authority over the whole world, though his boasts would make us believe that he thought so. But when Jesus speaks about global events, He did have the authority from God the Father to do so with accuracy and truth. So on one hand we have the emperor's point of view and what he believes is the "whole world," and on the other hand we see God's point of view and what He *knows* is the "whole world."

What I find confusing about Amillennialists is that often these same preachers and teachers will go to great lengths to prove that Noah's flood was a world wide catastrophe, but they would like to say that the Great Tribulation is local. With the way John describes the End Times scenario it seems to be global. It says a third of the world will die; a third of the life in the sea and a third of the animals will die. If it was localized, this information would not be relevant or even true, if it was only a third of the life in the empire, or country, etc. that died.

As a side note, the geological record and the fossil record both argue for a global flood, and match with what Jesus affirmed about the account in Genesis that Noah's flood encompassed the entire world.

Furthermore, we see Jesus and the book of Revelation describing earthquakes as ones whose magnitude are such that the world had never seen before. If it was a local phenomenon, God would not use that type of description, knowing that his people would be around 2,000 years from the event, and experiencing earthquakes that far outweighed any that happened during 70 AD.

And finally, Jeremiah, when speaking of End Times events at the end of chapter 25, speaks of God being angry with the entire world. When Jesus returns, it will be an event that impacts the entire world. There is no way it can be a secret.

It is true that Lot had to experience a localized tribulation, but that was not the case with Noah. And our Lord described the world as being like it was in the "days of Noah." And the world had degraded to such a wicked state that all seemed hopeless, so God poured out destruction on the inhabitants of the world. So, just as Noah had to endure a Global Tribulation, I am convinced that we will have to endure a Global Tribulation as well.

Will the Tribulation be 7 years long?

The short answer to your question is, no, the Tribulation period will be three and a half years.

The long answer to this question is, yes, if you consider the 3.5 buildup years as part of the Tribulation as a whole. Technically, the term "Great Tribulation" is only referring to the final 3.5 years of Daniel's final week of prophecy. To understand this we need to understand Daniel's week of prophecy found in Daniel chapters 9 and 12, where we see that the first half of the week long end time period shows the buildup leading to the Antichrist's power base being consolidated. The second half of the week is the period of time where the Antichrist is allowed to have his reign.

Most scholars agree that in Daniel's week each day represents a year. So, there is a 7 year time period at the end which is crucial. We see that Jesus refers to this time period as the Last Days in Matthew 24, which we often take to mean the time period of the end. What Jesus might have been speaking of when He used this particular phrase was the very last days of Daniel's prophetic week. He tells us that as the time of His second coming approaches, things will get dramatically worse, until the conclusion of those Days will be unlike any that have ever happened on the earth before. Whether he was referring to the Last Days as being the latter portion of time in general, or specifically to the last three and a half years when the Antichrist will reign, either way that time period will be unique in the history of the world.

The key to understanding this is found in the Book of Revelation in 13:1 which shows that the Antichrist only has full authority for three and a half years. The rest of the time leading up to that period of three and a half years is most likely when the Antichrist will be consolidating his power base. This will begin obviously before the Tribulation, because the Antichrist will be the one who makes the treaty with the Jews at the start of the seven year period. In order to be in a position to make such a treaty, he will have to be on the scene prior to the treaty. According to Daniel, he will break the treaty in the middle of the seven year period, and attack Jerusalem. The time period that follows is what Jesus is referring to in Matthew 24 where it is a time unprecedented in the history of the world.

It would not be unthinkable that the three and a half years leading up to the breaking of the Treaty would be a period that the “wars and rumors of wars,” the seismic activity and other signs would find fulfillment. As many of these global events would actually aid the Antichrist’s cause and give him a platform to show the people of the world how he can solve their problems, causing them to turn to him as the answer.

This is very similar to the world state at the beginning of WWII. Things were so bad in Germany that when Hitler came on the scene, he seemed like he had real solutions to the problems the German people were facing. Because he had tangible solutions that got people back to work, and put food on their tables, the people followed him all the way to the point of carrying out the atrocities that were performed in Hitler's name.

I often say two people changed the course of history dramatically: Jesus and Hitler. Jesus of course for the better, but look how much has changed for the worse just because of Hitler's influence. I believe Hitler was a type of Antichrist, a foreshadowing of things to come, and as much power as he wielded, the Antichrist will be far superior to him, and able to accomplish a great deal of evil in a very short period of time.

The church is the "Bride of Christ," so why would Jesus want to have His bride battered and bruised right before the wedding day?

This is a popular argument of Tim LaHaye. And it is completely unsound. The Church is the Bride of Christ. But it's not just the End Times church or even the "right before the End Times" church, that is the Bride. It is the entire church that is the "Bride of Christ," which includes the battered and bruised 1st century church. The Bride of Christ includes the bruised and battered Christians who fought against Muslim oppression during the Dark Ages. It includes those Christians who were martyred for their faith during the Reformation, as well as the Christians tortured and martyred during the Communist take over of the early 20th century in Russia and China. It includes Christians, like Dietrich Bonhoefer who died in the gas chambers and death camps of Nazi Germany, choosing to die with the Jews instead of shunning them. The Bride of Christ includes those Christians who even today are being condemned, tortured, burned and executed for their faith in countries like Algeria, Saudi Arabia, Iran, Burma, Vietnam and China, etc.

The Bride of Christ *will be bruised and battered* right before the wedding day, because Christ's return is the dramatic rescue of His bride from the clutches of the evil one who has set out to oppress and persecute her for the past 2,000 years. One way or the other, she already is battered, so if the Pre-Tribbers are right, which they are not, but suppose for a minute that they are, 90% of the church around the world is already battered and bruised. Just because of God's kindness and grace you might not be, doesn't mean that the rest of the church isn't.

Paul said that people will be living in a time of Peace and Safety, but the Tribulation is the worst time ever in the history of the world, how will they be crying "Peace and Safety" if we're still around when the Tribulation happens?

The passage being referred to here is found in 1st Thessalonians chapter 5:3.

For when they shall say, Peace and safety; then sudden destruction cometh upon them, as travail upon a woman with child; and they shall not escape. (KJV)

Some people say that there has to be a Pre-Trib Rapture of the church because the people aren't expecting it. But aside from failing to read the conclusion of this passage in 2nd Thessalonians chapter 2, they are also forgetting that Paul is referring to the situation on the earth immediately prior to the return of the Lord. Elsewhere in the Bible we see that this time is unparalleled in human history as the worst time ever. I see that they are crying out for "Peace and Safety," not saying that everything is peaceful and safe. This passage could very well be referring to the response of the masses to the Anti-Christ as a person they believe will be bringing peace and safety to the world.

In a presidential campaign, political demonstrations and even professional sports events, people chant slogans and call out things that they believe their side will accomplish. It very well could be that "Peace and Safety" here is a campaign slogan for the coming world leader. Or there is the possibility that the people believe since they now have their Great World Leader, they have now achieved world peace. And so in their exuberance at finally achieving the impossible they are rejoicing by crying "Peace and Safety."

We can see that there are globalists currently who think that by exterminating a third of the world, they can achieve peace and safety. There are websites and organizations and environmental groups that advocate abortion as a way to reduce carbon emissions and save the planet.

There are trans-humanists, such as Ray Kurzweil, who believe that we will be able to upload our brains into computers in the not too distant future, and achieve a virtual Utopia on earth.

What Christians need to believe is that these people are NOT in opposition to the coming Anti-Christ. They will be *overjoyed* when he arrives to lead the world into global harmony, *world safety and universal peace.*

The situation at the end of the Tribulation will be one in which all of the world opposed to Christians and Jews will be so happy because they think they have finally obliterated those who have opposed their schemes for so long. Of course they will be concerned by the catastrophic events that happen at that time, but they will believe they are just bumps in the road to progress, because their illustrious leader the Antichrist, who had delivered them from so many things, will be able to deliver them from these things as well.

They will be like the Nazi's of WWII who wanted a "Final Solution," to what they perceived as a global problem. The people who follow the Antichrist will be of the same mind-set and will be following the same demonic spirit.

So it makes sense that towards the end of the Great Tribulation they would be crying "Peace and Safety."

In an interesting aside note, on January 20th, 2012, a YouTube user named "Awakened2Truth" uploaded a video entitled "BIble Prophecy Happing NOW -Peace and Security" (sic). In the video there is footage of many world leaders giving speeches where they use the phrase "Peace and Security," in reference to the Middle East crisis. Apparently, this YouTube user believes that we are currently living in a time when the people are saying "Peace and Safety."

If God is loving, why would He hurt His children by making them go through the Tribulation?

Martyrdom. Deut 4:36, 11:2, Job 5:17, Ps 39:11, Ps 94:12, Prov. 3:11.

Also, there are a lot of people today, who think they are His children, just like the Pharisee's when Jesus told them they were children of Satan, who are not really God's children at all. They are not concerned with the things God is concerned about. They do not care about the things God cares about. They will be slain, and punished, and will not even know until the very end that they were never God's children. Jesus told us that we are to take up our cross and follow Him.

One thing that many do not understand is that Jesus uses hardship to discipline his people and to make them holy. In fact in Revelation chapter 3:19 Jesus says that

God disciplines and corrects everyone that He loves. He's saying this in the context of telling the church of Laodicea that He is angry at them. He says He loves them, but will spew them out of His mouth if they do not change.

Just put yourself in their shoes for a second. If you were in that church and Jesus said that to you, would you dare retort, "Yeah, but Jesus, Paul said nothing can separate us from the Love of God"? Of course not! I hope you would find your faith with fear and trembling, repent, and get on fire for Jesus!

Discipline is used by God to bring His rebellious people back in line. We live in a very rebellious time. There are theologians, pastors and teachers teaching all sorts of God-less heresy in the church today, excusing sin and claiming all sorts of doctrines that are contrary to sound Biblical principles. Many say we can "debate these things, but they are not essential to salvation." I would respond by saying, faulty views of many of these so-called peripheral doctrines reflect a faulty exegesis that often leads to a faulty understanding of salvation, because all scripture is God breathed and none of it is peripheral.

Jesus is very clear in this passage, and other passages, that those He loves are in danger of being disciplined and potentially spewed out. This is a really sad thing. Please if you are reading this, and find yourself in this position, please do not harden your heart, but turn from whatever sins you are harboring and chase headlong after our Lord. He loves you, but that won't stop Him from punishing you if you are being rebellious.

One final point here, many people ask this question, but this question really reflects our modern mindset that is preached to us by the likes of Dr. Phil, Oprah and other non-Christian sources. A loving parent disciplines their kids. A parent who does not love their kids allows them to grow up to be unruly. The same God who says He loves us, gave provision to the Israelites to turn their children over to the authorities to be stoned if they were evil lawbreakers. *(see Deut 21:18-21)* He wants us to live righteous lives before Him.

How can there still be saints that are raptured out before the Tribulation, and still be saints going through the Tribulation?

Good question. There can't. We see in Revelation 20:4-6 that the 1st Resurrection is after the Tribulation.

And I saw thrones, and they sat upon them, and judgment was given unto them: and I saw the souls of them that were beheaded for the witness of Jesus, and for the word of God, and which had not worshipped the beast, neither his image, neither had received his mark upon their foreheads, or in their hands; and they lived and reigned with Christ a thousand years. But the rest of the dead lived not again until the thousand years were finished. This is the ***first resurrection.***

Blessed and holy is he that hath part in the first resurrection: on such the second death hath no power, but they shall be priests of God and of Christ, and shall reign with him a thousand years. (Revelation 20:4-6, KJV)

We know that Resurrection is after the Tribulation because this passage includes the Tribulation martyrs who refused to worship the Beast or his image, or take his mark.

Now, during the Tribulation there can be no resurrection of the dead saints before this time because this passage says that this is the 1st Resurrection. We know from what Paul taught us that the 1st Resurrection of the dead happens when the Rapture happens.

And now, dear brothers and sisters, we want you to know what will happen to the believers who have died so you will not grieve like people who have no hope. For since we believe that Jesus died and was raised to life again, we also believe that when Jesus returns, God will bring back with him the believers who have died.

We tell you this directly from the Lord: We who are still living when the Lord returns will not meet him ahead of those who have died. For the Lord himself will come down from heaven with a commanding shout, with the voice of the archangel, and with the trumpet call of God. First, the Christians who have died will rise from their graves. Then, together with them, we who are still alive and remain on the earth will be caught up in the clouds to meet the Lord in the air. Then we will be with the Lord forever. So encourage each other with these words. (I Thessalonians 4:13-18, NLT)

Now if the resurrection of the dead happens at the end of the tribulation, and we know this because in Revelation it includes the Tribulation martyrs in the 1st Resurrection, there can therefore be no Pre-Trib Rapture. It is also important to note here that due to this fact, a Mid-Trib Rapture is impossible as well.

Further insight into this is given in Revelation chapter 7 where we see that the souls of the saints who were martyred during the Great Tribulation were standing before God's throne before the 1st Resurrection.

And all the angels stood round about the throne, and about the elders and the four beasts, and fell before the throne on their faces, and worshipped God, Saying, Amen: Blessing, and glory, and wisdom, and thanksgiving, and honour, and power, and might, be unto our God for ever and ever. Amen. And one of the elders answered, saying unto me, What are these which are arrayed in white robes? and whence came they? And I said unto him, Sir, thou knowest. And he said to me, ***These are they which came out of great tribulation****, and have washed their robes, and made them white in the blood of the Lamb. Therefore are they before the throne of God, and serve him day and night in his temple: and he that sitteth on the throne shall dwell among them. (Revelation 7:11-15, KJV)*

If the Rapture happens before the Tribulation, then these believers will have to wait until the end of the 1,000 years mentioned in this passage. But we can see in the Revelation 20 passage, that they do not have to wait until the Millennium is over.

Another passage to consider is Revelation 12:11 where we see that again the martyrs are mentioned. Almost everyone agrees that there will be martyrs during the Tribulation, but a Pre-Trib and a Mid-Trib explanation does not explain how they get to be included in the 1st Resurrection if it happens before all of their number is accounted for.

In 1 Thess. 4:16-18 we are told to encourage each other about Christ's Second Coming, but talking about having to endure the Tribulation is not encouraging.

This passage is talking about how to cope with grief and death when we lose loved ones. We encourage each other because we know that if we endure and continue to follow God in spite of the horrors we have to endure (similar to the horrors the early church was enduring at the hands of Rome) we will be reunited with our loved ones when Christ does return. See 2 Tim 2:10 that we must endure persecution to be reunited with those who have gone before.

Also, if I were to tell you that in a year your house would be hit by a tornado, but you have a chance to reinforce it to make it withstand the tornado, wouldn't that be an encouragement? Imagine, that instead, if I knew the disaster was coming, but decided not to tell you, wouldn't that be horrible of me?

Don't you think it's *an encouraging thing to be forewarned* that you can have the power and the ability to endure the worst that Satan has to throw at you? I believe it is. God was so kind to spend a great deal of time to warn us of what was to come. And when it is all said and done, He tells us through His word, that those of us who are slain, or who endure until the end will be saved, will be raptured to meet Jesus when He comes back and *will reign with Him though eternity*. That's GREAT news!!!!! How does that not encourage us when we are in the midst of struggle?!?

The fact is, one day, if you are reading this and you are a believer, you might be either persecuted or ridiculed for your faith, possibly jailed for your faith, or maybe even killed for your faith. But *if you endure*, if you survive, if you press on, if you keep going*, Jesus is coming for you!*

That's the encouragement Paul was talking about. In the midst of grieving, in the midst of trying to make sense of senseless slaughter, in the midst of hurting, remember what we have at the end. Don't forget. Encourage each other with the truth that there is hope at the end. One day Jesus will come back for us. He has not forgotten us. In fact, when you see all of these things happening, He said, Look up for your redemption draweth nigh! *(Luke 21:28)*

What does Luke 21:5-36 teach us about the Tribulation time period?

The following section of Luke is taken from the King James Version, and we can study it by sections to examine and see what we will learn about this period of time.

And as some spake of the temple, how it was adorned with goodly stones and gifts, he said, As for these things which ye behold, the days will come, in the which there shall not be left one stone upon another, that shall not be thrown down.

I think it is pretty clear from studying the history that this event happened in 70 AD when the Romans destroyed Jerusalem and drove the Jews out.

And they asked him, saying, Master, but when shall these things be? And what sign will there be when these things shall come to pass?

And he said, Take heed that ye be not deceived: for many shall come in my name, saying, I am Christ; and the time draweth near: go ye not therefore after them. But when ye shall hear of wars and commotions, ***be not terrified:*** *for these things must first come to pass; but the end is not by and by.*

This passage is most likely not referring to the immediate threat that was to happen thirty to forty years later with the Roman destruction of Jerusalem, because Jesus infers that there is a long period of time when many people will claim to be Him. As we see in the next section, Jesus describes events that are on a global scale, nations rising against nations, earthquakes, signs in the heavens, etc.

Then said he unto them, Nation shall rise against nation, and kingdom against kingdom: And great earthquakes shall be in divers places, and famines, and pestilences; and fearful sights and great signs shall there be from heaven. ***But before all these, they shall lay their hands on you, and persecute you, delivering you up***

to the synagogues, and into prisons, being brought before kings and rulers for my name's sake. *And it shall turn to you for a testimony. Settle it therefore in your hearts, not to meditate before what ye shall answer: For I will give you a mouth and wisdom, which all your adversaries shall not be able to gainsay nor resist.*

It seems here Jesus is combining the not too distant events with End Times events here, in the manner of the prophets. When He spoke to and through the prophets He used this technique, and when He spoke to the people when He was here on earth, He used this technique as well. We might not understand why He used this technique so frequently, but regardless of why He used it, it is something that we have to contend with when we study prophecy, and recognize.

In the above passage He is clearly pointing to details that have been a part of church history ever since. People even today are delivered up to authorities for proclaiming the name of Christ all over the world. But this is nothing new, as these events began immediately after Jesus ascended into Heaven.

And ye shall be betrayed both by parents, and brethren, and kinsfolk, and friends; and some of you shall they cause to be put to death. And ye shall be hated of all men for my name's sake. But there shall not an hair of your head perish. In your patience possess ye your souls. And when ye shall see Jerusalem compassed with armies, then know that the desolation thereof is nigh.

This is a fascinating passage. Jesus says here that many will be put to death, but not a single "hair of your head" will perish! This clearly shows that He was teaching about Resurrection, not some type of delivery from the trials.

Jesus also speaks, in this passage, about seeing "Jerusalem compassed with armies." Many amillennialists point to this passage as having been fulfilled during the siege of Rome in 70 AD. However, there have been many times in Jerusalem's history when it was compassed about with armies, many times during the crusades, and during the Israeli wars after the 1948 return to Israel. And even at the time of this writing, we are seeing things arise that very possibly could lead to us seeing Jerusalem compassed about with armies in our time.

I do not think we have to get overly technical here about the use of the word "armies," but it does seem to me that a possible understanding of the use of the plural by Jesus might denote not just one empire or nation, but several nations that assemble at Jerusalem for battle. But in the first century, though there were many nationalities represented by the Roman army, it was technically only one army that surrounded Jerusalem during the 70 AD siege.

Then let them which are in Judaea flee to the mountains; and let them which are in the midst of it depart out; and let not them that are in the countries enter there into. For these be the days of vengeance, that all things which are written may be fulfilled. But woe unto them that are with child, and to them that give suck, in those days! for there shall be great distress in the land, and wrath upon this people. And they shall fall by the edge of the sword, and shall be led away captive into all nations: and Jerusalem shall be trodden down of the Gentiles, until the times of the Gentiles be fulfilled.

It is important to note here that the early Christians did flee from Jerusalem during the 70 AD siege, taking this warning from Jesus literally and running into the mountains. In his book *"Many Infallible Proofs",* A.T. Pierson tells us, *"At this crisis, as we learn from church historians of the first century, all the followers of Christ took refuge in the mountains of Pella, beyond the Jordan, and there is no record of one single Christian perishing in the siege!" (Pierson, 67)*

This passage has to be referring to the 70 AD Roman siege , because He clearly states that the event will cause the time of the Gentiles to begin, and that time will continue until the time of the Gentiles is fulfilled. He also calls this the "Days of Vengeance," a phrase which Margaret MacDonald used to describe the Tribulation. It is very possible that the "Days of Vengeance" and the "Great Tribulation" are two different events. If this is true, then MacDonald was wrong about using that term to refer to the Tribulation as the Days of Vengeance.

However, some contend that these two terms are synonymous, by pointing out Jesus statement that "all things which were written" would be fulfilled during the "Days of Vengeance." If all prophetic events must be fulfilled during a time period known as the "Days of Vengeance," then that would mean that 70 AD wasn't that time period, and it is still to come, quite possibly coinciding with the Great Tribulation, and making them one and the same event.

Another question to consider is: "Who is exacting vengeance here?" The easiest answer would be "the gentiles," or the Romans, but we know that our enemy, as pointed out in the Bible time and time again, is Satan.

So Satan is taking vengeance against "this people," by using Gentiles to attack them.

It is also obvious who Jesus is referring to when He says "this people." He has to be describing the Jews, as they were the ones listening to Him. He had not gathered in many Gentile believers at this point, and He was at the Temple with His followers, the place where Jews worshiped. Unfortunately, this passage is what has lead many to believe that the Tribulation period is only for the Jews.

When we compare this with the rest of Scripture we see that this is clearly not the case, because many places show that the "saints" are persecuted during this time period as well. Again, I think it is possible that Jesus has combined very End Times things with soon to happen prophetic events, by showing what was going to happen with the Roman invasion, the Jews would be scattered, Jerusalem would be trampled under until the time of the Gentiles be fulfilled, and then they would be brought back. He is summing up approximately 2,000 years of prophecy in a single paragraph.

And there shall be signs in the sun, and in the moon, and in the stars; and upon the earth distress of nations, with perplexity; the sea and the waves roaring; Men's hearts failing them for fear, and for looking after those things which are coming on the earth: for the powers of heaven shall be shaken. And then shall they see the Son of man coming in a cloud with power and great glory. And when these things begin to come to pass, then look up, and lift up your heads; for your redemption draweth nigh.

Ok, so here we see Jesus switching to the End Times view again. This did not happen at the siege of

Jerusalem in 70 AD. Jesus isn't just arbitrarily jumping around in time though. He sets it up by explaining that the "time of the Gentiles," must be fulfilled, then He goes on to talk about things that will be signs of His return. It appears according to this passage that we will see signs in the heavens at the start of the Tribulation.

And he spake to them a parable; Behold the fig tree, and all the trees; When they now shoot forth, ye see and know of your own selves that summer is now nigh at hand. So likewise ye, when ye see these things come to pass, know ye that the kingdom of God is nigh at hand.

Many of us have been taught that the Fig Tree represents Israel's rebirth in 1948, as many prophecy scholars claim, but this passage does not give great clarity on that point. The fact is this passage could or could not be pointing to that event. It doesn't seem to be clear enough to use as a proof text for this theory without further support. But what we do learn from this passage that is very clear, is that when we see many of the aforementioned events coming to pass, the Kingdom of God is right on our doorstep.

Verily I say unto you, this generation shall not pass away, till all be fulfilled. Heaven and earth shall pass away: but my words shall not pass away. And take heed to yourselves, lest at any time your hearts be overcharged with surfeiting, and drunkenness, and cares of this life, and so that day come upon you unawares. For as a snare shall it come on all them that dwell on the face of the whole earth. Watch ye therefore, and pray always, that ye may be accounted worthy to escape all these things that shall come to pass, and to stand before the Son of man. (Luke 21:5-36, KJV)

This is perhaps the most important statement to unwrap in this section. Jesus says that "this generation shall not pass away, till all be fulfilled." Preterists claim that all of these events were fulfilled at the siege of Jerusalem in 70 AD, but this clearly isn't true, because Jesus didn't come back then. We're still waiting for Him to come back, so He could not have been referring to the generation that was alive and hearing His teaching that day. He had to be referring to the generation that would actually see the signs that He was referring to, namely those that directly preceded this enigmatic statement.

Then Jesus says a few things that are very important to our discussion here. First He declares that His words will never pass away. It's almost as if He is warning the people that these words are to be stored up for a future time period. Secondly, He issues a stern warning against the things of this world; that we should not get wrapped up in them, because we might not be paying attention. He commands us to watch for these signs. Why are we to watch; so that we can escape all of these things which shall come to pass.

Our pre-trib teachers would like us to believe He said this so we would be ready for the rapture beforehand, but this section clearly does not teach a pre-trib rapture, because it begins with the persecution of His followers, who if the pre-trib people were right, would not be there to be persecuted.

So it is clear that this passage is telling us that there is a chance that we can escape these dangers. *God wants His people to survive, and to be active on the earth during the time of the Tribulation*; to stand firm against the Antichrist and his minions, and to oppose Satan at every opportunity. Sure, there will be some of us who suffer and die, and all of us will feel the sting of persecution, but we have to *stand firm*, we have to continue to proclaim the good news of Jesus, because in just a little while, we will see Him face to face if we do.

Is the "Restrainer" mentioned in 2 Thessalonians 2:7 the Holy Spirit, and if so, if the Holy Spirit is removed during the Tribulation, how can anyone get saved during that time period?

MacPherson has an interesting comment on this topic in his book "The Incredible Cover-Up."

"Although there is widespread disagreement as to who the 'restrainer' is in II Thessalonians 2:7, many pre-tribs feel that he is the Holy Spirit. His partial removal from earth is accomplished, they argue, by the rapture of the believers whom He indwells. Thus they use even this passage in support of their doctrine.

"But if the Holy Spirit's indwelling is missing during the tribulation, it would constitute a return to the 'weak and beggarly elements' which Paul condemns as legalism (Galatians 4:9). The tribulation saints would then retreat from the Master to the schoolmaster. This would also mean that the 144,000, without the indwelling Holy Spirit, would better evangelize the world in seven years than the church has been able to do in nearly two thousand years with *the indwelling Holy Spirit and* without *tribulation intensity all around.*

If, on the other hand, pre-tribs concede that the tribulation saints are indwelt by the Holy Spirit, that damages their assertions about the Holy Spirit being the restrainer. If indwelt believers can't restrain the Antichrist later on, neither can the indwelt church now. All of which disproves the latter-day notion that the Antichrist can't appear while the church remains on earth." (MacPherson, 115-116)

I'd like to take this a step further. If one argues that the Holy Spirit is not necessary for evangelism as the Pre-Trib people who hold this view claim, then what they are really arguing is tantamount to Blasphemy of the Holy Spirit. Without the empowering of the Holy Spirit, we can do nothing of value for the Kingdom, and to say that any believer, in the current age, or during the End Times, can evangelize without His help, is wrong, and treading on very dangerous ground.

One other thing that I must point out is that the teaching that the Holy Spirit is removed in this time is in direct contradiction to Joel 2:28-29 which states that the Holy Spirit will be poured out on that day. While Peter states in Acts that the fulfillment happened at Pentecost, we also know that Joel is also speaking of the Day of the Lord, which as we will see in that chapter, happens at the very end of the Tribulation. So if the Spirit was poured out on Pentecost, as Peter states, then we should expect the Spirit to either continue to be poured out until Jesus returns, or as some argue, to be poured out in an even greater way, during the very end.

Will The European Union start the Tribulation?

The idea that the European Union represents the 10 horns of the Beast's Empire is one that is touted by many Pre-Trib and even Post-Trib theologians.

If a New Age or Occult or Illuminati type Antichrist is going to rise out of Europe, he'd better hurry up and get on with it, because Europe is rapidly becoming an Islamic state. France is over run by Muslims, and is currently trying to pass laws to curtail their spread. Denmark is completely overrun by Muslims, as is England. Germany is passing laws against Muslims. They are infiltrating every aspect of European society and if Jesus should tarry for another 10 years, I suspect that all of Europe will have fallen to the Crescent Moon of Islam.

But this really isn't surprising, because Europe has turned it's back against God, and are reaping the benefits of that decision. The takeover by Islam is really just another arrow pointing to the Apostasy that Jesus and Paul warned would come.

Islam is a great rebellion against God. Islam hates everything that Judaism and Christianity stand for. It is a religion founded by Satan, revealed to an illiterate madman who even claimed that he believed he was being possessed by demons when he first started receiving his visions. Islam is the religion of hate, murder and warfare. It is not a religion of peace, and it elevates and gives a place to all the things that we as Christians believe are evil. And it is on the rise throughout Europe.

Furthermore, the European Union is falling apart due to the bad financial decisions that came from embracing

Socialism. Greece has gone bankrupt, and we see the rise of the Nazi party in Greece. Ireland is in a financial crisis, and on and on it goes, like a wildfire spreading throughout the continent.

I believe we will see the fall of Europe before or around the same time as we see the rise of an Islamic Antichrist. But as I explain later on, I do see that there could be a Roman Catholic false Jesus that works in conjunction with the Antichrist. This could explain many of the theories of many prophecy scholars who see a place for the Roman Catholic church in the Antichrist Empire.

When Will The Tribulation Start?

That's an incredibly difficult question to answer, because there are variables, such as prophecies that we are still waiting to see fulfilled, and even using very accurate Bible chronology it is tricky, because we don't know exact dates when certain events in history happened. There is a margin of error that even the best scholars have a hard time figuring out.

That being said, there are some clues that will tip us off to the start of the Tribulation. When we see a 7 year peace treaty made with Israel that will allow the Temple to be rebuilt, we will have a good understanding of the timing.

There are some speculations that should be addressed and considered.

Daniel in chapter 8 gives us a prophecy about 2,300 days from the overthrow of the Medo-Persian empire as a clue to how long the Jews would be exiled from Israel.

In Daniel 8, he received a vision of a goat and a ram locked in mortal combat. The angel Gabriel gives Daniel some information about the meaning of the dream, how it relates to the End Times events, how it concerns the future history of the Jews, and also information that apparently relates to the coming evil king we now know is the Antichrist, though some argue that all of the info in this passage pertains to Antiochus Epiphanies. Scholars tell us that Alexander overthrew the Medo-Persian empire in 333 or 334 BC.

In the past many have incorrectly interpreted this time by various dates. 7th Day Adventists have incorrectly calculated the date of Christ's return based off of this prophecy coming up with the date of 1844 as the date when Jesus will return. Instead of correcting the error in prophecy that their founder made, they instead now come up with many strange theories to justify this false prophecy.

But it is very interesting to use this prophecy made by Daniel to come up with some interesting dates. In 1754, Thomas Newton came to the conclusion that the time period of Israel's exile would end in 1967. Also, in 1868, Milligan concluded that the period would end in the spring or early summer of 1967. Gabriel informed Daniel that after this period the sanctuary would be cleansed, which seems to imply that there is a time period from the date when the Jews return until they clear the ground to build the temple. Of course the Jews did regain the Temple Mount in June of 1967.

Some history books show that Alexander attacked the Medo-Persian empire in 333 BC, and that would give us a date of 1966 if we added 2300 years to that date. Adam Clark used this method to arrive at the date of

1966, but was off by one year. Others argue that the overthrow of the entire Medo-Persian Empire apparently did not take just one day, but spread over into the year 334 BC as well. And if we work from that year, we correctly arrive at 1967.

Some argue that if we add Daniel's prophecy of 70 years to 1967, it will give us the start of the Tribulation at 2037, however, we must account for the fact that the Tribulation is a time period of 3.5 years and 3.5 years of buildup. So if we subtract the 7 years that are also prophesied by Daniel we arrive at 2030 for the year that the Tribulation starts and 2037 as the year Jesus supposedly would return.

But the problem with this type of calculation is that is always open to different interpretations. For instance, it could be, using the above calculations, that the Tribulation would start at 2037 and bring Christ's return at 2044. This is why it is not very useful to engage in date setting.

Some people also point to Christ's words that "this generation will not pass away," to mean that the generation that sees the Jews take back the Temple Mount will not pass away, and if you add 70 years (the biblical generation) to that number you again get 2037 as the year of Christ's return.

The problem with this reasoning is that we do not know if what Jesus said means the generation that takes the mount, or the generation that is born in the year the mount. If it was the generation that takes the mount, then we'd have to subtract a certain amount to get that figure, but we don't know what number to subtract.

Which is a big reason why this type of speculation does not really get us anywhere. We can't know for certain the exact date of any of these prophecies. However, the careful study of these issues will give us a feeling of urgency as we approach these dates, and hopefully will spur us on to evangelism.

A couple other dates that have been supplied in the past include counting 70 years from 1948, the year Israel was reformed, which would give 2018 as the year Jesus would return, and would make 2011 the year the Tribulation started, though we can clearly see that it did not start then. However, from the fall of 2010 to the beginning of 2011, we did see a great increase in mass animal deaths, which could possibly be a "birth pang" that Jesus describes.

Or consider this, by adding 7 years to the 2018 date (which would meant the Tribulation would start in that year instead of Christ's return) we arrive at 2025 as a possible year when Jesus could return.

But as I just mentioned, this speculation gets us nowhere, and can really make us look foolish and get us branded as false prophets like it did Harold Camping, and many others who tried to place exact dates to Christ's Return. We see from the conclusions of Milligan, Newton and Clark that there can be some fruit in studying the timing of these events, but we can also be incorrect as well, and shouldn't cling dogmatically to our math.

I will recommend Tim Warner's interesting series on the subject of Bible Chronology and End Times events located on his website at www.answersinrevelation.com, where he ties in the Year of Jubilee with many of the End

Times events, for more information on this subject. While I do not agree with all of Warner's conclusions, he does provide a very thought provoking discussion on the topic. The bottom line, however, is keep watching the signs, and expect to go through some hard times ahead before Jesus comes back.

During the End Times "The Love of Many Will Grow Cold." Why Is That and How Will We Over Come Letting Our Love Grow Cold?

Matthew 24:9-14 "Then they will deliver you to tribulation, and will kill you, and you will be hated by all nations because of My name. At that time many will fall away and will betray one another and hate one another. Many false prophets will arise and will mislead many. Because lawlessness is increased, most people's love will grow cold. But the one who endures to the end, he will be saved. This gospel of the kingdom shall be preached in the whole world as a testimony to all the nations, and then the end will come…" (NASV)

Jesus says in this same passage that it is because of the persecution that we endure that the love of many will grow cold. But He also says elsewhere that people will know we are Christ's disciples by our love one for another. We are happy when people say, "That church is full of nice people." But how many times do we hear people say, "Those people at that church really love each other." It is worth the concerted effort to prepare our hears to continue to be filled with love even in the midst of persecution.

Here are a few things to consider. We continue to love each other by:

1. Staying close to God (How do we stay close to God?)
    a. Pray
    b. Give
    c. Fast

These three things are things God told us to do both Publicly and privately (Matthew 6 tells us about private praying, giving and fasting, but other passages call for group praying, giving and fasting)

A couple things to keep in mind. Praying is not just talking to God. It can also be singing to God. Singing can be a powerful way to get through tough times. Remember the Father is looking for worshipers who worship in spirit and in truth (John 4:24). Worship is an act of praying, praising and preparing our hearts to hear from God, all wrapped in one event. It's one of the most powerful weapons we have against discouragement. Consider Paul and Silas singing in jail.

Giving to others and sharing is one of the best ways to reach others in turbulent situations.

Fasting teaches us that our bodies belong to God, and also without God's provision we literally would die. The end result of fasting is thanksgiving, a greater focus on God and more of His power working through our lives.

2. Study God's Word – Study to show yourselves approved (2 Tim 2:15)

It is exciting when you learn something new about God, His love for you, and His way of working in the world.

God's truths revealed when going through persecution will enlighten, encourage and embolden us as we continue to follow Him through hard times.

3. Reach Out – Go into all the world and make disciples (Matthew 28:16-20). It encourages us, and others when we see new people come to Christ. In a time such as the Great Tribulation we will be afraid to do so, but think of the greater reward we will reap if we continue to reach out to others with the Gospel!

4. As we continue to stay close to God, His love flow through us, and it keeps our love from growing cold.

Just what makes the Tribulation the Tribulation?

The Tribulation is God's last ditch effort of showing compassion on a lost world. We see this clearly reflected in Revelation chapter 16, where we see the phrase "but they refused to repent..." repeated several times. God's desire throughout the Tribulation is that lost people would repent and turn to Him.

The Tribulation is a time when the powers of God are manifest in the world, and so are the powers of Satan. These two powerful forces clash in such a way that it spills over into our world, and people (notice even lost people as described in Revelation 16) see it and know where it is coming from.

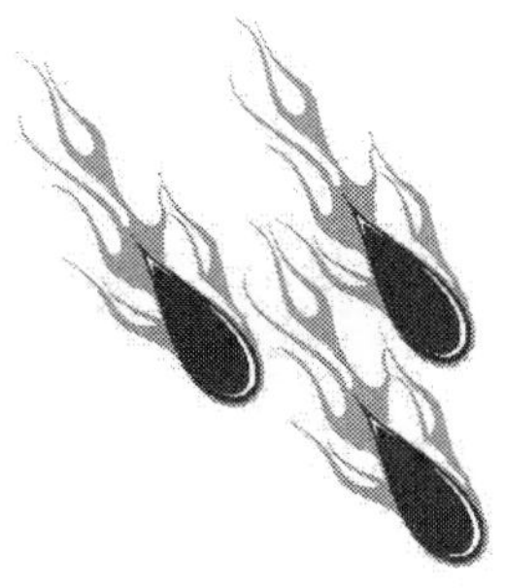

Israel In The End Times

Isn't the Tribulation just for the Jews? Doesn't Jeremiah 30 call the Great Tribulation the "Time of Jacob's Trouble?"

Actually no, the Tribulation is not just for the Jews, and no where in the Bible does it say that. In fact, the passage mentioned here, in Jeremiah 30, is not even talking about the Great Tribulation at all. It is specifically talking about the Diaspora of Israel which happened in 722 BC by the Assyrian army, and the final destruction of Jerusalem and the deportation of Judah to Babylon in 586 BC. I often find that the more I learn about history, the more I realize that Pre-Trib theology is an unacceptable lie. Some people after coming to this conclusion make the vast jump to Amillennialism, throwing out 90% of prophecy. They don't need to do that, because Amillennialism/Partial-Preterism is really a lot like throwing up their hands and admitting defeat, that they can't understand prophecy. They might concede that the easiest way to understand it is to deny its existence, and say that it was all historical.

The fact is there remains a great deal of prophecy left to be fulfilled, and recent events in the Middle East are proving every day that prophecy is being fulfilled. God the Father knew full well when He ordained it that prophecy would be a tool used to bring about the Bible that readers would need it in every generation. It speaks to many events that happened in Israel's past, the present at the time of the writing, the immediate future, and the distant future. We know this because there are Messianic prophesies given as far back as Genesis. So there is the possibility that God can give prophesies for close events such as the Diaspora which was just a few years away from when Jeremiah was prophesying, and as far away as the distance between Adam and Christ when God spoke of the seed of the woman crushing the head of the serpent.

As important as it is to understand that some prophecy is for the far future and some is for the near future of the original audience, it is equally as important to understand as much about the history of the Jews as we can, so we can discern which prophecies were fulfilled, and which ones were to be fulfilled in the future. The return of the Jews, those descendants from the tribe of Judah, began in 438 BC, when Ezra the scribe led a group back to rebuild the temple, but the so called "Lost Tribes" of Israel are only now just starting to come back into the land, as many Jewish Messianic organizations attest to.

If you read the rest of Jeremiah 30, 31 and chapter 32, you will see that God prophesied a coming time when the Jews as well as the rest of the tribes of Israel would return to the Land, and in that day, they would never again be driven out of their land. That day came on May 14th, 1948. So, I believe this passage shows that even during the Great Tribulation, the Jews will remain in their land and will not be driven out, though they will be at war with the rest of the world, and the Anti-Christ.

As a matter of fact, 2 Chronicles 36:21 explains that a lot of Jeremiah's prophecy was fulfilled with the deportation and reestablishment of the Jews after the exile to Babylon. This is also stated again in Ezra 1:1.

Ezra 1:1 (NLT)

Cyrus Allows the Exiles to Return

In the first year of King Cyrus of Persia, the LORD fulfilled the prophecy he had given through Jeremiah. He stirred the heart of Cyrus to put this proclamation in writing and to send it throughout his kingdom:

Furthermore, the whole concept that the Tribulation is only for the Jews seems to be based on racism and anti-Semitic, and goes against Paul's teaching in Galatians 3:28 and Colossians 3:11 that in Christ there is neither Jew nor Greek, and Peter's teaching in Acts 15:8-9 that both the Jew and the Greek are purified by faith in Christ.

Also, the teaching that the Tribulation is a time when the Jews will come to know Christ is faulty, as currently there is going on in Israel the biggest Christian revival ever since the first century, with many Jews coming to Christ. Even whole towns in Israel are now Messianic today. All of this is happening *before* the Great Tribulation.

There is another side of the argument which stems from a faulty theology known as Replacement Theology, which claims that the Jews have no place in God's plan anymore, but there are numerous passages in the Old and New Testaments that say that God will never revoke his promises to Abraham, Moses and David. Replacement Theology is also racist, completely not biblical and unfounded.

Romans 11:17-18 teaches us that we are grafted into the vine of Israel, and have received their blessings. Paul used this imagery for a particular reason. When a farmer grafts onto an olive tree for instance, the tree is hacked off at the stump, but then new branches from a productive tree are inserted in place of the old growth. The new branches essentially become the old tree. The old tree is not replaced, it gives life to the new branches.

There are several important questions we should ask ourselves:

"What about Jewish believers now? Will they be raptured in a Pre-Trib scenario, or will they be left behind to preach to their brothers?"

Of course, they would be raptured as well because they are believers. It is interesting that Jeremiah 30:7 calls the

Tribulation the "Time of Jacob's Trouble," but He goes on to say that they will be saved "out from it," using the same type of phrasing that Jesus gives in Revelation that so many Pre-Trib people use for the Rapture. Now if Israel is saved out from it, why aren't they raptured too? The logic is faulty here.

Another question to consider: "But if current Jewish believers are not left behind, who will preach, because the Bible tells us that 'faith comes from hearing the word of God?'"

This is a good point that we discussed briefly in an earlier section. If the current messianic Jewish believers are left behind, they would then most likely fulfill the 144,000 Jews that are mentioned in Revelation. So there would be no need for other Jews to become saved during the Tribulation, which would mean that if the purpose of the Tribulation is so the Jews will become Christians, then it would be pointless.

Of course the Tribulation is not only for the Jews. But the truth is some Jews today argue that the Pre-Trib doctrine is highly anti-Semitic and racist just because of this idea. The fact is some Jews will accept Jesus (many already do) and some won't. Just like some Gentiles will accept Jesus and some won't. But this has nothing to do with the Tribulation. The Tribulation is a time of trial on the *entire world*, as it says in Revelation 3:10. It's not just for Jews, not just for Christians, we see in Revelation 16:11 that even the purpose of God's wrath is so people of the world will repent. The Tribulation is a time to bring repentance upon anyone who needs to repent. We know from John 3 that God's desire is for all the world to be saved.

The book of Revelation was written for and directed to the 7 churches, so in a very real sense, we see from the very start of the book that the entire book of Revelation is for the church, not only for Tribulation saints, not only for End Times Jews. And furthermore, Revelation is said to be the only book that comes with a blessing for those who read it. *What is that blessing? It is the warning that comes from reading the book for those who must go through the Tribulation, to be prepared.*

But aren't the "elect" that are referred to in Matthew 24 just the Jews who are around in the Tribulation?

No, every reference to "elect" in the NT refers to the Saints, not to unbelieving Jews, or to only believing Jews. Almost every time we see the word "elect" used in the NT, whether in a gospel, epistle or in Revelation, it refers to believers.

The notion that some Pre-Trib theologians claim that this word is only referring to Jews is really baseless. There are three things that could be happening here:

Either Pre-Trib teachers are just passing information on without studying it for themselves…

They are performing incredibly bad exegesis of the text…

Or they are just out right lying because they know there is no way this could ever be taken this way.

Any way you look at it, any theologian who would claim this is either a mistaken theologian, or a false teacher. Either way true believers do not want to listen to anyone who would make this claim.

But isn't the point of mentioning 144,000 that there will be 12,000 Jews from each tribe of Israel saved in the Great Tribulation? Why isn't the Tribulation just for the Jews?

The calling out of the 144,000 is only one event that happens during the Tribulation, not the entire point of the Tribulation. We are told in James 1:1-9 that trials and tribulations are used to purify us and make us patient, and we are also told that God will purify Christ's bride, i.e. the church, in 1 Peter.

We're also told that "it rains on the just and the unjust," implying that good and bad both come to those who are good and bad, but one day we can be sure there will be a reckoning. However, that day isn't until the very end of the Tribulation when Christ *physically* returns. We have been here for all sorts of calamity, and yes, God has delivered a great number of us from calamity and disaster, but some of us have perished and gone on to be with Him. That doesn't mean He doesn't love us. There is no reason for the Tribulation to be only for the Jews. All believers are part of the Bride of Christ, not just the Gentile believers. The early Jewish believers and the early Gentile believers are part of the Bride of Christ too. Modern day Gentile believers and modern day Jewish believers are also part of the Bride of Christ. To argue that the later Jewish believers are out of luck and have to endure the Tribulation makes no sense. Tribulation happens to all of God's people.

When the Babylonians came in and conquered Jerusalem, some did escape, while others who were righteous were brought to Babylon, among them Daniel, Shadrach, Meshach and Abednego. And God raised them up as seers, prophets and righteous men even while in captivity.

Now among these were of the children of Judah, Daniel, Hananiah, Mishael, and Azariah: Unto whom the prince of the eunuchs gave names: for he gave unto Daniel the name of Belteshazzar; and to Hananiah, of Shadrach; and to Mishael, of Meshach; and to Azariah, of Abednego.

But Daniel purposed in his heart that he would not defile himself with the portion of the king's meat, nor with the wine which he drank: therefore he requested of the prince of the eunuchs that he might not defile himself. (Daniel 1:6-8, KJV)

There will be 144,000 believers from all of the tribes of Israel called out to serve God during the Tribulation, but just because that is an event that is mentioned, we are nowhere told that the 144,000 believers are the only believers left alive on the earth.

The context of this passage shows that in addition to the 144,000 believers from the tribes of Israel, there are countless others who are Gentile believers.

And after these things I saw four angels standing on the four corners of the earth, holding the four winds of the earth, that the wind should not blow on the earth, nor on the sea, nor on any tree.

And I saw another angel ascending from the east, having the seal of the living God: and he cried with a loud voice to the four angels, to whom it was given to hurt the earth and the sea, Saying, Hurt not the earth, neither the sea, nor the trees, till we have sealed the servants of our God in their foreheads.

And I heard the number of them which were sealed: and there were sealed an hundred and forty and four thousand of all the tribes of the children of Israel. Of the tribe of Judah were sealed twelve thousand. Of the tribe of Reuben were sealed twelve thousand. Of the tribe of Gad were sealed twelve thousand. Of the tribe of Asher were sealed twelve thousand. Of the tribe of Nephthali were sealed twelve thousand. Of the tribe of Manassas were sealed twelve thousand. Of the tribe of Simeon were sealed twelve thousand. Of the tribe of Levi were sealed twelve thousand. Of the tribe of Issachar were sealed twelve thousand. Of the tribe of Zebulon were sealed twelve thousand. Of the tribe of Joseph were sealed twelve thousand. Of the tribe of Benjamin were sealed twelve thousand.

After this I beheld, and, lo, a great multitude, which no man could number, of all nations, and kindreds, and people, and tongues, stood before the throne, and before the Lamb, clothed with white robes, and palms in their hands; And cried with a loud voice, saying, Salvation to our God which sitteth upon the throne, and unto the Lamb. (Revelation 7:1-10, KJV)

The context of this passage reflects what Romans 1 and 2 says, "to the Jew first, and then to the Gentile." First the Jewish believers are sealed, and then the Gentile believers are sealed, and they all worship God.

Some would like to say that this second paragraph included here reflects the raptured saints in heaven rejoicing over their Jewish brothers who are saved, but it doesn't say that. It says that *all* of these people, including the Jews, are standing before the throne, but we're told in Hebrews 4:16 that we can go boldly before the throne of grace. When we pray we are already before the throne of God. So this passage more likely refers to the entire group of believers crying out in praise.

There are two parallels to this passage. One is found in Ezekiel.

And the glory of the God of Israel was gone up from the cherub, whereupon he was, to the threshold of the house. And he called to the man clothed with linen, which had the writer's inkhorn by his side; And the LORD said unto him, Go through the midst of the city, through the midst of Jerusalem, and set a mark upon the foreheads of the men that sigh and that cry for all the abominations that be done in the midst thereof. And to the others he said in mine hearing, Go ye after him through the city, and smite: let not your eye spare, neither have ye pity: Slay utterly old and young, both maids, and little children, and women: but come not near any man upon whom is the mark; and begin at my sanctuary. Then they began at the ancient men which were before the house. (Ezekiel 9:3-6, KJV)

The other passage is found in Exodus.

And they shall take of the blood, and strike it on the two side posts and on the upper door post of the houses, wherein they shall eat it. And they shall eat the flesh in that night, roast with fire, and unleavened bread; and with bitter herbs they shall eat it. Eat not of it raw, nor sodden at all with water, but roast with fire; his head with his legs, and with the purtenance thereof. And ye shall let nothing of it remain until the morning; and that which remaineth of it until the morning ye shall burn with fire. And thus shall ye eat it; with your loins girded, your shoes on your feet, and your staff in your hand; and ye shall eat it in haste: it is the LORD's passover.

For I will pass through the land of Egypt this night, and will smite all the firstborn in the land of Egypt, both man and beast; and against all the gods of Egypt I will execute judgment: I am the LORD. And the blood shall be to you for a token upon the houses where ye are: and when I see the blood, I will pass over you, and the plague shall not be upon you to destroy you, when I smite the land of Egypt. (Exodus 12:7-13)

This demonstrates a biblical pattern that God has used this method of delivery for His people in the past. He marks those who are His followers so that when disaster strikes, they can be delivered out of the situation.

At this point in the Revelation narrative God's wrath is brewing and is about to be unleashed upon the world that has rejected Him and His people. As we see in verse 1 of this chapter. Four mighty angels were holding back the four winds of the earth. They are spoken to by the angel who is bearing the seal of God, and commands these other angels not to harm the earth, yet, because he is getting ready to mark all of those faithful to God.

What follows in the next chapter is the opening of the seventh seal, and then after that the catastrophe is loosed upon the earth for the next several chapters. And in chapter 9 we see that the beasts that are unleashed upon the earth do not have authority to hurt those with the mark of God on their foreheads.

So even in the midst of the Great Tribulation, God is looking out for His people, and protecting them through the evils that are ahead.

I heard that Israel isn't important to End Times events. I was taught the Church took over all of the promises God gave to Israel because we are grafted in. Weren't the Jews cut off from God's promises?

Nowhere does it say that the church replaced the Jews as God's chosen people, or that the people of the church usurped the promises that He made specifically to the Children of Israel. In fact, we are told in the Scriptures that God never revokes His promises. (See 2 Samuel 22:31, Nehemiah 9:8, Psalm 12:6, etc.) We're also told by Paul that God isn't finished with the Jews. He says in Romans 11:1 that "God has not rejected His people." God has a plan for Israel that will connect the beginnings of time all the way to the end, from Abraham, to the 2nd Coming. Paul even goes on to say that God still loves Israel. Replacement Theology outright contradicts the Bible.

Furthermore, some would say that God's promises to Israel will not be fulfilled, because the Jews didn't keep the terms of God's covenant, so He rejected them. But what about all the faithful Jews that did keep His covenant, such as Simeon and others who were looking for the Messiah to come? Almost all of the earliest converts were Jews. So how can anyone say that God's promise to Abraham was revoked, when those Jews were faithful? We see in many places that God was willing to start over with the faithful people He had, such as Noah, Lot, Moses, etc. So this information coupled with Paul's declaration that God is not finished with the Jews destroys so-called Replacement Theology.

Way back in Genesis, God promised a great deal of land to Abraham. When God made His promise to Abraham, there was no conditional clause in the promise. Over the years, the Jews never did anything to revoke that promise. Even killing Jesus was not enough to condemn the Jews. The crucial part of this that some Christians forget is that Jesus was destined to die for our sins. If the Jews didn't hand Him over, the prophesies would not have been fulfilled, and none of us would have been saved. So in a way, we have the 1st Century Jews to thank for playing their part in God's marvelous plan of salvation.

Yet foolish theologians do not understand this, though God saw it all before the foundation of the earth. These theologians somehow think that the Jews surprised God by the part they played in Jesus' crucifixion. God wasn't surprised. He knew when He made His promise to

Abraham that his descendants would deny Him and reject His Son. But He chose to make that promise anyway. And He did so in such a way that there can be no doubt as to the length of the terms of the contract. In Genesis 13:14-15 God tells Abraham that it is an "everlasting promise." Everlasting seems like a long time to me. God didn't say, "Abraham, I'm making you an everlasting promise that will last about… well, never. I'm never really going to give you all the land that I promised you. Let's just say it's spiritual. Here's the land. You can have it all. Spiritually. In your heart. It's all yours."

That isn't what God said. He said it was an everlasting promise. So there will come a day when God fulfills it. What God says He will do, He will bring about.

Furthermore, some say God's promise is fulfilled, because all of the Arabs are descendants of Ishmael. However, Genesis 21:12 teaches us that the covenant will be fulfilled through Isaac, not Ishmael. So the Muslims and Arabs are not the fulfillment of this promise.

Others argue that God fulfilled it during the reign of Solomon, but archeology doesn't demonstrate any veracity to this claim.

Some claim that based on our being grafted in that Jesus is the fulfillment of this promise, but again that goes back to the spiritual fulfillment, but not the physical fulfillment.

I believe this promise to Abraham will be completely fulfilled spiritually and physically in the Millennium, as we will see in the section on the Millennium.

Jeremiah 7:7 says that when God finally gives Israel to the descendants of Abraham, nothing will ever take them away from that land, because they will live in that land forever. I believe this is true, and I believe that since we

A picture of the entire land of Israel as promised to Abraham. Some scholars debate the full extent of the borders, but this picture represents the entire possible land that was promised. The Nile River

is on the left, travels through Egypt all the way down to Ethiopia and Somalia. The Wilderness is the entire land covering Modern Day Saudi Arabia and all of the countries to the south, the Euphrates is on the right and goes from the Persian Gulf up to Turkey, and the land of the Hitites covered the bulk of the modern country of Turkey. These promises were given in Genesis 15, Exodus 23:22, and Deuteronomy 11. Some scholars argue that the Hittite kingdom extended all the way down to Jerusalem at the time Abraham received the promise, and so the northern portion of Israel, should be cut off not much farther than modern day Lebanon. However, the text says that the land occupied by these various nations would be given, therefore, I have concluded that God meant the entire portion of those kingdoms would be given to Abraham.

saw the re-birth of Israel on May 14th, 1948 we will never see Israel destroyed completely or the Jews completely kicked out of the region. There will be tribulation, hardship and what seems like absolute disaster, but the day will come when they call for the messiah to rescue them from the Antichrist, and then Jesus will come.

Some theologians argue that Jesus fulfilled everything promised to Abraham, but did Jesus really fulfill *everything* that was promised to Israel and Abraham? Of course not! Jesus did not conquer the land that was given to Abraham. He didn't stay in the land forever. He moved on to heaven!

Also some theologians like to say that the word "everlasting" doesn't always mean forever, because some things mentioned, such as sacrifices, etc. were said to be "everlasting," but they clearly aren't because they were ended. I would argue that the animal sacrifices ended, but we see the reason why in Hebrews 13:15

where it tells us that they were replaced by Jesus as a continual sacrifice to God. So the sacrifices are "everlasting." And in the same way, we can believe that God's covenant with Abraham, and the other promises He gave to Israel are still good.

The fact is the Bible is clear that we are grafted into Israel's blessings. God didn't provide the image of grafting flippantly. He specifically chose that on purpose. Grafting is a process where the original plant is hacked off, but the roots are retained. Then new branches are placed into the cut and sealed with a sealant. The plant then begins to grow from that point. This does not stop the original plant from producing more branches. And we can see this clearly in the revival that is taking place in Israel right now, where many Jews are becoming Messianic Believers. It is obvious to anyone who will just take the time to look, that God is not finished with Israel yet.

When examining this subject, we should ask ourselves if we believe anti-Zionist propaganda because it's biblical, or because we don't see how God can bless a very secular nation like Israel? I believe that God will turn Israel into a very Holy Nation, and as a Believer shouldn't that be your hope too?

I use the word propaganda above, because much of this propaganda stems from the Palestinian terrorists who are trying to say they are segregated and have no place, when in reality they are Jordanian, and have a country that they could go to. The fact is that before modern

Israel was given to the Jews the entire area belonged to the country of Jordan. The British took control of the area and gave the historic region that had belonged to the Jews back to them. Many Jordanians refused to leave and began to call themselves Palestinians. I would challenge any one who doubts to look into the history for yourselves. God is not finished with the Jews.

What is the Significance of the 3rd Temple?

The 3rd Temple will be built, and it will be the temple mentioned in a great deal of the End Time prophesies. At some point the Antichrist will seat himself in the Temple and declare that he is God and demand worship. This has never happened, and though some events came close, the prophecies that are pointed to as belonging to a 3rd Temple by dispensationalists, have yet to be fulfilled.

There are several questions that should probably be addressed about the 3rd Temple and they are listed below.

I think it is very interesting to note that the 3rd Temple is actively being discussed even now. In an article found at http://www.israelnationalnews.com/News/News.aspx/164007 entitled "Israel Planning To Build Holy Temple, Claims PA Official," which was published on January 9, 2013, we see that talk of building the 3rd Temple is thrust into the spotlight in recent weeks as tensions mount in the middle east over the Arab Israeli conflict. Of course, the person claiming that Israel is planning on building the

Temple is a Palestinian, but that just goes to show that the topic is hot right now, and is only getting hotter as we move towards the Day of the Lord.

Another interesting thing about the Temple Mount that is relevant here is brought out by L.A. Marzuli in "The Cosmic Chessmatch," where he points out that the Dome of the Rock (as well as Mecca and Medina) is controlled by the King Hussein of Jordan, one of the last remaining Hashemite kings (Bani Hashem), kings that are considered direct descendants of Abraham. Hashemites trace their lineage from the Arab chieftain Quraysh, to their prophet Ismail (Ishmael) and to Abraham. They get their title "Hashemite" from a descent of Quraysh, Qurayy bin Kilab, who ruled Mecca in the year 480 AD. His grandson was named Hashem, and he was supposed to be Mohammed's great grandfather. And so they claim direct descent from Mohammed from his daughter Fatima and her husband Ali bin Abi Talib who was Mohammed's first cousin. *(more info on this can be found in Marzulli's book, as well as www.kinghussein.gov.jo/has_intro.html which gives a great deal of info on King Hussein.)*

As a direct descendant of Abraham and Mohammed, he wields great power in both the Suni and Shia'a Islamic worlds. He is a key player to watch in the rebuilding of the 3rd temple, and even makes him a possible candidate for the Antichrist in the current geo-political climate.

One final thing to include here is that the 3rd Temple will most likely be destroyed during the final onslaught of the

Antichrist. There are several passages that point to this, but one that stands out to me is Amos 9:11, where God says He will raise up the tabernacle of David that had fallen down. What tabernacle did David make? Well, it was David's plans that were put into action by Solomon and became Solomon's Temple. So it is quite possible that though the temple will be rebuilt, it may just as well be destroyed in the conflict caused by the Antichrist.

Was the Pig Sacrificed on the Holy Altar in 170 BC by Antiochus Epiphanes the Abomination that Causes Desolation spoken of by Daniel the Prophet?

No, it was not. I know there seems to be some confusion about this out there, but we know that it was not because Jesus speaks of the Abomination that causes Desolation again, as something that would happen in the future, as a sign that His coming was at hand. But the Antiochus Epiphanes event happened 170 years before Jesus was born. So how is it possible that it could be a sign of His 2nd Coming? It couldn't. It was, however, one of the events that Daniel prophesied would happen, and is most likely a foreshadowing of the Abomination of Desolation that is going to come.

Was the sacking of the Temple by the Roman 10th Legion the Abomination that Causes Desolation? –

No, because they completely destroyed the temple, and does not fit in with the details of the prophecy. It was however, a fulfillment of Jesus' prophecy that not a stone would be left standing of the Temple. In fact, only a small portion of the wall around the Temple remains to this day, known as the "Wailing Wall," but not one stone of the Temple was left standing.

Is The Dome of the Rock, also known as the Al Aqsa Mosque, the Abomination that Causes Desolation?

It most certainly is an abomination, as it sits enthroned on the mountain where Abraham offered Isaac as a sacrifice to God, exalting the Arabian moon god which was originally called Sin *(which is where our word "sin" came from originally)* but who is often referred to as Allah and commonly mistaken to be the same God as the Bible. *(Incidentally, "Allah" comes from the word "Al-ilah - the Diety;" Steve Quayle does a great job discussing this topic in his well documented book "Angel Wars," on pg 211, as well as Walid Shoebat in "Why I Left Jihad," both must have books in my opinion.)* So an abomination the Al Aqsa Mosque clearly is.

However, is it the Abomination that Causes Desolation? We can't be sure that it is. For one thing, Paul tells us in 2 Thessalonians 2 that the "man of lawlessness" is the one who causes desolation by sitting in the temple and proclaiming that he is God. Mohammed, as evil as he was, never claimed to be God.

However, one could argue that the spirit of lawlessness is certainly present in the Muslim religion as their Sharia law has many aspects that we would consider lawlessness. Consider, for example, how one of the various types of jihad *(Islamic holy war)* calls for deception when dealing with anyone one they consider an infidel in order to prosper and eventually take over, which of course most Christians would consider lawlessness. This type of jihad comes in two forms *taqiyya*, saying something that isn't true, and *kitman*, lying by omission, two tactics practiced by Mohammed in his dealings with people of other religions.

While I am not completely convinced that the current mosque is *the* abomination, some argue that a close reading of Daniel 9 points to the idea that perhaps the Dome of the Rock could be the abomination desolation.

Consider for instance these very different translations of Daniel 9:27:

The King James

And he shall confirm the covenant with many for one week: and in the midst of the week he shall cause the sacrifice and the oblation to cease, and for the overspreading of abominations he shall make it desolate, even until the consummation, and that determined shall be poured upon the desolate.

The New Living Translation

The ruler will make a treaty with the people for a period of one set of seven, but after half this time, he will put an end to the sacrifices and offerings. And as a climax to all his terrible deeds, he will set up a sacrilegious object that causes desecration, until the fate decreed for this defiler is finally poured out on him.

The New American Standard

And he will make a firm covenant with the many for one week, but in the middle of the week he will put a stop to sacrifice and grain offering; and on the wing of abominations will come one who makes desolate, even until a complete destruction, one that is decreed, is poured out on the one who makes desolate.

The NIV

He will confirm a covenant with many for one 'seven.' In the middle of the 'seven' he will put an end to sacrifice and offering. And at the temple he will set up an abomination that causes desolation, until the end that is decreed is poured out on him.

The NIV Footnotes

Daniel 9:27 Or: *And one who causes desolation will come upon the wing of the abominable temple, until the end that is decreed is poured out on the desolated city.*

The Septuagint

And one week shall establish the covenant with many: and in the midst of the week my sacrifice and drink-offering shall be taken away: and on the temple shall be the abomination desolations; and at the end of time an end shall be put to the desolation.

By looking at all of these texts, we begin to see the possibility that the Abomination Desolation is in fact a temple that is dedicated to evil.

The KJV gives us the idea that after a certain amount of time passes the Abominable thing will be destroyed, or made desolate. The NLT makes it appear that the one being destroyed is the one who makes the sacrilegious object, but it appears from the context that both the one who makes the object and the object are destroyed when the time comes.

The NASV makes it appear that the abominations are brought along with the one who defiles the temple, but that he will be destroyed when his time comes. And the NIV seems to agree with the NASV and the NLT. But the NIV footnotes and the Septuagint seem to point to the fact that it is a temple that IS indeed the Abomination Desolation, and that it will remain in place until the time of the end, when it will be destroyed.

So what conclusions can we draw from this study? Well, for one thing, it appears that there is some disagreement with the translators over what this phrase really means in the Hebrew. But we can see that one could argue that the Abomination that causes Desolation is a Temple, and it will be set up by either the Antichrist, or an antichrist figure.

The Dome of the Rock is a sacrilegious object (temple) dedicated to a demonic entity, not YHWH, or Jehovah of the Bible. It was set up by a culture that was founded by an antichrist type figure. In order to build the 3rd Temple, it would need to either be taken out of the way, or the Temple would have to be built in such a way to incorporate it into the design structure, causing it to be possibly on the "wing of the temple." And it will most certainly be destroyed by Jesus when He returns or before, as it does not belong on God's holy mountain.

In a scenario where the Antichrist is also the Muslim Mahdi, it is very reasonable to imagine him sitting in the Dome of the Rock and proclaiming that he is God.

Is the Third Temple Being Built now?

As of this writing, no. However, plans are in preparation to rebuild the Temple. You can find out a great deal of information from the Temple Institute. They have a large menorah and all of the other articles that are needed to outfit the temple.

It appears that the building pieces of the temple are being built now, and when they are ready, the Temple could be assembled in a matter of months.

Now, for those who do not believe that Jerusalem belongs to the Jews, that the Jews have no place in prophecy, and that the Temple referred to in prophecy is the one destroyed by the Romans, why is God allowing them to progress so far in their plans to rebuild it? The fact remains, God still has a plan for the Jews.

Are Jews Returning To Israel?

I find it interesting that recently pressure on Jews to stop performing circumcisions seems to be increasing in many countries. At the time of this writing, groups in Germany, Sweden, San Francisco and several other places are trying to get legislation passed to ban circumcisions based on the faulty reasoning that it is inhumane to children. On message boards under several articles that I have read, many Jews from Israel are recommending that Jews in these places return to Israel. I find this very interesting because another prophecy is that in the end times all the Jews will be living in Israel. We could find in the very near future a great migration of Jews from all over the world returning to Israel.

In fact, while I was working in New York, I worked part time delivering large boats to different parts of the state. I remember driving through several towns that were almost ghost towns, and asking my boss what happened. He explained that the towns we passed were once Jewish towns, and that most of the people had moved to Israel. So, I think the chances are good that more and more Jews will return to fulfill prophecy in the very near future.

At the time of this writing an article was released where Israel was asking the Pope to return several articles from the Temple that are known to be housed in the Vatican. Only time can tell what will come of this interesting development.

Who are the Two Witnesses and when do they arrive on the scene, and are they Elijah and Enoch, or Elijah and Moses or Enoch and Moses?

In Revelation 11 we are introduced to two witnesses who are released at the End of Time. Some people want to pick out which two prophets these two individuals will be, but the fact is we just do not have enough information. Some claim that the prophets will be Enoch and Elijah because they were two prophets who were "Raptured," but usually the people who claim this are Pre-Trib. If God returns these prophets that Pre-Tribbers use to point to a Pre-Trib rapture, then it actually would defeat their Pre-Trib argument, because the very prophets they point to in an attempt to prove their viewpoint would be going through the Tribulation.

Some claim that these two prophets are symbolic, representing the church and Israel, or many other possible symbols, but we simply do not know for sure. I believe they will literally be two prophets, but that is because, as mentioned earlier, I hold to a more literal interpretation of Revelation than many other writers.

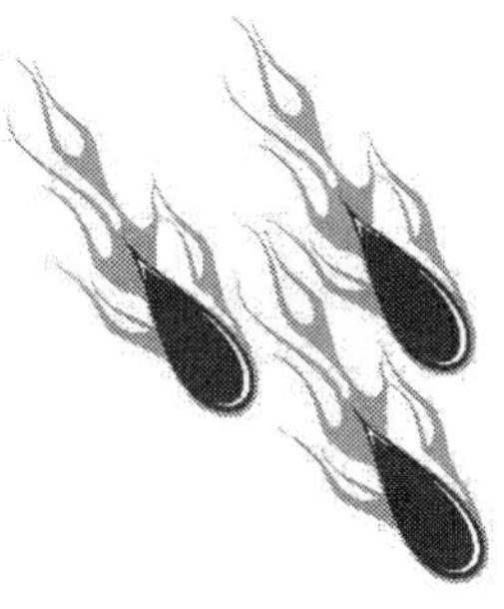

The Resurrection

What is the difference between the 1st Resurrection and the 2nd Resurrection, and when do both of these events take place? Also, who will be at these two events?

This is an interesting question. You are referring to two different events. The first Resurrection happens when Jesus returns, when the dead in Christ rise first, as Paul tells us in I Cor. 15 and 1 Thess. 4. When this happens, Revelation 20 shows us that at this Resurrection we see the ones given authority to judge sitting on thrones (we see in Matthew 19:28, that it is the apostles sitting on these thrones), we also see the souls of those who were beheaded during the Tribulation in the same scene.

There is a curious phrase here that tells us that the rest of the dead did not come alive again until after the thousand years had ended. Many people think this means that only certain people are resurrected at this point. This is not true. What this is referring to is that there are people who die after the Millennium starts. Those people who are the descendants of the survivors from the Tribulation into the Millennium will continue to live normal lives, under the rule of Christ. We will talk about this more in the section on the Millennium, however for the sake of clarity here, you should know that there will be people who live after the Tribulation, who are not resurrected/glorified. These people are described by Joel and Isaiah and referenced by John.

The 2nd Resurrection is at the end of the Millennium when all of the souls of people who lived out their lives during the Millennium are resurrected. Then they (along with all of the non-Christians who lived before the Tribulation) will be judged at the Great White Throne of Judgment, referred to at the end of Revelation 20.

This is also another powerful example of why we are not raptured before the Tribulation. If we were raptured before the Tribulation, these tribulation martyrs would not be included in this number, because they would have missed the rapture, missed getting glorified bodies, etc. But we see in this passage that they do have glorified bodies and are included in the number of other saints (such as the Apostles who are there, who as Paul tells us would have to be included in that number), so the Rapture has to happen after the tribulation because the Tribulation Martyrs are there.

When do we receive our Resurrection Bodies?

We read in Philippians 3:20 and 21:

"For our citizenship is in heaven, from which also we eagerly wait for a Savior, the Lord Jesus Christ; who will transform the body of our humble state into conformity with the body of His glory, by the exertion of the power that He has even to subject all things to Himself." (NASV)

We read here that we are waiting for Jesus to return to do this miraculous thing that will make our bodies like His. The New Living Translation demonstrates this even more.

"But we are citizens of heaven, where the Lord Jesus Christ lives. And we are eagerly waiting for him to return as our Savior. He will take our weak mortal bodies and change them into glorious bodies like his own, using the same power with which he will bring everything under his control." (NLT)

So we can see in this passage that when Jesus returns He will transform us. Another passage makes this clear as well. In 1 Corinthians 15:52 we read that this transformation will happen immediately, "in the twinkling of an eye…"

"In a moment, in the twinkling of an eye, at the last trump: for the trumpet shall sound, and the dead shall be raised incorruptible, and we shall be changed." (KJV)

When Jesus returns, at the Last Trump, which we will talk about more later, we will be raised up to meet Him in the air, as described in I Thessalonians 4, and at that moment we will be changed. So we can see that when Jesus Returns, it will happen when the Last Trump sounds, at the moment of His return, we will be raised into the air, and at that moment, we will be changed into our Resurrection Bodies.

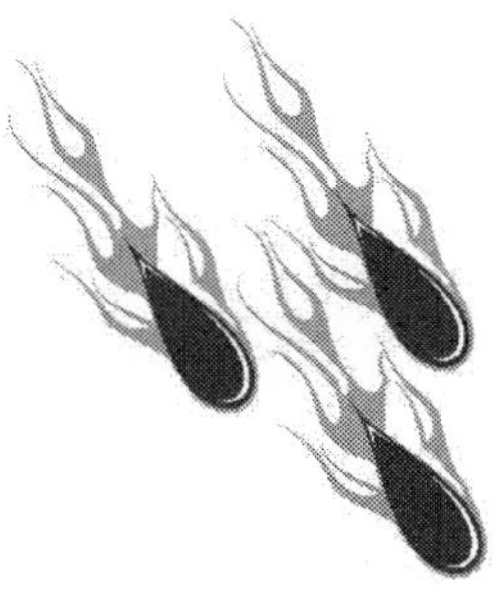

The Return

Matthew 24:44 teaches that Jesus will come unexpectedly, so isn't Christ's return imminent, in other words, couldn't He come at any time?

Why did Jesus warn his disciples about this if He didn't want them to be looking for it and expecting it? The mere fact that He taught about it means that He wants the Church to expect it. He means that the *World* won't expect it. He wouldn't be giving us signs to watch for if we weren't to expect it. See Matthew 24:29-30, also Rev. 3:3 *(if you wake up you will know when He's coming)* also 1 Thess. 5:4-5. The Matthew passage shows that the prophecy of Joel concerning the moon, stars and sun turning black must happen first so believers will expect His coming. Also in Joel it talks about people calling on His name to be saved and He will save them. This would seem to show that some people who had heard about the Second Coming recognized that it was happening and repented at the very end.

Christ's return is NOT imminent in the sense that He could come at a moments notice. This statement should be removed or rephrased from every Christian church that includes it in their statement of faith. See Daniel 9:25-27 and compare it to Matthew 24, as well as 2 Thessalonians 2:1-4.

Daniel 9:25-27 (NLT)

Now listen and understand! Seven sets of seven plus sixty-two sets of seven[a] will pass from the time the command is given to rebuild Jerusalem until a ruler—the Anointed One—comes. Jerusalem will be rebuilt with streets and strong defenses, despite the perilous times.

"After this period of sixty-two sets of seven, the Anointed One will be killed, appearing to have accomplished nothing, and a ruler will arise whose armies will destroy the city and the Temple. The end will come with a flood, and war and its miseries are decreed from that time to the very end. The ruler will make a treaty with the people for a period of one set of seven, but after half this time, he will put an end to the sacrifices and offerings. And as a climax to all his terrible deeds, he will set up a sacrilegious object that causes desecration, until the fate decreed for this defiler is finally poured out on him."

Matthew 24:9-16 (NLT)

"Then you will be arrested, persecuted, and killed. You will be hated all over the world because you are my followers. And many will turn away from me and betray

and hate each other. And many false prophets will appear and will deceive many people. Sin will be rampant everywhere, and the love of many will grow cold. But the one who endures to the end will be saved. And the Good News about the Kingdom will be preached throughout the whole world, so that all nations will hear it; and then the end will come.

"The day is coming when you will see what Daniel the prophet spoke about—the sacrilegious object that causes desecration standing in the Holy Place." (Reader, pay attention!) "Then those in Judea must flee to the hills.

2 Thessalonians 2:1-4 (NLT)

Now, dear brothers and sisters, let us clarify some things about the coming of our Lord Jesus Christ and how we will be gathered to meet him. Don't be so easily shaken or alarmed by those who say that the day of the Lord has already begun. Don't believe them, even if they claim to have had a spiritual vision, a revelation, or a letter supposedly from us. Don't be fooled by what they say. For that day will not come until there is a great rebellion against God and the man of lawlessness is revealed—the one who brings destruction. He will exalt himself and defy everything that people call god and every object of worship. He will even sit in the temple of God, claiming that he himself is God.

Many scholars believe that this means the Temple must be built first, since the Holy Place that existed in Jesus' time was the Temple. Half way through the Tribulation, the AC will break his treaty with Israel, set up the "Abomination that causes Desolation" for 3 and a half years. See also Daniel 11:31-32. In Daniel 12:11 he says the very end will be 3.5 years after these things happen. *(As a side note, as you can see in the Daniel passage, it doesn't seem that the Dome of the Rock fits this profile, because it's been there for far longer than 7 years.)*

We also see in Matthew 24:15-25 Jesus said that the Tribulation was cut back so that there would be survivors.

Survivors for what? He gives the answer in 24:30; His Second Coming. And Survivors from what? Obviously there had to be something they were surviving. The Second Coming is the capstone that signals the very end, so it cannot happen 7 years before the end. And since the Rapture is preceded by a Great Devastation that some would survive, it makes sense that the only event causing such devastation mentioned in Scripture is the Tribulation. Therefore, the Rapture has to be after the Tribulation.

The Tribulation, and End Times events are imminent, and if statements of faith were to be updated to say *the events* that lead to Christ's return are imminent then that would make a whole lot more sense and be a great deal more Biblical.

What Does It Mean When It Says "These Things Must Soon Take Place?"

Revelation 1:1 (KJV) - The Revelation of Jesus Christ, which God gave Him to show to His bond-servants, the things which must soon take place.

Revelation 22:6 (KJV) - These words are faithful and true"; and the Lord, the God of the spirits of the prophets, sent His angel to show to His bond-servants the things which must soon take place.

It is odd that Jesus uses the phrase that He is coming soon, or these things must soon take place. Some argue that because Jesus used the word "soon" we must be wrong in our study of End Times events because if Jesus was telling the truth, then these events had to happen during the first century. Unless Jesus was wrong. One might get the impression that Jesus either didn't know what He was talking about, or was deceiving people by using this type of terminology. But we know that He was perfect and would never lie to us. These statements seem to contradict each other, but we know that the Bible doesn't contradict itself, so we have to dig a little deeper to find the answer.

Just because He used the word "soon" doesn't mean that everything in Revelation is meant to happen soon. It also doesn't mean that Jesus is using our time schedule. The fact that many events described, that Amillennialists would like to call figurative, were given as signs by Jesus and the prophet Joel and repeated in the Book of Revelation such as the Sun going dark, the moon turning blood red, the stars falling from heaven, these things did not happen in 70 AD.

(For events that happen in the heavens, such as dealing with the Mazzaroth and how the ancient Jewish Zodiac pertained to prophecy see Tim Warner's book "The Mystery of the Mazzaroth," or Larson's www.bethlehemstar.net, which gives a very good overview of ancient astronomy and how it relates to prophecy.)

Many would like to claim that these events are allegorical, but there is no proof that they are. In fact, there is far greater evidence that these events will be literal. One example, but which demonstrates this point perfectly is that the Jews were expecting many of the events that amillennialists claim are allegorical to actually happen before the Messiah made His appearance. Since none of these things happened, they rejected Jesus.

One of the big reasons many scholars believe Judas betrayed Jesus was because He was not engaging in war against the Romans. Some speculate that Judas thought that if he were to place Jesus in a desperate position, it would force Jesus to act and begin the wars that Isaiah, Joel and the other prophets prophesied.

Some scholars claim that "Iscariot" is a derivation of the word "sicari," which was both the name of a group of Zealots and the dagger that the group was known to carry on them at all times in the event that the Messiah would appear and He would need their services to overthrow the oppressing foreigners. This group of Jews believed in the literalness of these events so much that they were constantly prepared for these events to begin at any moment.

The fact is these prophetic End Times events will most likely come to pass just as described, and some might be reflected in both the heavens and on the earth as a warning for people to repent. Throughout the book of Revelation, we see that the tumultuous events are sent by God as a means of getting people to repent, often to no avail.

One final thing to consider when studying this portion of Revelation, many scholars point to strong evidence that the first three chapters of Revelation are a separate vision given for the seven churches in the first century, and that the rest of the book of Revelation is meant to show what will happen throughout the rest of time until Jesus physically returns. So the second half of Revelation might not be related to the "I am coming soon," warnings that Jesus gave the 7 churches.

"I Am Coming Soon…" What does this mean?

Most of the seven churches do not exist today. As far as I have been able to research, none of these churches are still there, though in these cities there still may be some Christian influence, even after all of these years of Islamic domination. And there appears to be some evidence that they are being rebuilt, as we discuss elsewhere. So what can it possibly mean when Jesus said to them, "I am coming soon." Jesus repeated this to the 7 churches, several times in different contexts. I have found that when God repeats something in the Scriptures it must be important!

To the Ephesus church, He says, "If you do not repent I will come to you…" Then he says something curious, "He who has an ear, let him hear what the Spirit says to the churches."

To the church of Smyrna, He does not say He is coming soon, but He says trials and persecution are coming soon to them. Again He repeats Himself, and when Jesus repeats Himself we should listen, "He who has an ear, let him hear what the Spirit says to the churches."

To the church of Pergamum, He tells them to repent, "otherwise I will come to you soon and fight against them with the sword of my mouth." Again He repeats "He who has an ear, let him hear what the Spirit says to the churches."

To the church of Thyatira, He says "only hold onto what you have until I come." He encourages them to overcome until the end, and then He makes a reference to His rule over all the earth, and how He will make them rulers. And He ends Thyatira's message with, "He who has an ear, let him hear what the Spirit says to the churches."

To the church of Sardis, He doesn't mention when He is coming, but He does say, that His coming would be like a thief, and they might not be ready if they do not “strengthen what remains.” He also says, “He who has an ear, let him hear what the Spirit says to the churches.”

To the church of Philadelphia, He commends them for keeping His command to endure patiently, and tells them that He’s coming soon. But will keep them from the hour of trial that will come upon the whole world, to test those who live upon the earth. Then again He says, “He who has an ear, let him hear what the Spirit says to the churches.”

Finally, to the church of Laodicea He says, “Here I am.” So apparently He already is at their church, standing at their door and knocking, testing them and trying them to make them either hot or cold, instead of lukewarm. He also says, that “those I love, I rebuke and discipline.” And He also says, “He who has an ear, let him hear what the Spirit says to the churches.”

What does this all mean?

I believe that when Jesus says, I am coming soon to these churches we see that He is not talking about His second coming to earth. How could he be? He did not return to the earth in 70 AD, as Full Preterists would like us to believe. And He did not complete the entire vision of Revelation in 70 AD, as partial Preterists would have us to believe. The fact that the Revelation was most likely written 20 to 30 years after the destruction of Jerusalem around 70 AD, and the fact that John never included the church in Jerusalem in the letters to the churches, just shows that this event was already past.

So Jesus was not talking about His return. In fact, I believe we are clued into what He was talking about by what He repeats. First He repeats that the Spirit is saying something to the churches. I believe when Jesus says He is coming soon to the churches, He is referring to something spiritual. I think this is demonstrated by what he says to the church of Laodicea. To most of the other churches, He says, "I am coming," or "I will come," and it doesn't sound like a pleasant thing. But to the church of Laodicea He says, "I'm already here!"

It sounds like when a dad says to the kids on a long road trip, "Knock it off! You don't want me to come back there do you!?!" These churches need discipline because they are getting sidetracked by Satan.

He further explains to the church of Laodicea that discipline and rebuke are from Him. I believe what He means by "I am coming soon," in the context of the opening part of Revelation is that His Spirit will bring persecution to them to discipline them to make them be the people He wants them to be. I know in my life, when I have strayed off the path that God has for me, He will often bring hardship to teach me to cling to Him. I can imagine that His methods haven't changed much in 2,000 years, especially since we're told Jesus Christ is the same yesterday, today and forever.

One final thing that I notice: there seems to be a split after the messages to the churches, as John goes into his longer vision that comprises the rest of the book of Revelation. Many scholars claim that Revelation is a collection of two different visions. I believe this is true, because Jesus brings John up to heaven and then says that the events that he is about to see take place "after this," which we can take to mean, "…after this present time."

I believe this second part of the Revelation is Jesus showing John the long term plan, most likely in an effort to explain to the churches that He is not physically coming soon, but that there is a lot to be done before He does physically return.

When we study the book of Daniel we see this pattern again. God gives Daniel visions of some things that will happen over the course of his lifetime, such as the overthrow of the Babylonian empire, and the return from captivity. But he also is shown many things that will come about 500 and 2500 years into the future. So like Daniel, God is showing John the short term and the long term plan of prophecy.

Is there a difference between the "Marriage Supper," and the "Wedding Feast?"

Some pre-trib teachers claim that there is a difference between these two statements, but when you look at it in the Greek, there is no difference. They are one and the same event.

The Apostasy

What does the Bible teach about the Apostasy?

Matthew 24:4-10 (NLT)

Jesus told them, "Don't let anyone mislead you, for many will come in my name, claiming, 'I am the Messiah.' They will deceive many. And you will hear of wars and threats of wars, but don't panic. Yes, these things must take place, but the end won't follow immediately. Nation will go to war against nation, and kingdom against kingdom. There will be famines and earthquakes in many parts of the world. But all this is only the first of the birth pains, with more to come.

"Then you will be arrested, persecuted, and killed. You will be hated all over the world because you are my followers. And many will turn away from me and betray and hate each other.

"Apostosia" comes because "many are offended" because of the afflictions, killings and hatred because of

Jesus' name sake. The offense, the apostasy comes from persecution. It's coming. Get ready. Love one another. Even as you see the day approaching meet together and Pray!

The Rapture has to happen *AFTER* the "Apostasia," or Great Falling Away because it specifically says that the Apostasy is one of the signs to look for in 2 Thess. 2 and in Matthew 24:10 *before* Jesus returns.

Some ministers mistakenly use the reference in 2 Thessalonians 2:3 to the apostasy to mean the rapture has to happen first. They use the King James Version of the Bible which reads: "*Let no man deceive you by any means: for that day shall not come, except there come a falling away first, and that man of sin be revealed, the son of perdition,"* and then they tell people that this falling away is our falling away from the earth into heaven at the rapture. This is not what it means.

The use of the King James as "the only Bible" is a modern version of a very old tactic that Satan has used countless times in the past. He did it with the Latin Vulgate with the Catholic Church, and he's using it now in America with the KJV. He tricks people into being sold on the idea that the King James Version of the Bible is the only acceptable version of the Bible, and then uses their ignorance of King James English to distort and pervert what the text actually says.

Let me make this clear, the King James Version of the Bible is a fine translation if you can understand the

English of that time period. English has changed a lot over the years, and we have seen many words that originally meant one thing, take on new and completely different meanings. Some words have changed so much that reading the King James without a background in this can cause great confusion.

As you can see in this book, I use the King James, but it is in no way the only translation, or even the most accurate translation. It is a translation into English of the Latin Vulgate which was a translation into Latin from *some* of the Greek texts that they had at the time of the translation. But the King James is not a direct translation from the Greek, and it is not the most literal or accurate translation based on all of the ancient texts available.

In my personal Bible study, I use the KJV because it is the version that I memorized most scripture from as a kid, and I use it in my writings because it is copyright free. I also use the New Living Translation because it uses a different translation method that of translating, basically a paragraph at a time, so that a modern English vernacular meaning can be achieved. And I also use the English Standard Version and the New American Standard Version, both great literal word for word translations.

There are three ways to translate from one language to another, as any foreign language student knows. One can translate things literally, sentence by sentence, or thought by thought. If the target language does not match up with the way the original language places different parts of speech then there can be confusion when one uses a literal approach.

For instance, one language might put the verb first and say something like “Eat dog cat.” Where another might put the verb at the end such as “Dog cat eat.” But neither of these word orders give an English reader the gist of what is being said. Is the speaker telling us that we should eat dogs and cats? Or is the speaker telling us that the Dog ate the cat? When we translate the phrase, we might understand within the context of the paragraph that “the Dog eats the cat.”

Now if there is a modifying sentence that explains why the dog ate the cat, in a thought for thought translation we might get a sentence that reads, “The dog eats the cat because he was hungry and the cat looked tasty.” The original translation might have appeared like: “Dog cat eat. Tasty Cat was. Hungry Dog.” Thus the thought for thought translation comes across very differently from a literal translation. We are not trying to sound like Yoda, the fact is, many languages are very different from English. Greek and Hebrew both happen to be vastly different from English.

So this is why we have different translations of the Bible, to take care of these subtle nuances in translation methods. The only way to do away with these translation problems is by becoming an expert in Greek and Hebrew, which is time consuming and difficult, and beyond the scope of most Christians who have a job and a family. The fact that there are crooked ministers out there who use this translation problem as a way to manipulate their congregations is reprehensible, but one that will only get worse as we get closer to the fulfillment of End Times events.

In King James time the phrase "falling away," meant literally the same thing as the Greek word from which it comes "apostasia," which gives English the word Apostasy, which means literally *to fall away from faith.* In other words: *a renouncement of the faith that one was raised with, once claimed as their own, or a turning away from God.*

There is no way at all that this means the rapture comes before the Tribulation, and it just goes to show that some ministers out there will out right lie about what Scripture says just because of their evil pride. Because otherwise it would mean that they would have to humble themselves to admit that they were wrong their whole lives. Some pastors have humbled themselves and mad such an admission. These are the pastors that we should support and encourage, rather than the pride filled ones that will not consider what the Bible actually says.

Another interesting thing about the Matthew passage, Jesus mentions the Antichrist in that passage, which shows that he will be on the scene at the time of the falling away. Paul confirms this in the 2 Thessalonians passage.

Daniel 7:25 says the Antichrist fights and defeats Israel (or possibly the saints, or both, if compared to Revelation

12) for 3.5 years. Daniel says here that all of the End Time events will be completed after that final 3.5 years. Revelation 12:13 says there will be a place of safety prepared for “her” (either the church or Israel) in the Desert (not heaven), out of the Antichrist’s reach. Remember that Satan and the Antichrist are not divine and are not omnipresent. They take up a specific place both in material and in the spiritual realms.

So it is very possible there could be a place on earth that they cannot reach and influence. After Matthew 24:10 Jesus speaks of the Gathering (a.k.a. the Rapture) in 24:31. Also, Daniel says that the final kingdom will be one of “iron and clay” which shows that there are very strong parts of the kingdom, but also some very weak parts. No one has ever been able to sustain a completely totalitarian reign in history, not even Hitler or Stalin. Therefore, there must be some places where people will be able to hide or be safe.

How and when will the apostasy happen?

We can’t know for sure when these events will happen, but it seems from the spiritual climate in America, we might be seeing the beginnings of the Apostasy even now. Many churches that were formerly solid Bible teaching churches have accepted a great deal of false doctrines and social evils into their congregations, and it appears to only be getting worse. Just explore the faulty doctrines of popular preaches such as Rob Bell, Joel Olsten, Rick Warren and others to find that some ministers have fallen far away from what the Bible teaches.

What we can say is that there will be a predictable pattern that the Apostasy takes. *It will be a progression from a secure stance against evil, to an apathy against it, and apathy will lead to a tolerance of evil. Tolerance of evil always leads to false doctrine, false doctrine leads to apostasy, apostasy leads to acceptance of an evil situation, acceptance leads to destruction.*

When you see this pattern gaining more and more ground until there is very little solid orthodox doctrine left, then you will be able to tell that the Apostasy is in full swing.

If nothing can separate us from the Love of God, then how can we be in danger of the apostasy?

Many people believe that being "saved" is equivalent to having a relationship with God. However, everyone has a relationship with God: good, bad or indifferent. The question is does everyone have a right relationship with God? And the answer to that is no. We see in Revelation that even Christians can have a relationship with God that isn't right. He tells the church in Laodicea that He was prepared to spew them out.

It is interesting to me that the so-called "Once Saved Always Saved" doctrine propagated by groups such as Dallas Theological Seminary, is also a doctrine that was popularized by the Scofield Bible, which popularized the Pre-Trib teaching. I find it very strange that many of the

Wesleyan groups that descend from a more Arminian slanted doctrine buy into the Pre-Trib idea at all. Without the "once saved always saved" stance, the Pre-Trib argument falls apart.

For you Pre-Trib Arminians out there, follow my line of thinking here: You claim that a person can lose their salvation. You teach that we are warned not to fall away when facing trials and temptations, etc. And yet you believe that when the greatest trial ever to hit the earth comes, to purify the people and make them holy, the church gets to skip the exam? It makes no sense from an Arminian perspective. One would think that Arminians would be the most Post-Trib of anyone out there.

As to the question of losing salvation, it is true that Paul tells us in Romans 8 that nothing can separate us from the love of God, but what do you do if He spews you out? Apparently, God can separate us from Himself, and does. That's the purpose of Hell. Some scholars point out that God's ever present gaze would be Hell to people who do not want God in their lives. Either way, eternal separation from God, or the eternal focus of God's displeasure is an apt description of Hell. But I will leave the academic debate over the salvation issue to the theologians.

As for our study, the key thing to keep in mind here is that Paul said "nothing can separate *US*." So who is the "us" he is talking about? He's talking about people who are wholeheartedly following after God. He tells us earlier in Romans Chapter 6 that we shouldn't keep on sinning. He makes a distinction that we have died to sin. We are not to keep on sinning. There are too many churches today that teach that we are all just a bunch of sinners, and we should overlook our sins and encourage each other.

This is not the message that Paul preaches here. We need to repent of our sins and STOP doing them! Otherwise, *we are not saved*. It's really that simple. I used to go to a church where the pastor was a very strong proponent of the "once save always saved," doctrine, but he always added "but once saved changed." I'll make a distinction between Calvinists and Arminians and Once Saved people and Wesleyans, because they differ on other issues that we're not covering here, but this is a point where Once Saved people and Wesleyans can reach an agreement.

The bottom line of this discussion is this: there are a great deal of people who populate our churches who are most likely not saved, or who are dabbling way too much in the world and demonstrate that they have never made a true commitment to Jesus.

So when Paul warns us in 2 Thessalonians 2 that the Apostasy must come first before the 2nd coming, who is he talking about? He's talking about all of the lukewarm "Christians" who will not stand for Christ when the heat is on. I feel such an overpowering burden of the Lord to share this:

IF YOU ARE ONE OF THESE "CHRISTIANS," YOU NEED TO BE STRONG IN HIM. YOU CAN NOT LIVE WITH ONE FOOT IN THE WORLD AND ONE FOOT IN THE CHRUCH. YOU CANNOT PERSIST IN YOUR SIN. WHEN THE SHAKING COMES, IF YOU ARE NOT ROOTED IN HIM, YOU CAN FALL AWAY.

The church in America today might as well be the Laodicean church. We are so sinful, and we excuse the sins of everyone else as well. What we are mistaking here is that we can have security as believers in Jesus, but that doesn't mean that all of the people in our churches are really believers. It doesn't mean that many won't think "submitting to our authorities" is more important than standing firm against evil, even when the authorities are evil.

One thing that I would like to point out to any American Christian reading this; when the time of shaking comes to our country, remember: YOU are the authority in this country, the Constitution of the US is the only authority over you in this country. "We the people…" If a president, governor, city council, judge or police officer or military personnel, or any other person goes against the Constitution, you have absolutely NO obligation to follow their orders. You are biblically free to follow whatever you believe the Bible commands you to do in any and every situation in the United States of America, no matter what the government might like to tell you otherwise. I pray that you remember that when we get into the Tribulation. We are under no obligation to follow the corrupt orders of evil politicians.

What Is "The Coming Great Deception?"

In Matthew 24 the very first thing Jesus warned about was to be on guard against Deception. So it is very important that we keep watching for something that will try to deceive us from the truth. We see a great deal of deception on so called Christian television even today, but I believe that the "Great Deception" will be something incredibly confusing even for the "very elect." Though after searching the scriptures, study and prayer, the "very elect" will not be taken in by the deception.

In 2 Thessalonians 2:11, Paul tells us that a day is coming when the world will be sent a "strong delusion," or as some translations have it a "great deception" that will cause many to be damned eternally.

And with all deceivableness of unrighteousness in them that perish; because they received not the love of the truth, that they might be saved. And for this cause God shall send them strong delusion, that they should believe a lie: that they all might be damned who believed not the truth, but had pleasure in unrighteousness. (2 Thessalonians 2:10-13, KJV)

First of all, I'd like to give a warning to us all, myself included, we need to beware the very end part of this verse, "...but had pleasure in unrighteousness." How many times have we watched an unrighteous movie, laughed at an unrighteous joke, cherished an unrighteous thought or acted on an unrighteous motive? I know that I am certainly guilty of these things. This should be enough to make us fall on our knees i beg God not to include us in this group that falls for the great deception when it comes.

What we do know about the Great Deception Paul described is that it dovetails very well with what John tells us about the Beast and the False Prophet in Revelation.

In Revelation, we see that the Antichrist and the False Prophet are given the power to perform great signs and wonders that the Bible refers to as “lying signs and wonders.” So these miracles that they perform are in some way fake, or else they appear to be divine in origin, but in fact are rooted in some other type of ability, science or power. They are not in fact divine. But unless we are watching and remaining close to the Lord, we will be taken in by these signs. The best advice is to be humble before God and stay as close to Him as possible in order not to be deceived.

Many wonder what exactly the Great Deception will be. The Bible doesn’t give us exact details on the particulars of this deception, but we do know that it will have something to do with how the Antichrist deceives many and convinces them to follow him.

One of the things that the False Prophet is said to do, both in Christian circles, and by inference from Islamic sources where they reference the return of Isa, their Jesus, is to enforce a one world religion devoted to the Antichrist. We see from Islam that the Antichrist is aided by the wonders that their Jesus can do that will convince Christians to follow the Antichrist.

We also see in Revelation that False Prophet lends a great deal of power and credibility to the Antichrist when he comes. Certainly this will have to be something incredibly miraculous in order to convince many people who grew up in Biblical homes, states and areas. But we know that it will because the Bible warns that a great deal of people will fall for his lies. We see in Revelation 16 that the Beast of the Earth is also the False Prophet.

One thing to keep in mind is that all false prophets are said to have an unclean spirit that guides them. We see this in Zechariah 13:2 - *"And on that day," says the Lord of Heaven's Armies, "I will erase idol worship throughout the land, so that even the names of the idols will be forgotten. I will remove from the land both the false prophets and the spirit of impurity that came with them."*

To find our more information about the False Prophet also called the Beast out of the Earth, and the Antichrist, called the Beast out of the Sea, let's turn to Revelation chapter 13 and examine it further…

Revelation Chapter 13 (NLT)

The Beast out of the Sea

Then I saw a beast rising up out of the sea. It had seven heads and ten horns, with ten crowns on its horns. And written on each head were names that blasphemed God. This beast looked like a leopard, but it had the feet of a bear and the mouth of a lion! And the dragon gave the beast his own power and throne and great authority.

Many scholars agree that the 10 horns referenced here relate to Daniel's vision where the 10 horns represent 10 kingdoms that are overtaken by the Antichrist, which make up his empire.

I saw that one of the heads of the beast seemed wounded beyond recovery—but the fatal wound was healed! The whole world marveled at this miracle and gave allegiance to the beast. They worshiped the dragon for giving the beast such power, and they also worshiped the beast. "Who is as great as the beast?" they exclaimed. "Who is able to fight against him?"

This is an interesting passage, we see here the power of the Antichrist comes from the Dragon, Satan, and people begin to worship the dragon openly. I see a parallel to this in Islam, where they praise Satan openly under the name of Allah, and are looking for the Mahdi which they will also worship in some respect.

Then the beast was allowed to speak great blasphemies against God. And he was given authority to do whatever he wanted for forty-two months. And he spoke terrible words of blasphemy against God, slandering his name and his dwelling—that is, those who dwell in heaven. And the beast was allowed to wage war against God's holy people and to conquer them. And he was given authority to rule over every tribe and people and language and nation. And all the people who belong to this world worshiped the beast. They are the ones whose names were not written in the Book of Life before the world was made—the Book that belongs to the Lamb who was slaughtered.

Here we see another parallel to the book of Daniel, and we also see that the Antichrist has power for 3 and a half years. We also see here that he conquers God's people. Also at this point, he apparently conquers most of the world, or at least has power to exert authority over them, if he doesn't directly enfold their countries into his empire.

Anyone with ears to hear
should listen and understand.

Anyone who is destined for prison
will be taken to prison.
Anyone destined to die by the sword
will die by the sword.

This means that God's holy people must endure persecution patiently and remain faithful.

"This means that God's holy people must endure persecution patiently and remain faithful." This is a very important reminder that, yes, we will have persecution. Stand strong!

The Beast out of the Earth

Then I saw another beast come up out of the earth. He had two horns like those of a lamb, but he spoke with the voice of a dragon. He exercised all the authority of the first beast. And he required all the earth and its people to worship the first beast, whose fatal wound had been healed. He did astounding miracles, even making fire flash down to earth from the sky while everyone was watching. And with all the miracles he was allowed to perform on behalf of the first beast, he deceived all the people who belong to this world. He ordered the people to make a great statue of the first beast, who was fatally wounded and then came back to life. He was then permitted to give life to this statue so that it could speak. Then the statue of the beast commanded that anyone refusing to worship it must die.

This passage is very interesting also. Notice that the Beast out of the Earth speaks with the voice of a dragon. What do prophets of God do? They speak with the voice of God. But here we see that False Prophet speaking with a voice of a dragon, which we see in chapter 12 is

Satan. We also see that he can do astounding miracles, such as fire flashing down from the sky. So the False Prophet, most likely even more so than the Antichrist, will have great power and will do miracles.

He required everyone—small and great, rich and poor, free and slave—to be given a mark on the right hand or on the forehead. And no one could buy or sell anything without that mark, which was either the name of the beast or the number representing his name. Wisdom is needed here. Let the one with understanding solve the meaning of the number of the beast, for it is the number of a man. His number is 666.

We will talk more about this in the section on the Mark of the Beast, but we should give it some consideration in this passage.

Many people out there have done a lot of speculation as to what the mark of the Beast will be. Muslims claim that Beast of the Earth is a good thing. They call him al-Dabbat al-Arḍ (الأرض الدابة, in Arabic), the Beast of the Earth, and he will mark all good Muslims with the staff of Moses. They claim that it is a good thing to receive this mark.

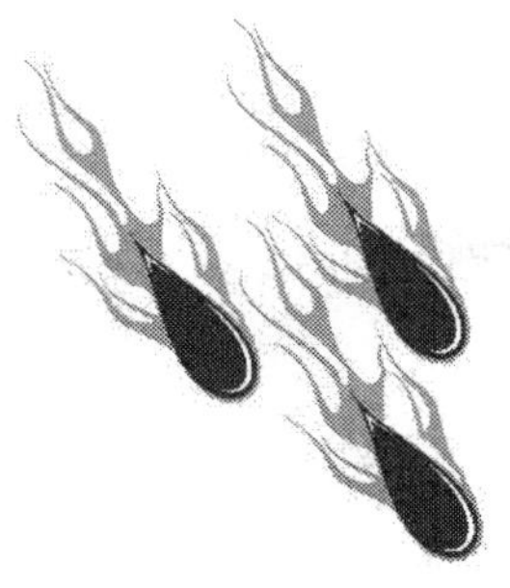

The Day Of The Lord

What is the "Day of the Lord?"

2nd Peter chapter 3 tells us that the Day of the Lord, the Second Coming and the Burning of the Earth by Fire all happen at the same time.

A great deal of what Jesus taught pointed to evil doers being taken out from the world. See Matthew 13:41. *The Son of Man will send his angels, and they will remove from his Kingdom everything that causes sin and all who do evil. (NLT)* In the parable of the wheat and the tares, the angels are sent to take out the evil doers and throw them into the fire.

Also, when you look at Joel and Revelation, when the Messiah comes, He will destroy all of the evil doers. According to Joel, He rides over the whole earth with His army, that destroys all the evil people like locusts destroying crops, but whoever calls upon His name will be saved. And survivors will be assembled to come up and pay tribute to him with what little wheat crop they have left over. It appears that His army is assembled at the time of His coming, and then He calls the rest of the evil doers to assemble in the valley of Megiddo where the last battle takes place.

Another important thing to consider is that the "Day of the Lord," mentioned in 1 Thess. 5:2, is associated with the Rapture.

For yourselves know perfectly that the day of the Lord so cometh as a thief in the night. (KJV)

Matthew 24:27-31 corresponds to Joel 2:31 which says the darkening of the Sun, Moon and Stars precede the Day of the Lord, which also includes the appearing of the Son of Man, the sending out of angels, the blast of the trumpet. All of these events are events of the Day of the Lord, not a multi-staged rapture event.

For as the lightning flashes in the east and shines to the west, so it will be when the Son of Man comes. Just as the gathering of vultures shows there is a carcass nearby, so these signs indicate that the end is near. Immediately after the anguish of those days, the sun will be darkened, the moon will give no light, the stars will fall from the sky, and the powers in the heavens will be shaken. And then at last, the sign that the Son of Man is coming will appear in the heavens, and there will be deep mourning among all the peoples of the earth. And they will see the Son of Man coming on the clouds of heaven with power and great glory. And he will send out his angels with the mighty blast of a trumpet, and they will gather his chosen ones from all over the world—from the farthest ends of the earth and heaven. (Matthew 24:27-31, NLT)

The sun will become dark, and the moon will turn blood red before that great and terrible day of the Lord arrives. (Joel 2:31, NLT)

In Acts 2, Peter applies this same passage to the Church, not to a select group of "Tribulation Saints."

Then Peter stepped forward with the eleven other apostles and shouted to the crowd, "Listen carefully, all of you, fellow Jews and residents of Jerusalem! Make no mistake about this. These people are not drunk, as some of you are assuming. Nine o'clock in the morning is much too early for that. No, what you see was predicted long ago by the prophet Joel: 'In the last days,' God says, 'I will pour out my Spirit upon all people. Your sons and daughters will prophesy. Your young men will see visions, and your old men will dream dreams. In those days I will pour out my Spirit even on my servants—men and women alike— and they will prophesy. And I will cause wonders in the heavens above and signs on the earth below— blood and fire and clouds of smoke. The sun will become dark, and the moon will turn blood red before that great and glorious day of the Lord arrives. But everyone who calls on the name of the Lord will be saved.' (Acts 2:14-21, NLT)

Also in 2 Thess. 2:2 and 3, it says the Antichrist must be revealed first before the Day of the Lord.

Don't be so easily shaken or alarmed by those who say that the day of the Lord has already begun. Don't believe them, even if they claim to have had a spiritual vision, a revelation, or a letter supposedly from us. Don't be fooled by what they say. For that day will not come until there is a great rebellion against God and the man of lawlessness is revealed—the one who brings destruction. (NLT)

All the events of the Day of the Lord mentioned in Joel are associated with Christ's actions when He returns to set things right. He does not return just to get us, He returns to subjugate the entire world under His rule so He can turn it over to His Father. See 1 Cor. 15:25.

For Christ must reign until he humbles all his enemies beneath his feet. (NLT)

This passage teaches Christ must reign until all things are subjected under Him. It is in a tense that implies that there will be a long term period of conquering everything, which explains why there is a 1,000 year reign and then a final rebellion of Satan.

When the thousand years come to an end, Satan will be let out of his prison. He will go out to deceive the nations—called Gog and Magog—in every corner of the earth. He will gather them together for battle—a mighty army, as numberless as sand along the seashore. And I saw them as they went up on the broad plain of the earth and surrounded God's people and the beloved city. But fire from heaven came down on the attacking armies and consumed them.

Then the devil, who had deceived them, was thrown into the fiery lake of burning sulfur, joining the beast and the false prophet. There they will be tormented day and night forever and ever. (Revelation 20:7-10, NLT)

It also explains why it seems that, in several passages, including Joel, Zechariah and Isaiah, there are a group of people who were not believers coming up to pay homage to Christ who are not transformed saints.

But everyone who calls on the name of the LORD will be saved, for some on Mount Zion in Jerusalem will escape, just as the LORD has said. These will be among the survivors whom the LORD has called. (Joel 2:32, NLT)

In that day five of Egypt's cities will follow the Lord of Heaven's Armies. They will even begin to speak Hebrew, the language of Canaan. One of these cities will be Heliopolis, the City of the Sun. (Isaiah 19:18, NLT)

Any nation in the world that refuses to come to Jerusalem to worship the King, the LORD of Heaven's Armies, will have no rain. (Zechariah 14:17, NLT)

This also explains why some Jews won't come to know Christ until He returns. The Jews will be His people, but glorified saints will be their governors, leaders, etc. This also coincides with Matthew 25:31-33 which states clearly that the same day that Jesus comes back is the same day when Jesus returns to judge the wicked.

Some would argue that "Day of the Lord" does not mean a literal 24 hour day, and this may be true, but they are also often the same people who like to argue that "Day" in Genesis 1:5 is a literal 24 hour day. The point is whether it lasts for 24 hours or several days, weeks or even a year, the Day of the Lord starts the very day He returns.

There are several passages that speak about the Day of the Lord, here are several below, for you to study. These are all from the New Living Translation, so as to give you a quick overview in plain English. As you can see, the Day of the Lord is the time of Christ's vengeance upon the evil doers, which shows a stark difference from the time of Satan's vengeance upon the church. Notice who is being hurt in these passages, it is the evil ones, not the church. If you compare these passages with the ones that describe the persecutions of the church, it is very easy to see that the Day of the Lord is a day of rejoicing for the church, as Jesus brings the vengeance that He has said is His alone.

1. Isaiah 13:6 Scream in terror, for the day of the LORD has arrived— the time for the Almighty to destroy.

2. Isaiah 13:9 For see, the day of the LORD is coming— the terrible day of his fury and fierce anger.

The land will be made desolate, and all the sinners destroyed with it.

3. Isaiah 34:8 For it is the day of the LORD's revenge, the year when Edom will be paid back for all it did to Israel.

4. Jeremiah 46:10 For this is the day of the Lord, the LORD of Heaven's Armies, a day of vengeance on his enemies. The sword will devour until it is satisfied, yes, until it is drunk with your blood! The Lord, the LORD of Heaven's Armies, will receive a sacrifice today in the north country beside the Euphrates River.

5. Ezekiel 7:19 "They will throw their money in the streets, tossing it out like worthless trash. Their silver and gold won't save them on that day of the LORD's anger. It will neither satisfy nor feed them, for their greed can only trip them up.

6. Ezekiel 13:5 They have done nothing to repair the breaks in the walls around the nation. They have not helped it to stand firm in battle on the day of the LORD.

7. Ezekiel 30:3 for the terrible day is almost here— the day of the LORD! It is a day of clouds and gloom, a day of despair for the nations.

8. Joel 1:15 The day of the LORD is near, the day when destruction comes from the Almighty. How terrible that day will be!

9. Joel 2:1 Sound the alarm in Jerusalem ! Raise the battle cry on my holy mountain! Let everyone tremble in fear because the day of the LORD is upon us.

10. Joel 2:11 The LORD is at the head of the column. He leads them with a shout. This is his mighty army, and they follow his orders. The day of the LORD is an awesome, terrible thing. Who can possibly survive?

11. Joel 2:31 The sun will become dark, and the moon will turn blood red before that great and terrible day of the LORD arrives.

12. Joel 3:14 Thousands upon thousands are waiting in the valley of decision. There the day of the LORD will soon arrive.

13. Amos 5:18 What sorrow awaits you who say, "If only the day of the LORD were here!" You have no idea what you are wishing for. That day will bring darkness, not light.

14. Amos 5:20 Yes, the day of the LORD will be dark and hopeless, without a ray of joy or hope.

15. Obadiah 1:15 "For the day of the LORD draws near on all the nations. As you have done, it will be done to you. Your dealings will return on your own head.

16. Zephaniah 1:7 Stand in silence in the presence of the Sovereign LORD, for the awesome day of the LORD's judgment is near. The LORD has prepared his people for a great slaughter and has chosen their executioners.

This passage seems to say that many of God's people will be killed prior to the coming of the Lord. It says in this context that the day is near, which means that it hasn't arrived yet.

17. Zephaniah 1:14 "That terrible day of the LORD is near. Swiftly it comes— a day of bitter tears, a day when even strong men will cry out.

18. Zephaniah 1:18 Your silver and gold will not save you on that day of the LORD's anger. For the whole land will be devoured by the fire of his jealousy. He will make a terrifying end of all the people on earth.

19. Zephaniah 2:2 Gather before judgment begins, before your time to repent is blown away like chaff. Act now, before the fierce fury of the LORD falls and the terrible day of the LORD's anger begins.

20. Zechariah 14:1 Watch, for the day of the LORD is coming when your possessions will be plundered right in front of you!

21. Malachi 4:5 "Look, I am sending you the prophet Elijah before the great and dreadful day of the LORD arrives.

22. Acts 2:20 The sun will become dark, and the moon will turn blood red before that great and glorious day of the LORD arrives.

23. 1 Corinthians 5:5 I have decided to deliver such a one to Satan for the destruction of his flesh, so that his spirit may be saved in the day of the Lord Jesus.

24. 1 Thessalonians 5:4 But you aren't in the dark about these things, dear brothers and sisters, and you won't be surprised when the day of the Lord comes like a thief.

25. 2 Thessalonians 2:2 Don't be so easily shaken or alarmed by those who say that the day of the Lord has already begun. Don't believe them, even if they claim to have had a spiritual vision, a revelation, or a letter supposedly from us.

26. 2 Peter 3:10 But the day of the Lord will come as unexpectedly as a thief. Then the heavens will pass away with a terrible noise, and the very elements themselves will disappear in fire, and the earth and everything on it will be found to deserve judgment.

Some Other Passages To Investigate

In that Day…

The phrase "in that Day…" is often used as a prophetic device, most of the time in conjunction with judgment or as a reference to the "Day of the Lord." Here are several other passages that you can investigate on your own that are prophetic, sometimes for events that happened to Israel in their history, or that will happen in the future still to come, some describing the Tribulation and some the Millennial Reign of Christ.

Deuteronomy 31:17-18
1 Samuel 3:12
1 Samuel 8:18
Isaiah 2:11-20
Isaiah 3:18
Isaiah 4:1-2
Isaiah 5:30
Isaiah 7:18-23
Isaiah 10:20-27
Isaiah 11:10
Isaiah 12:4
Isaiah 17:4-9
Isaiah 19:16-24
Isaiah 20:6
Isaiah 22:8-25
Isaiah 23:15
Isaiah 24:21
Isaiah 25:9
Isaiah 26:1
Isaiah 27:1-13
Isaiah 28:5
Isaiah 31:7
Isaiah 52:6
Jeremiah 4:9
Jeremiah 48:41
Jeremiah 49:22-26

Jeremiah 50:30
Hosea 2:16-21
Joel 3:18
Amos 2:16
Amos 8:3-13
Amos 9:11
Micah 4:6
Micah 5:10
Zephaniah 3:11-16
Zechariah 2:11
Zechariah 3:10
Zechariah 9:16
Zechariah 12:3
Zechariah 13:1-4
Zechariah 14:4-21
Mark 2:20
Luke 6:23
Luke 10:12
John 14:20
John 16:23-26

Joel's Great Battle at the "Day of the Lord"

There are over 20 references to the "Day of the Lord" in the Bible. This is the day when God will pour out His vengeance and make everything right. We learned earlier that the "Day of the Lord," is the same day that Jesus raptures the church.

We see in Joel 2 that Jesus will physically be at the battle referred to on the "Day of the Lord." And since we also see in Revelation that since Jesus returns at the

Battle of Armageddon, they must be one and the same battle. But if some are right in their understanding that Armageddon is actually a military campaign, then it might be that the Day of the Lord is more than just one physical day and one battle.

Is the "Day of the Lord Jesus Christ," the same as the "Day of the Lord" mentioned elsewhere in Scripture?

Yes, in fact it is. There are several pre-trib teachers that claim otherwise, but there is no scriptural support for this teaching. The details that surround the "Day of the Lord Jesus Christ," and the "Day of the Lord," are identical, and are obviously the same events. There is no way the Bible is citing multiple examples of events that occur just a couple years apart. They are the same event, just called two different names.

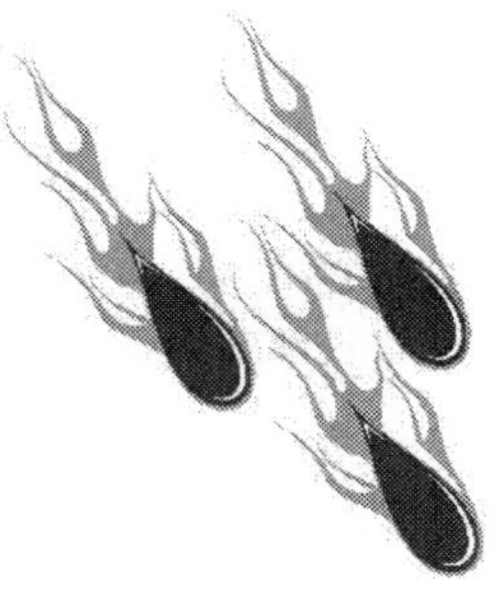

The Last Trump

What is the significance of the Last Trump?

But let me reveal to you a wonderful secret. We will not all die, but we will all be transformed! It will happen in a moment, in the blink of an eye, when the last trumpet is blown. For when the trumpet sounds, those who have died will be raised to live forever. And we who are living will also be transformed. For our dying bodies must be transformed into bodies that will never die; our mortal bodies must be transformed into immortal bodies. 1 Corinthians 15:51-53 (NLT)

1 Cor. 15:51-53 teaches us that the Rapture happens at the time of the Last Trumpet. We also see in Matthew 24: 29-31 that there is a Trump sounded to signify the end of the Tribulation (i.e. the Last Trump). Just for clarification *"Trump"* and *"Trumpet"* are synonymous terms.

"Immediately after the anguish of those days, the sun will be darkened, the moon will give no light, the stars will fall

from the sky, and the powers in the heavens will be shaken." And then at last, the sign that the Son of Man is coming will appear in the heavens, and there will be deep mourning among all the peoples of the earth. And they will see the Son of Man coming on the clouds of heaven with power and great glory. And he will send out his angels with the mighty blast of a trumpet, and they will gather his chosen ones from all over the world—from the farthest ends of the earth and heaven. Matthew 24:29-31 (NLT)

Furthermore, 1 Thessalonians 4:15-18 teaches us that the Resurrection of the Dead happens with the Trumpet call of God.

We tell you this directly from the Lord: We who are still living when the Lord returns will not meet him ahead of those who have died. For the Lord himself will come down from heaven with a commanding shout, with the voice of the archangel, and with the trumpet call of God. First, the Christians who have died will rise from their graves. Then, together with them, we who are still alive and remain on the earth will be caught up in the clouds to meet the Lord in the air. Then we will be with the Lord forever. So encourage each other with these words. 1 Thessalonians 4:15-18 (NLT)

I believe that a complete understanding of the "Last Trump" is perhaps the most damaging blow to the Pre-Trib argument. Many people teach that we are raptured before the Tribulation, however, the Rapture *cannot* possibly happen before this Trump, otherwise it wouldn't be the "Last" Trump.

Therefore, since the "Last Trump" signifies both the End of the Tribulation of the Church and the Rapture, not to mention that it also signifies Christ's Second Coming, it shows that these three events happen at the *same time*. Thus again, proving that the Pre-Trib point of view is totally false.

This all coincides with what Jesus said in John 6:39, 40, 44 and 54 that He would raise us up on the "Last" day, not seven years before nor three and a half years before.

And this is the will of God, that I should not lose even one of all those he has given me, but that I should raise them up at the last day. For it is my Father's will that all who see his Son and believe in him should have eternal life. I will raise them up at the last day."

Then the people began to murmur in disagreement because he had said, "I am the bread that came down from heaven." They said, "Isn't this Jesus, the son of Joseph? We know his father and mother. How can he say, 'I came down from heaven'?"

But Jesus replied, "Stop complaining about what I said. For no one can come to me unless the Father who sent me draws them to me, and at the last day I will raise them up. As it is written in the Scriptures, 'They will all be taught by God.' Everyone who listens to the Father and learns from him comes to me. (Not that anyone has ever seen the Father; only I, who was sent from God, have seen him.)

"I tell you the truth, anyone who believes has eternal life. Yes, I am the bread of life! Your ancestors ate manna in the wilderness, but they all died. Anyone who eats the bread from heaven, however, will never die. I am the living bread that came down from heaven. Anyone who eats this bread will live forever; and this bread, which I will offer so the world may live, is my flesh."

Then the people began arguing with each other about what he meant. "How can this man give us his flesh to eat?" they asked.

So Jesus said again, "I tell you the truth, unless you eat the flesh of the Son of Man and drink his blood, you cannot have eternal life within you. But anyone who eats my flesh and drinks my blood has eternal life, and I will raise that person ***at the last day.*** *John 6:39-54 (NLT)*

Another interesting thing to note, the feast of Trumpets, one of the special feasts that the Jews celebrated, was the feast of Harvest, and the Second Coming is also described as the final harvest of the believers. As American Christians we often forget that God gave the feasts to Israel for a reason. They are not arbitrary festivals, but each had a significant meaning. The spring feasts all represent aspects of Jesus' first coming to earth, and the final fall feasts also represent aspects of His second coming. The Last Trump relates to the last trumpet that is blown during the Feast of the Trumpets, and it signifies the Harvest of the believers mentioned in Revelation 14.

Some people wonder if the "Last Trump" is also the final of the 7 Trumpets mentioned in Revelation. It seems very likely that this is the case. In the book of Revelation, there are seven stars, seven churches, seven seals, seven trumpets, seven bowls of wrath, seven songs, and even seven golden lampstands. The number seven has great significance to God.

It does seem to be highly likely that they are one in the same trump. Paul tells us in I Corinthians 15:52, that when the last trumpet is blown, we will all be raised. We see in I Thessalonians 4:15-16 that with the "Trumpet call of God" the dead will be raised first. In verse 15 Paul tells us that this doctrine does not come from John, or from John's revelation, but it comes from the "Lord Himself." What could this mean? Did Jesus teach about a final trump? Well, as we can see, yes, He did.

In Matthew 24:31 we see that when Jesus returns there will be a blast of a trumpet, and then the angels will gather the elect from all the corners of the earth and heaven, to be with Jesus.

So when John talks about the seven trumpets in Revelation, He is not talking about something new to the believers. They were all aware that there would be a trumpet at the very end to signify Christ's return. Furthermore, they also were well aware of the seven feasts of the Biblical calendar. They were also aware that the final feast, the 7th one, was the feast of Succoth, also known as the feast of Tabernacles or the Harvest feast. The Israelites were commanded to observe this feast in Deuteronomy 16. So the early church was well aware of the connection between the Harvest Feast and the Final Harvest of the Saints, and the Trumpets in connection with this Festival. *(A side note: Succoth is the 7th Feast, in the 7th month of the Jewish calendar, and it lasts for 7 days! Talk about a lot of 7's!)*

So to determine if the 7th trump mentioned in Revelation is the same as the "Last Trump" of the Feast of Harvest we need to determine when this trumpet sounds, and what follows. We see in Revelation chapter 11 the sounding of the 7th trumpet. This trumpet signals to the entire world that Christ's reign has begun. Now what does the trumpet mentioned by Paul signify? Does it also signify that Christ's reign has begun? We can see that, yes, it does signify the beginning of Christ's reign. Because as we have already established, when the Last trump sounds, we are resurrected and raptured. So why then does the rapture not happen until Revelation 14, if the trumpet is sounded in Revelation 11?

In order to understand this we must remember that many events can happen at once. Right as you read this there are many things transpiring perhaps in your home, in your town, in your state, in your country, in your continent, and in your hemisphere of the world, not to mention all of the events that are happening around the entire world.

It seems that Revelation 12, 13 and the first part of 14 are all explaining many of the events that lead up to the trumpets sounding, and are transpiring while the trumpets are sounding. As if John takes a pause to fit in all of the important details so that the reader doesn't miss some of the key things that happened in his vision.

This is a very typical way to relate multiple simultaneous events even now. We can only describe one detail at a time. Our language is limited in this respect. So it is no surprise that John would have to do this as well. We read in the Gospel of John where he says there is a great deal more that could be said about Jesus, and it would fill up volumes. So we already know that John's writing style is to give important details as he remembered them. In Revelation it is similar, which is one of several reasons why I believe it is the same John who wrote the Gospel, the Epistles and the Revelation.

So I do believe that the 7th trumpet of Revelation is also the Last trump that is mentioned by Paul and Jesus. Furthermore, there is no mention for the rest of Revelation of any significant trumpet. The only other reference to a trumpet is in a collection of musical instruments that will never again be heard in Babylon in Revelation 18. So I think the likelihood of these two trumpets being the same is very high. But at the "glorious appearing" passage in Revelation 19, there is no trumpet mentioned, and if Revelation 19 represents a different event from the Rapture, there would have to be a trumpet mentioned there as well. But since a trumpet is not mentioned there, we can be confident that the 7th Trumpet of Revelation is indeed the "Last Trump."

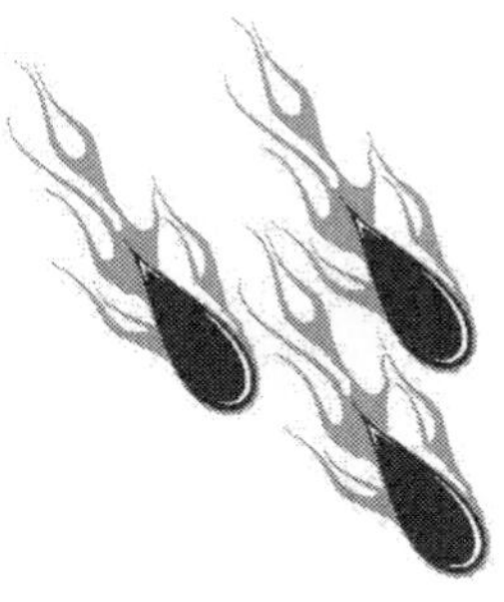

The Antichrist

What Do We Know About The Antichrist?

An entire book could be written on just the subject of the Antichrist alone, and in fact, I do have plans for such a book in the future. Some of the things that we want to cover in the upcoming edition include a study of the world conquerors of the past, and how their methods lead us to a better understanding of the Antichrist's conquests as well. However, for the purpose of this book, we do need to cover a few things about Him.

The Bible tells us a great deal throughout all of the prophets and the New Testament about the individual commonly called the Antichrist. In fact in Ezekiel 38:17, it says that all of the other prophets have been telling about his coming. It seems that the two most important figures in history, Jesus the Messiah and the Antichrist have been the most talked about figures in prophecy.

First of all, we see throughout Scripture that he has many titles, and though there is debate as to the singularity of some of these titles, most Christian scholars seem to be in agreement on many of them. He has been referred to as the seed of the Serpent all the way back in Genesis. He was also called Gog, the Assyrian, Pharaoh and the King of Tyre. Other titles include: the Wicked Man, the King of Babylon. Daniel called him the Little Horn and the Profane and the Stern-faced King. And he also referred to him as the Coming Prince. Zechariah referred to him as the Worthless Shepherd, which points to his ties to a world religion. He's also called the Oppressor by Isaiah. Paul called him the Man of Lawlessness in 2 Thessalonians, and John called him the Antichrist and the Beast.

A complete study on just his titles would reveal a great deal about his personality, history and the areas that he conquers. There are several other things we've been taught about him in church, and some of these teaching line up and some of them conflict, so it is important to sort through what we do know about the Antichrist, including:

He will wage war against the most powerful military power on earth, Daniel 11

He will deny the Father and the Son – 2 John 1

His empire will be made up of 10 countries, or 10 countries will surrender their allegiance to him – Rev 13:1, 17:7-16, 20, Dan 7:24, Some use Daniel 2, but after much study, I do not believe Daniel 2 is a reference to the Antichrist's empire, as all of the things mentioned in the prophecy have already come to pass, exactly as

Daniel predicted. The only part of that prophecy yet to be fulfilled is that the mountain, which represents Christ's church, founded on Christ the Rock, will never be taken from the earth.

He will be the embodiment of Lucifer, who is described in Isaiah 14

His empire will control the whole world – Revelation 13:12

His empire will not control the entire world – Daniel 11:40-45, Rev. 16:10, Rev. 12:14

He does not honor the gods of his fathers – Daniel 11:37

He does not honor the desire of women – Daniel 11:37

Jesus will fight against him and his armies – Habakuk 3, Isaiah 10:34 and Joel 3

He is called the Man of Lawlessness – 2 Thessalonians

Most of these attributes are pretty straight forward, however a couple probably need a little more clarification.

Some teach that his empire will control the entire world, based on what Revelation describes about the mark of the beast, and his world wide influence. Others teach that his empire will not control the entire world but will influence the entire world, based on Daniel 11, Rev 16:10, and on the fact that his kingdom is apparently made up of only 10 kingdoms. They argue that since his empire is limited to only 10 kingdoms he cannot control the entire world. Some argue that since his reign is marked by warfare, he can't control the world for the entire time if he's constantly at war. It is difficult to know exactly which of these teachings is correct. But it is conceivable that he could dominate the globe, in fact he would have to in order to wield the power that he is said to wield. Whether he has complete control is a subject of debate. Based on Revelation 12, I do not believe he will have total control of the globe, but will have some weak places, because Jesus said that a place would be prepared in the wilderness (or the desert depending on the translation) where God's people would be safe.

He does not honor the gods of his fathers – This could mean that he will attempt to change the religion of his forefathers. Or that he will not be polytheistic, where his ancestors were. Could he be a convert to his new religion? I do not know. This passage seems to me to strongly describe Mohammed. Mohammed grew up in a polytheistic society, but picked one, the moon god Sin, also know as Allah (the diety), to worship. John tells us that the spirit of the antichrist is already at work in the world. If this is so, I pose the question to you, would we have seen some of the prophetic events fulfilled in the lives of other people who were possessed by this spirit? Do we need to see all of these prophetic events fulfilled within one in the same demonic individual? Those are questions for further study. Perhaps instead of looking for one world leader at the end to embody every single prophecy about him, we should be looking for the activity of his spirit throughout the centuries since Jesus left.

We do know from Revelation that he creates a one world religion, which either means that he will in some way create an ecumenical movement that will unite the religions of the world, deifying himself, or he will use religion as a means of enslavement. This is the big debate currently between the "Rome is the Antichrist's Kingdom" and "Islam is the Antichrist's Kingdom" stances. Is the Antichrist's religion some sort of New Age/Occult religion or is it Islam? Or maybe it is it some new form of an ecumenical hybrid religion? Currently, looking at the rapid growth of Islam in Europe and throughout the world, and since it fits in with Revelation's descriptions of the final religion (i.e. one that beheads people, one that requires a mark or badge of servitude to it, etc.) I am far more convinced that it will be Islamic.

He does not honor the desire of women (Daniel 11:37) - This doesn't necessarily mean that he will be a homosexual, but he will hate women, and he will also not care about their pleas. Perhaps, like Herod before him, he will be a murderer of innocent children. Since he is the embodiment of Satan he will hate the woman, just like Eve is hated by Satan. In Satanic cults, like Islam, the woman is hated. We can see in a similar manner that Hitler was like this, and killed Jewish men, women and children indiscriminately.

Jesus Will Fight Against him and his armies (Habakuk 3 Isaiah 10:34 Joel 3) – (incidentally, all places where the Messiah fights Islamic countries) In Isaiah 63 we see the war against Edom, and in Zechariah 14 we see that Christ will fight for Israel against the Antichrist.

He is Gog - Ezekiel 38:17 is pretty convincing that Gog and the Antichrist are one and the same person, though there is some confusion here, because after the Millennium, Gog comes back on the scene for one final battle with Christ, but the Antichrist is thrown into the lake of fire forever. If this is the same individual or another, the Bible is unclear, and it's hard to come to any hard and fast conclusion on this issue. Perhaps after the Millennium a group of people from the land of Gog will rise up, but we cannot make any definitive judgment on this yet. The good news is when Jesus returns, we can ask Him for clarity on these enigmatic passages!

He is called the Man of Lawlessness – 2 Thessalonians shows us this title.

Some scholars contend that Gog and the Antichrist are two different individuals because both Daniel and Ezekiel use the phrase "the King of the North," to describe possibly two different individuals.

Most scholars agree that Daniel is talking about the battle between the Seleucids and the Ptolemys after Alexander the Great's empire was divided upon his death.

The strongest defense of this position is that exactly as Daniel described it, there was an attack of Antiochus Epiphanes against Ptolemy VI around 168 BC. This was during the inter-Testamental time period described by the book of Maccabees, found in the Apocrypha. During the Maccabean Revolt, the Jews revolted against Antiochus' authority. Daniel's description of this even is so accurate that many liberal and secular scholars believe that the Book of Daniel had to be written after this event, in spite of overwhelming evidence to the contrary.

But many prophecy scholars point to patterns of prophecy, where history often repeats itself, and we can sometimes gauge the prophetic nature by the repetition of similar events throughout history. In their view, many historical events are similar. In defense of this view, I would like to point out that if we are dealing with the same enemy, i.e. Satan, in different guises, then not only are his goals exactly the same as they have always been, his strategies would most likely be similar each time he is seen to operate in the world. Satan is a finite being. He is limited in the creativeness and intelligence that God created him with (though far superior to our own), and he also is dealing with humans who often repeat the same mistakes over and over and over again.

This could also refer to the same land occupied by two different empires. We see that the Seleucid territory was ruled over by many different kingdoms since the time period directly before the New Testament.

But then again, the distinction between the two mysterious southern and northern kings could be that there are kings of countries that are even further north than the Antichrist's "north of Israel" country. In a scenario where the Antichrist is Islamic, then perhaps a country such as Russia might attack him, and that would explain why a king of the North could attack The King of the North.

I tend to lean towards Gog and the Antichrist being the same individual, but I do not think that Armageddon and the Gog/Magog war are the same event, as some people teach. I believe they are two events, and I cover that more in the section on Armageddon.

How will I recognize the Antichrist when he arrives?

I think we can be fairly convinced that the Antichrist is not Robert Owen, the founder of the 19th Century commune of New Harmony, Indiana. Why do I mention Robert Owen you might ask?

Because in the same night that Margaret MacDonald had her Pre-Trib vision, that so many continue to cling to, she proclaimed that Robert Owen was indeed the Antichrist, according to the biographer of the Catholic Apostolic Church, Robert Norton. You can read more about this in Dave MacPhearson's book, *"The Incredible Cover-up."*

This is clearly a case of a false prophecy. The Scripture is very clear that we are not to listen to false prophets, yet countless Pre-Trib teachers still cling to her false teaching without realizing it. But though they cling to her false interpretation about a Pre-Trib Rapture, how many cling to her false teaching about who the Antichrist will be, which came to her in the very same night?

Though the Antichrist most certainly will not be Robert Owen incarnate, there will be a way to spot him when he arrives. In order to recognize the Antichrist there are several things that must be discussed which I intend to include in my next book about him. But for sake of reference here we should go over a few of the things that will help us identify the Antichrist when we see him.

First he will have a false prophet accompany him. The false prophet will claim to be the true Jesus, and will be a powerful figure in and of himself. The false prophet will help the Antichrist consolidate his power.

The Antichrist will be a person who makes a peace treaty with Israel for a period of seven years. In the middle of that peace treaty he will break it and invade Israel, attack Jerusalem, send many Jews off into slavery, kill many and take over the third temple.

He will be a very warlike man, and will wage war across the Middle East, and will carve an empire out that will resemble the 7th empire, which is the empire that followed the Roman Empire. The empire that followed Rome was most likely, the Ottoman Empire or one of the Islamic empires that followed in uniting the former Roman lands, so most likely the Antichrist will be of Middle Eastern descent, or at least very interested in the area of the Middle East possibly due to the power that oil has over the world.

He will use his wealth and station to influence the rest of the world to acquiesce to his demands.

His empire will be very degenerate, and will have a powerful capital that will follow John's description of Mystery Babylon. Whether it is actually set up where Babylon was or not, is not clear. My opinion is that it will not because the name is Mystery Babylon, not Babylon

Reformed, or Babylon Reborn or anything like that. And the fact that Babylon was still a place at the time of John's writing, makes me think that it isn't Iraq. It might include ancient Babylon, but it will overshadow ancient Babylon. John is showing us that his city is in many ways glorious like ancient Babylon, but also just as evil and corrupt.

Aside from Biblical references, we can also look at previous world leaders to get an idea of some of his characteristics. There have been many men who have set out to conquer the world, the first being *Nimrod* around the time of the Tower of Babel. Some believe that the Antichrist spirit will be the spirit of Nimrod coming into the man. Ancient sources point to Nimrod possibly being one of the Nephilim referred to in Genesis, and that he was a man of giant proportions. The Nephilim were wiped out by God in the flood, but apparently came back as the children of Israel had to deal with them when they came back to the Promised Land from Egypt. You can see this in the account of the spies who crossed over into the land, and also in the account of the fall of Jericho in the book of Joshua.

Nimrod was the first world conqueror, conquering the known world at the time, and subjugating fealty and worship under him. Of the most prominent men to study in comparison, Nimrod is the first place to begin any study on the Antichrist.

After Nimrod, there was a great world leader known as *Nebuchadnezzar* who had the drive to conqueror. During Nebuchadnezzar's reign, the Jews were deported to

Babylon, and Daniel was able to give the interpretation to Nebuchadnezzar's dream about the statue with various body parts of different metals. This dream is found in Daniel chapter 2.

You looked, O king, and there before you stood a large statue – an enormous, dazzling statue, awesome in appearance. The head of the statue was made of pure gold, its chest and arms of silver, its belly and thighs of bronze, its legs of iron, its feet partly of iron and partly of baked clay. While you were watching, a rock was cut out, but not by human hands. It struck the statue on its feet of iron and clay and smashed them. Then the iron, the clay the bronze, the silver and the gold were broken to pieces at the same time and became like chaff on a threshing floor in the summer. The wind swept them away without leaving a trace. But the rock that struck the statue became a huge mountain and filled the whole earth. (Daniel 2:31-35, NLT)

Daniel explains to Nebuchadnezzar that the head of Gold represented the Babylonian empire. The rest of the empires represent various kingdoms and empires that tried to take over the world. But there is great debate as to who the empires actually were or if there is one that will be to come.

First there are 5 materials represented here: Gold, Silver, Bronze, Iron and Clay. Daniel says that these 5 materials represent 4 empires, though some prophecy teachers point to the iron and clay mix as a 5th empire: Babylon, and then three or four others. I believe these empires were the Medo-Persian Empire, Alexander the Great's

Macedonian Empire and the Roman Empire. I believe this dream was fulfilled, and came to pass, and the final Mountain was Christ. He established a kingdom that will never end, which gives me great comfort as a Post-Trib teacher, because it means that even in the harshest time of the Antichrist's rule, he will never be able to break the mountain that is Christ.

I'm not convinced that Nebuchadnezzar's vision shows a gap between the legs and the feet, and it is quite possible that this vision has nothing to do with the end times, though many Pre-Trib people like to claim that it does. Many Pre-Trib teachers claim that there is a gap between the legs and the feet and toes which are Iron and a mixture of Iron and Clay.

But this vision follows too closely the pattern of what actually happened historically. So closely, in fact, that many liberal and secular scholars believe that it couldn't have been predicted before hand. But as I mentioned before, the documentation is overwhelming in favor of it actually being prophecy. Furthermore, some of the details in the vision (such as the intermarriage of the various parts of the iron and clay mixture) actually happened in modern history. From the time of the fall of the Holy Roman Empire, principalities and sovereign cities did in fact intermarry so frequently that it eventually lead to various strains of diseases known to royal families because of the inbreeding. In fact, we know that the Roman Empire, which was the Empire of Iron, did indeed split into two sections, the Roman Empire and the Byzantine Empire. We also know that the Roman Empire morphed into the Holy Roman Empire and continued up until very recent times, though it has been on a long and slow decline.

Many Biblical scholars link the 10 toes of the feet with the 10 horns, and perhaps there is a link, but it is important to point out here that there is no direct Biblical connection. Any connection is speculation on the part of the prophecy teachers, and not contained within the text. Remember we need to go to the Bible for Truth, not to support our man made theories. And also we must read what the text actually says before we start making theories or connecting dots that might not connect. Because this vision shows not just once, but twice, that multiple body parts seem to represent specific details of prophecy, I will not rule out the ten toes as a possibility of being connected to the prophecy of the ten horns, but I see no internal textual support.

Nearly every scholar I have studied believes that the silver represented the Medo-Persian empire that came next and overthrew the Babylonian Empire.

The Medo-Persian Empire was composed of both the empires of the Medes and of the Persians. Some argue that these were in fact two separate Empires, but their transitions and areas of influence seem to be of such a nature that most scholars connect them as one and the same. It is interesting to note that the arms and the chest portion are of silver, and just as there are two legs to the Roman portion (the Roman and Byzantine), there were two portions to the Medo-Persian empire.

Many years later, this world conquering spirit was seen in the ambition of Alexander the Great. According to most Biblical scholars, Alexander's empire was the one Daniel explained would be the empire of Bronze. Alexander the Great, as a world conqueror, demonstrated a great deal of tactical ability and was able to put an entire swath of land from Southern Europe to India under his control. But like Nimrod, he was unable to unite the entire world under his authority.

When Alexander died, the remnants of his empire did not go to a descendant because he didn't have any, so it was left to his generals. His generals were very able people, and carved out and left some smaller empires in their own right. The Seleucid Empire was the dominating empire of the northern portion of Alexander's empire from 312 BC until 64 BC when it was overthrown by Roman general Pompey. It was the Seleucid Empire which controlled Israel during the time between the Old and New Testament when the Book of Maccabees, found in the Apocrypha, was written. The Book of Maccabees details the Maccabean Rebellion against Antiochus IV Epiphanes, who earned the nickname Epimanes "The Mad One" due to his erratic and irrational behavior.

Some might wonder why Antiochus' Seleucid Empire is not one of the empires represented by Nebuchadnezzar's dream. But most scholars attest, the Seleucid Empire was really just a continuation of Alexander's empire, and not really another empire. Daniel was given more information about these empires in both Daniel chapter 8 and also in chapters 10 and 11. Most scholars agree that Daniel referred to the Seleucid Empire as the Kingdom of the North, and the Ptolemy kingdom as the Kingdom of the South in Daniel 10 and 11. These chapters are concerned a great deal about the war between the Seleucid and the Ptolemy Empires, the latter portion of Daniel 11 shifts to talking about the Antichrist, who is here compared with Antiochus Epiphanes. "Epiphanes," by the way, is Greek for "manifested god," or "god manifest." He obviously thought highly of himself, as will the Antichrist.

But the final empire of Nebuchadnezzar's dream I believe is Rome. We see a conquering spirit yet again with Julius Caesar, and the Roman emperors who followed him. Many scholars agree that Rome represented the next empire, the 4th, in Nebuchadnezzar's strange dream, and is the empire characterized by iron. Many scholars believe that the iron in this vision represents that the empire would be one that was very harsh, and Rome certainly fits the bill with its reputation of the terrible Pax Romana, the Roman Peace. Rome inflicted heavy tribute from the territories they subjugated, and certainly ruled with an iron fist.

But while the Roman empire was one of Iron, Daniel also says that the feet of it would be miry clay, and when studying the fall of the Roman empire, and its transition to the Holy Roman Empire (HRE), we see a great deal of weak elements mixed in. What I see here is that the Roman Empire has technically existed from its inception with Julius Caesar until the present day. It has been on a slow and steady decline from the time of Rome's glory until the incredibly weakened state of the Catholic Church today.

Many scholars will separate out the Catholic Church from the Roman Empire, but history bears witness that the church existed as an empire, and it is a verifiable fact that it was just a continuation of the Roman Empire. In fact, Constantine was the last Roman emperor and first HRE emperor. When one does a study of all of the atrocities of the Roman Catholic Church on the world, there really is no debate that they fit the bill of an empire of Iron and Miry Clay. So of all the empires mentioned in the dream of Nebuchadnezzar, the Roman Empire is the only one that continued into the modern era.

However, we see that the true church is represented by the mountain of Christ who establishes His Kingdom that will ultimately destroy the other empires entirely. We also see that this kingdom will always be represented on earth forever. This shows again that there will never be a time when the church is not present in the world, again going against a Pre-Trib argument.

But Nebuchadnezzar wasn't the only one who had a vision of the coming empires of the world. Daniel also had a vision and some information given to him from the angel Gabriel in chapter 11. Currently there is a great debate as to whether the Antichrist Empire will be a revived Roman Empire, or a Middle Eastern Empire, based on Daniel's vision detailed in chapter 11.

Many Christian scholars in modern times have claimed that the Holy Roman Empire is the last Empire. But in actuality, the Holy Roman Empire was technically not another empire, but a continuation of the original Roman Empire. An empire did rise out of the ashes of the Roman Empire, and yet was entirely distinct from the Roman Empire. That empire was the *Ottoman Empire*, which lasted from early medieval times, up until almost modern times. The Ottoman Empire was ruled by a harsh ruler as well, and took over a large portion of the world. And it too was characterized by ruling with an iron fist.

Daniel shows us that the last empire will be a *revival* of the 7th empire. For those theologians that still point to a resurrection of the Roman Empire, I would point out that nearly everyone agrees that the Roman Empire was the 6th Empire in Daniel's vision of the empires. And according to some scholars the 7th was the Holy Roman Empire, and the 8th would be a restored Holy Roman Empire. However this cannot be the case. The Holy Roman Empire was technically formed by Constantine, who was also an Emperor of the Roman Empire, which as I mentioned before makes the Holy Roman Empire just a continuation of the Roman Empire. So the 7th Empire cannot be Rome.

Therefore, since the final Antichrist Empire cannot be a resurrection of Rome, it must be a resurrection of some other Empire. The only other Empire that remains is either the Ottoman Empire or one of the European Empires like the British or French Empires. As far as I can tell, no one argues that the Antichrist Empire will be a revival of the British or French Empires, as they would technically both be a portion of the Holy Roman Empire, and they were both, at least nominally, Christian.

I have to side with those who believe the Antichrist Empire will be an Islamic Empire. Also looking at the current world events, and the fact that Islam, not Catholicism is sweeping through Europe, really seals the deal in my mind. I do not foresee a rise of Catholicism, in spite of what many theologians argue. And John specifically stated in his epistles, that to deny both the Father and the Son is the antichrist spirit. (John 1:22)

Catholics, for all of their potentially heretical teachings, do not deny the Father and the Son, and do not fit the warning given by John. The one thing that could lead Catholics completely astray is their doctrine of Papal Authority. If an Antichrist type leader ever ruled the Papacy, then many Catholics could be lead astray.

Though I believe the Antichrist will be Islamic, some theologians, such as Martin Luther, taught that the Antichrist Empire would be a two pronged empire composed of both an Eastern and a Western half, based on the fact that there are two horns mentioned in Daniel's the vision of the horns. If the Antichrist were to revive the Ottoman Empire, and the False Prophet were to revive the Roman Empire, and then unite them into one Empire, then we would see both a two pronged Empire.

In order for this to happen, we are looking for someone who is very good at diplomacy, scare tactics and power brokering. This person will probably be very likable and charismatic, seeming to have a lot of answers, and will be able to unite diverse groups of people quickly.

If the Antichrist Empire is two pronged as Luther suspected, and the Roman Empire portion is ruled by the False Prophet, then the Antichrist will be a middle easterner, possibly a Turk, since Turkey was the seat of the last Caliphate during the Ottoman Empire, and Turkey is directly to the north of Israel. *Furthermore, Magog, Gomer, Meshech, Tubal and Togarmah are also places in ancient Turkey, and these places are linked with the Antichrist.*

Others argue that possibly the Antichrist could be a Syrian, since Syria is also to the north of Israel, and also the Antichrist is known as "the Syrian." But again, this would be an Islamic Antichrist, and not a Catholic one.

If the Antichrist is Islamic, which seems highly likely due to his areas of influence., he will also claim the title of Caliph (kind of like an Emperor/Pope of the Islamic religion) and will unite all the Islamic nations into one group.

At some point He will have a sort of treaty with the Jews, and most likely with someone posing as Jesus. If this so called "Jesus" is sitting as the Pope in Rome then it would fulfill the two pronged theory. If this Jesus is not in Rome, then it is very likely that some sort of overthrow of Rome could be in order.

Some argue that the Antichrist will not be able to overthrow Rome, and that Rome will not be part of the Antichrist Empire because of the prophecy found in Daniel 11 that says that the "Ships of Kittim" will oppose the Antichrist ("Kittim," meaning "the west"). While many scholars believe this prophecy was fulfilled when Roman ships opposed Antiochus Epiphanes, there are those who see a replay of this happening in the End Times scenario.

However, this does not necessarily mean that modern day Italy will oppose the Antichrist (though modern day Italy does have an impressive navy). Some scholars claim that these "Ships of Kittim" are a prophecy about American ships that oppose the Antichrist. It is certainly a possibility in an End Times scenario including America, that since America has always sided with Israel in the past, it could side with Israel in a war against the Antichrist. But unfortunately, we are told in Scripture that "all of the countries of the world," will oppose Israel. This is dire news for US citizens who are Christian. The future for our country would not be good in such a scenario.

But since we do not know for sure if this prophecy will be repeated again, we cannot be sure that either Rome or America is part of the End Times scenario.

Other world leaders have arisen since Julius Caesar, including men like Genghis Kahn, Charlemagne, Napoleon and Adolph Hitler, all men who have tried in one way or another to conquer the entire world. All have failed, and the Antichrist will fail as well, but all of them had a strong charisma, incredible battle tactics, and a curious ability to foresee danger and disaster in time to avoid it. But like Napoleon, who had his Waterloo, each one of them had a tipping point, where they reached too far, and were thrown down from their high and lofty position, to embrace defeat and become just a name in the history books.

Whoever the Antichrist will be, we can be safe to assume he will be in many ways like his predecessors before him, greedy, overreaching though highly intelligent and skilled in both diplomacy and warfare, and evil beyond all possible understanding.

Doesn't the Bible teach that the church will depart before the Antichrist is revealed according to 2 Thess. 2:7 and 8?

2 Thessalonians 2:3 (NLT)

Don't be fooled by what they say. For that day will not come until there is a great rebellion against God and the man of lawlessness is revealed—the one who brings destruction.

This passage is interesting because it specifically says that first the ἀποστασία (apostasy, or the loosing of the faith) and the ἄνθρωπος τῆς ἀνομίας (man of lawlessness), the υἱὸς τῆς ἀπωλείας (son of destruction) is ἀποκαλυφθῇ (revealed.) Here we have the word apocalypse, which is another term for Revelation. Revelation is about several revealings. Christ is revealed when He comes again. The Antichrist is also revealed to the people who are following God (notice the unbelievers are deceived, therefore nothing is revealed to them, they are blind, *compare this to Daniel 12:3 and 10*), and also information that is important to those who will live in those days is revealed to the reader. In verse 2 Paul lets us know that he is talking about the coming of Christ (which he links with his teaching in 1 Thessalonians 4 and 5 about the Rapture), but notice in this passage, verse 3, that first the apostasy has to happen, and then the man of lawlessness will be revealed.

Read 2 Thess. 2:3. It specifically states that the Antichrist must be revealed first before the Second Coming. The teaching that the church will be raptured before the Antichrist is revealed is completely unbiblical, and one could make a strong argument that it is even heretical, because it outright completely contradicts direct verses from the Bible.

Furthermore, the beasts that represent the major End Times players in Revelation are introduced before the “harvest” passage in Revelation 14. Either way you look at it, the Antichrist is revealed first.

“Is the Antichrist destroyed before the rapture of the church.” This is clearly not the case. We see that the Battle of Armageddon happens around the time of Christ’s return. The Antichrist is captured at the Battle of Armageddon, which the raptured and glorified church will be present for. So at the time of the Rapture the Antichrist must still be alive, and already deeply enmeshed in ruling his empire, not just starting out, or

even not on the scene yet, as some Pre-Trib teachers will have you believe.

What the Bible teaches is that the church will *endure through the Great Tribulation* which is the Antichrist's appointed time to try to take over the earth. He will cause many to be imprisoned, many to be executed, but a great many others will escape according to Revelation 12. When his time is up, and the people of Israel have turned to cry for deliverance from Jesus, then Christ will return, rapture the church, glorify their bodies, and descend into the Land to free the people from tyranny. This is the picture that Paul teaches here in 1 and 2 Thessalonians.

Will the Antichrist's empire be global?

There is ample evidence that the Antichrist's empire will not be global. Examples include the many wars that oppose him from Ezekiel's description of the Gog/Magog war, and the passages in Daniel's description of those that attack him in chapter 11, and also the fact that Revelation describes a limited scope of his kingdom like where only his kingdom goes dark during the bowls of wrath, and that chapter 12 specifies several areas that he will not overthrow.

The fact that his empire will be one that has a global impact, however can not be disputed. We see that many nations have dealings with him, as attested to in Revelation chapter 18, where we see the fall of his capital city, known only as Mystery Babylon.

In Revelation chapter 13 we see that the first beast, the Antichrist, and the second beast, the false prophet, have been given authority over all of the earth. Yet we also see in Daniel 11 and other places that many kingdoms will wage war against the Antichrist. For those who believe that Daniel chapter 2 has some relevance to the Antichrist's kingdom (which I personally doubt) even the miry clay mixed with iron suggests certain aspects of his empire are not well controlled as other parts. From these two pieces of information we can deduce that though his empire will have power in all the earth, and influence every nation in one way or another, his empire will not be completely global. We know that he will only have total control of 10 countries. But these 10 countries have something the other countries need or want.

It makes a great deal of sense that these countries might be oil producing countries, as every country in the civilized world needs oil to continue to sustain itself.

Many scholars theorize that the Antichrist's empire will be a revival of the Ottoman Empire which includes many of the world's largest producers of oil. These countries already hold a great sway in the world's economy, and it makes sense that if they were to unite they would be a force to be reckoned with.

So his empire will most likely not be completely global, but it will impact the entire world in its reach and influence.

There is a theory that does deserve mention here. Many claim that secluded Occultist/Free Masonic movers and shakers of the western world are currently behind the scenes controlling and shaping the world into a New World Order that will lead up to unleashing "Lucifer" to control the world. I put "Lucifer" in quotes because what they mean by Lucifer is different than what the Bible means by Lucifer. They believe that Lucifer is the "architect of the universe" and is basically God. We disagree, and believe that Lucifer is Satan.

Many claim that the ultimate plan of these nefarious people is to divide the world into 10 regions and then hand it over to Lucifer when he arrives.

There seems to me to be a great deal of support that there are people out there who would like to do such a thing. Proponents of this theory point to proposals such as the UN's "Agenda 21," and there can be no doubt that measures are currently being proposed that fall in line with such a plan. But the real question is will these people be allowed to rule in the Antichrist's kingdom, or will they ultimately be stabbed in the back by Satan and have their hard work handed over to someone they did not expect? It wouldn't be unlike Satan to do such a thing, and I can foresee such an event as the current world leaders, after getting so close to their own goal of a one world government, being forced to hand it all over to an Islamic Mahdi.

Will the Antichrist be Russian?

Map detail based on several maps in many of the popular Bible dictionaries that show where the lands mentioned in Ezekiel's prophecy about Gog and Magog existed.

Probably not. This theory comes from two misunderstood passages in the Bible. The first is because some older theologians thought that Magog was another word for Moscow. However, there is little proof of this. There is the theory that descendants of Magog settled in and around Moscow, and there does seem to be support for this, but one who holds this theory must contend with the fact that descendants of Magog settled in several other places as well, including what is now modern day Turkey.

There is also the misinterpretation of the Hebrew "rosh" found in Ezekiel 38:2. Some claim that this word should be interpreted as a proper noun, i.e. a specific place called Rosh, however there is no real support for this theory, as the word "rosh" literally means "Chief Prince," as it is translated in many translations of the Bible. This translation makes perfect sense since the Antichrist will be the chief prince of whatever Empire he rules.

The second passage links the Antichrist with the kingdom of the north. The thought process is that since Russia is north of Israel, and Moscow must be the farthest northern city above Jerusalem, and sense some of Magog's descendants settled in and around what is now Moscow, it must be that the Antichrist will be Russian. However, there is no validity to this either, as there are many cities north of Jerusalem, and there are several cities north of Moscow, including the capitals of Finland and Norway. Currently, Moscow is still a world power that produces many weapons, but this does not mean that it will be the Antichrist's seat of authority.

Furthermore, Daniel 11 specifically describes the Antichrist being attacked, or at least threatened, from both the North and the South. There are no countries north of Moscow that would be a major attacking force against a Russian Antichrist.

What many Pre-Trib teachers do not understand is that Bible scholars point out that Magog was actually a place in Turkey, which, incidentally, is the most likely country to the north of Israel that would have a reason to attack her.

For years many pointed to the fact that Turkey was an ally to Israel, indeed one of the only allies Israel had in the Middle East, with Egypt being a close second ally. Sadly, these two countries have both turned against Israel in recent times and are no longer allies.

While Russia would benefit from strong ties to oil producing Middle Eastern countries, Russia is not threatening Israel, at the present time. The neighboring countries such as Syria, Jordan, Saudi Arabia and yes, even Turkey (the former seat of the Islamic Caliphate), has been threatening Israel since it's very inception in 1948. Furthermore, when it is determined that "rosh" is not a proper name, and that Magog is most likely in modern day Turkey, then the logic used to deduce that Moscow is the seat of the Antichrist, falls apart, and makes no sense.

In any End Time scenario that should happen in the near future, the most likely culprit for an Antichrist kingdom would not be a New-Age Vatican ruled by a Russian. Russians most likely have backgrounds either as atheists or else Russian Orthodoxy, not the Roman Catholic Church. And as far as New-Age religion goes, most New-Agers lean more towards a peace, love and drugs mentality. If by "New Age" one means "occult" then that would make more sense. But the Antichrist must be someone from the revived 7th Empire of Daniel's vision, which would be the Ottoman Empire (not the Roman – the Roman was the 6th Empire). And since the Ottoman Empire had its seat of power in Turkey, a revived Ottoman Empire most likely will have its seat of power in

Turkey as well. And since Islam already is hateful to the Jews, it only makes sense that *Turkey is the "country of the North," not Russia.*

Will The Antichrist come out of Europe?

Some point to the mechanizations of Occult and Freemasonic type organizations to manipulate the outcomes of many things, and say that the evidence of the occult dealings of groups such as the Illuminati prove that the Antichrist will come out of Europe. I do not deny at all that occult groups exist, and have a hierarchy that has tried to influence and control the world, and indeed very well might control the world even now. But I would like to point out that throughout the Bible and history, we see that people who have dealings with Satan are often lied to by him, manipulated by him, given great power for a short period of time by him, but then ultimately abandoned by him because of his deceptive nature. Any group that thinks they will remain in power when Satan ultimately sees the fruition of his plans will most likely be disappointed.

I believe there is a lot of evidence that points to the existence of occult groups, but I believe they are being used by Satan, and will be abandoned and enslaved by the Antichrist in the end. It will be the final *coup de gras* by Satan against these groups who followed him so faithfully. We can see a hint of this in Revelation 17:13 where the kings of the earth hand over their power and authority to the Beast. Those who currently rule will be forced to give over their authority. So those who spent so much time manipulating the world political scene will be brought to a subservient position under the Antichrist.

Furthermore, many people will point to Daniel 2 to try to explain that the Antichrist will be from Europe, but no where in Daniel 2 does it say this. In fact, what it does say has nothing to do with End Times prophecy as all of the events have been fulfilled, as I explained earlier. But if by some chance it does have something to do with the Antichrist's kingdom, we can see that the final kingdom, the Antichrist kingdom will be a mixture of Iron and Clay. Daniel says this represents two separate groups coming together with intermarriage to try to strengthen their positions. I believe what we will see is the rebirth of the Islamic Ottoman Empire, and somehow it will be linked with the West's powerbrokers. I believe this is the case, because the West is made of Clay. The west is weak, we want peace, we want comfort, we are not willing to fight for anything we believe in, and we're always trying to make deals with people, while the Islamic world is hard and demanding, they take what they want, and they profit off of everything.

If Daniel 2 has anything to do with End Times prophecy, something to watch for will be the intermarriage of someone important in the reborn Islamic empire with someone prominent in the west. Or else we might see some sort of special treaty that could symbolically be a "marriage" of sorts.

Another passage that people often point to is Daniel 9:26 to prove that the Antichrist will be European, since the Romans destroyed the Temple and Jerusalem. But it goes on to say that a treaty will be made. Now we know that the Romans do not fulfill the prophesies that were made about the End Times, in spite of what people like Hank Hanegraaff want to tell you, as is demonstrated earlier in this book.

First of all, Partial-Preterists are missing the global nature of the prophecies. Secondly, Daniel shows that the same Ruler who destroys the temple will make a treaty with the people. After the temple was destroyed, the Romans never made a treaty with the Jews they simply dispersed them to the four winds.

The Antichrist and the Temple

I believe that a possible scenario could be: when the Antichrist sits in the temple and declares that he is God, immediately following that event he will destroy the 3rd temple and sack the city. Or a war could break out in rebellion causing the Temple to be destroyed. This could be why the people will have to flee through the newly formed passageway that will appear after the great earthquake, mentioned in Ezekiel 38:19, Zechariah 14:4-5, Matthew 24:16, Mark 13:14 and Luke 21:21.

Currently there is great debate among Jews about whether they should build the Temple or if the Messiah builds the Temple when He comes. Some Jews point to Isaiah 66:1 in an effort to say that when Messiah comes there will not be a house for him. However, the debate seems to be swaying towards building the Temple. Because the Isaiah passage does not say that there would be no house, a better understanding of the passage is that even a beautiful Temple is not glorious enough to fully house God.

I also see in Revelation that a new Temple descends with the New Jerusalem. Though it seems to imply that part of the Temple is on earth, and part of it remains in Heaven. So it is possible that there will be a 3rd and even a 4th temple, when the New Jerusalem descends from Heaven.

Why the Antichrist Could Be Islamic

I think the Antichrist will be the Islamic Mahdi for a variety of reasons. They share many of the same things in common. They both are said to be the ruler of a world dominating empire, they both are said to lead a world dominating religion, they're both supposed to be on the scene for 7 years and they both are said to have a treaty with the Jews, they are both described as riding white horses, they are both said to invade and rule from Jerusalem, they are both said to persecute Christians, they are both said to try to change the times and the calendar, both will be assisted by a prophet with miraculous powers (a fake Jesus), both have power to perform wonders, and they both arise during a period of great chaos, and both have a symbol that people must take on their foreheads or hands to follow him.

You can find more about this in Joel Richardson's book *"Islamic Antichrist,"* where he devotes a great deal of time showing the similarities between the Antichrist of the Bible and the Mahdi of the Muslims.

I was told that the Antichrist was the emperor Nero because the number 666 spells out "Nero Caesar" in Greek.

That theory popularized by "the Bible Answer Man" Hank Hanegraaff, is not correct for a number of reasons. First of all, the number 666 in Greek spells "neron," not Nero.

Secondly, using special codes and hiding names in numbers is a divination practice engaged in by Gnostics and necromancers known as gammatria or numerology, and is condemned in the Bible.

There shall not be found among you any one that maketh his son or his daughter to pass through the fire, or that useth divination, or an observer of times, or an enchanter, or a witch. Or a charmer, or a consulter with familiar spirits, or a wizard, or a necromancer. (Deut. 18:10-11, KJV)

Finally, John, who wrote the Revelation, spent the bulk of his gospel and epistles defending the faith against Gnosticism, so why would he engage in Gnostic practices to hide that he was talking about Nero? Remember, this is the same John who after being beaten and commanded to stop preaching in the name of Jesus, went on and continued preaching in the name of Jesus. (Acts 4:18, 5:28-29) This is also the same John who because of his public preaching about Jesus earned the honor of being boiled in oil for his testimony of Jesus Christ. Why would he resort to such tactics? It doesn't fit his personality profile.

Furthermore, John was exiled to the Isle of Patmos most likely in the 90's. Nero died in 68 AD. If you go with the early date of the Revelation, which some believe was the mid to later 60's there is no way Nero could be the Antichrist John was referring to, because he would have died before the 3.5 years that he was supposed to reign. Furthermore, he reigned for a total of 16 years which eliminates him as a candidate from the pool of candidates for the Antichrist anyway.

The fact is Revelation was written sometime between the mid 60's AD and the late 90's AD, so Nero as the Anti-Christ simply doesn't fit the timeline, nor the prophesies. And if he was somehow the Antichrist John was talking about, by the time John's sentence was over on the Isle of Patmos for him to deliver his message, Nero was most likely dead. Frequently, in the ancient times sentences of exile lasted at least the lifetime of the official that ordered the exile, or caused a refugee to flee into exile. An example of this is when Jesus was taken to Egypt by Joseph and Mary to escape the wrath of Herod. They returned to Judea after Herod was dead.

Most likely, even if John was on Patmos during Nero's reign, which seems highly unlikely according to most scholars, John's prison time on Patmos would have ended with Nero's death. This is perhaps one of the most compelling arguments, for the early date of the writing of the Revelation, but it also defeats the Preterists who would like to use it to bolster their erroneous belief that Nero was the Antichrist, not that he wouldn't have made a good candidate for the Antichrist, the man was a lunatic, and a potential antichrist figure, but he wasn't the final End Times Antichrist.

Some other partial-preterists argue that Vespasian was the Antichrist, but again his rule was not 7 years or 3.5

and his name does not spell out "neron." He doesn't completely fit the profile.

One might ask, "Why is it so important that candidates for the Antichrist fit the profile?" The answer to this is related to the authority of scripture. If God makes a prediction and we have to twist and bend the events to fit the prediction then it is less than a perfect prediction made by a perfect God. But those of us who believe in an omniscient perfect God understand that when His prophecies come true, they are perfect and one doesn't need to twist Scripture to make the events fit. The prophetic passages that relate to Jesus' first advent line up exactly with the details. And we should expect the same of the latter day prophecies.

What is the mark of the beast, and what is the significance of 666?

Islam has all of the traits of the Biblical antichrist system.

Many people are currently discussing the significance that the number 666 in the Greek looks a lot like Arabic writing that actually spells out "Bismillah," which literally means "in the name of Allah," with the crossed swords of Islam included. The original Greek letters are Chi, Xi and Stigma, and have also been used for numerals.

Several books detail this. The first one I read was "Why I Left Jihad," by Walid Shoebat. Another book, though I don't agree with his Pre-Trib stance, is "Unleashing the Beast" by Perry Stone. And then another popular book out there, and one of the best I've read on the subject, is "Islamic Antichrist," by Joel Richardson.

Read these and they will have a lot more information about this. However, in Shoebat's book, he describes how he became a Christian and left Islam. He says that when he began to study the Bible and decided to learn how to read Greek, he saw a scroll with the book of Revelation written on it, and saw the passage referring to 666 and recognized it immediately in Arabic.

The Bible says that the mark will be either in the hand or on the forehead. Shoebat claims that Muslims pray five times a day and lay their hands and forehead onto a prayer rug which has this phrase "Bismillah," on it. As they pray diligently every day, 5 times a day, this phrase becomes imprinted in their forehead and into their hands. Shoebat has a picture in his book of an Imam, an Islamic preacher, with these marks clearly visible on their forehead. Furthermore, a quick google search will reveal pictures of Muslims wearing the phrase or some variant of it on their arms or foreheads. There are also several pictures of older Imams with what appear to be bruises on their forehead and hands from praying.

This blew me away when I saw this. I was always taught that the mark of the beast would be either a credit card, or a microchip, or some such. But it never really made sense to me. I find it quite interesting that the Islamic paradigm is almost a completely perfect picture of what the Bible says the Antichrist's world system will be like. It ties up all of the loose ends that are left from a traditional Pre-Trib end times view point.

It is possible that this isn't the totality of the story. There are other things happening in the world now that other writers such as L.A. Marzulli, and Steven Quayle and Tom Horn discuss that relate to transhumanism that I believe could have a prominent place in the coming Antichrist empire.

Tom Horn has shown very clearly in many of his books that the next arms race will be a so-called "super-soldier" race. There's also a growing new age obsession with demonic activity and Satanism associated with Free Masons and others cultic groups. The nightmare that could be unleashed when such humans at the peak of human ability are "improved" with genetic material from animals is truly staggering.

The thing that I am not hearing yet in all of my studies is how these things will connect. While it is possible we might see something that will unite both Islam with some of the darker forms of cultic worship, how it will merge is still a mystery to me, because currently the Islamic world is just as opposed to the New Age, Masonic cultic ideology, as Christianity. I do not understand how it can all connect, but it is definitely something to look for. More likely, however, as I mentioned above, Satan is notorious for using "puppets" to get his way, i.e. people he grooms and manipulates and then deserts after his plans begin to formulate. It would not surprise me in the least to see the fall and annihilation of the New Age and the Masonic cults once the Mahdi gains power.

It is interesting that a lot of early theologians believed that the Antichrist would have a two pronged or two horned system, where part would be the western half of the empire and the other half would be the Eastern half of the empire. Or in other words, the Antichrist Empire would be made up from a Roman descended portion and an Ottoman descended portion. I believe this deserves more exploration as well. Is it possible that we will see a hybrid of the Pope and the Mahdi? Most likely what we would see in this event is, as I mentioned before, a false Jesus and an Islamic messiah.

It is interesting that Catholic tradition teaches that the current pope will be the last, and the final pope will be Petrus Romanus, Peter the Roman, who will possibly be the Antichrist or False Prophet.

I do think it is very interesting that during the writing of this book, Pope Benedict retired, the first pope to ever do so in modern times. Several hours after the Pope announced his retirement, lightning hit St. Peter's basilica in Rome. A picture of the lightning strike appeared on the Drudge Report shortly after it happened, where it has been seen by millions of people. Pope Benedict was followed in succession by Pope Francis, originally from Argentina from Italian parentage.

Why is this significant? The Catholic Church has a prophecy given by St. Malachy, an Irish Bishop some 500 years before the Reformation, which describes each and every Pope from his time until the end, when Christ should return. So far he has had an incredibly high success rate. The last pope is supposed to be known as Peter the Roman, or Petrus Romanus, and is supposed to lead the church during the Tribulation.

I don't know if this will have any significance to us Protestants, but it is a very interesting development in prophecy circles.

In the Book of Revelation we see there is a dual nature of the End Times Empire by the fact that the Antichrist is backed up by the False Prophet. The Muslims believe that the Mahdi will be supported by Jesus Himself. But their Jesus, or Isa as they call him, will not be the same as our Jesus, and bears close resemblance to the False Prophet of Revelation. One of the things they expect their Jesus to do is to correct the Christian church and lead many Christians to embrace Islam.

Could it be that the Antichrist will rule over a 10 nation empire in the east, while a false Jesus rules from Rome? I don't know, but it seems plausible. If this will be, then it is conceivable that the mark of the beast in the East might be something different than the mark of the beast in the west. Perhaps some type of microchip could be in store for those of us in the West. The strongest argument against this theory, however, is that the word is "mark" not "marks," of the beast.

I do not understand how all of this will play out, but I am convinced that whatever the mark of the beast will be revealed to be, those of us who are clinging to Christ will recognize it immediately. I also believe that it will be something that if we accept it, we will have to at the same time renounce our faith in Jesus to get it. Unless we renounce our faith in Jesus Christ, the true Jesus Christ, we will not be a candidate for the mark, whatever it is. And the powers that will be ruling will leave those of us who refuse out in the cold to fend for ourselves to find food and shelter. But we will not be able to buy or sell as Revelation clearly states. But I think it is important to point out here that we will be able to barter, trade and freely give to one another, because this type of transaction is not described as being forbidden under the beast's mark.

I could see a scenario arise in the west where an economic system dominated by the East (not entirely unlike the power oil has over us now) controls who can receive food and supplies after our Western countries have been hurt by economic and political collapse, natural disasters and war. If such a scenario came about, then someone ruling in the Middle East could proclaim that unless people in the west are marked in some way they cannot receive aid from them. Perhaps in the East the mark is "bismillah," where as in the war-torn and economically ravished west, the mark could be some sort of tracking device showing submission to the global power of the East, and insuring that some type of uprising against their power would not happen.

We will have to wait and see, and pray that God will reveal it to us in good time.

The False Prophet

Who Is The False Prophet?

Revelation 13:11-18 tells us a great deal about the False Prophet.

The Beast out of the Earth

Then I saw another beast come up out of the earth. He had two horns like those of a lamb, but he spoke with the voice of a dragon. He exercised all the authority of the first beast. And he required all the earth and its people to worship the first beast, whose fatal wound had been healed. He did astounding miracles, even making fire flash down to earth from the sky while everyone was watching. And with all the miracles he was allowed to perform on behalf of the first beast, he deceived all the people who belong to this world. He ordered the people to make a great statue of the first beast, who was fatally wounded and then came back to life. He was then permitted to give life to this statue so that it could speak.

Then the statue of the beast commanded that anyone refusing to worship it must die.

He required everyone—small and great, rich and poor, free and slave—to be given a mark on the right hand or on the forehead. And no one could buy or sell anything without that mark, which was either the name of the beast or the number representing his name. Wisdom is needed here. Let the one with understanding solve the meaning of the number of the beast, for it is the number of a man. His number is 666. (NLT)

It seems conceivable to me that the false prophet will be a fake Jesus. I believe this for two reasons. Jesus specifically told us not to believe it if other Christs appear in Matthew 24, and secondly, already built into the Islamic Eschatological system is a Jesus figure, called Isa, who will "teach" Christians that they had it all wrong, and that Jesus was a prophet pointing to Mohammed.

Like I mentioned before with the Antichrist, the False Prophet has a lot of things in common with Isa of the Muslims. They both take a supportive role to the one world leader, yet they both have great power in the world, they both are said to enforce the religion and laws of the world leader, they both perform signs and wonders, they both are said to persecute Jews and Christians, they both are said to outlaw any religion that isn't the one they endorse, they both look like a lamb yet speak like a dragon, and both are associated with a Beast out of the Earth, and they both enforce a type of mark.

I believe a key way to recognizing the false prophet will not only be in the way he claims to be Jesus, and these other identifying signs, but also in his appearing. The Bible says that he performs lying signs and wonders. I wonder if there will not be some sort of strange event, not necessarily a rapture event, but some sort of event that he will use to try to confuse and con people who have been raised in church but who are not really following God.

Furthermore, whatever the mark of the beast is, once we recognize who the false prophet is, it will be easy to spot what the mark of the beast truly is.

Another possibility worth considering is related to his title, "the false prophet." Muslims still refer to Mohammed as "the Prophet." I often wonder about the chronology of prophecy. Could the false prophet precede the Antichrist by several years? Even generations? I doubt it, but Mohammed is very much alive and well in the Muslim mind. Everything is done in his name and according to his teachings. In a very real way, there is a false prophet alive and well in the world, even though he's been dead for years. I do not really think the false prophet is a spiritual prophet, i.e. not a physical person, but it isn't unreasonable to wonder if some sort of resurrected Mohammed could fulfill this prophecy.

People Claiming to Be the Messiah

According to Wikipedia there have been over 70 claimants to the title of Messiah down through the ages.

Dating all the way back to Simon the Sorcerer mentioned in the book of Acts.

In Matthew 24:23, Jesus said that if people tell you that He is in the desert don't go there, or if He is said to be over here or there, don't believe them. So the idea that there would be a lot of people claiming to be the Messiah is something we should look for as a sign that the end is near. But of the short list that Wikipedia compiled, almost half of them have lived during my lifetime! I'm sure that the list is not complete, because there are names that I know about that are not mentioned on the list. But the fact that there have been so many people claiming to be the Messiah in recent years is staggering.

This Messianic complex that some people have developed deserves a book on its own, but for our purpose here in this book, it is important to note that this sign is definitely active and being fulfilled in our day.

Parables

How do we understand the role of parables when we study End Times events?

It is important to study the parables that Jesus gave in order to get a better understanding of End Times events. But we must be careful not to keep in mind that parables are designed to illustrate points, not to be literal play by play accounts of what is going to happen in the End Times.

Prophecy is a proclamation of what God said will happen.

Visions are a prophets best description of the events that He foresaw. It doesn't mean that he understood what he was seeing. So the prophet gave a description.

Parables are stories that Jesus told to try to illustrate a point that He was making. The parable is not fact, never really happened, and is primarily a teaching tool.

If we keep these things in mind, it will help us as we study these portions of the Bible.

What is the significance of the "Gathering from the Four Winds?"

"People say before there's a tribulation he will rapture. But it doesn't say that. It says he will gather his elect from the four winds. If they were already gathered with a Pre-Trib rapture, then he wouldn't need to do it again at the end of the tribulation." Pat Robertson, from a 700 Club broadcast, August 25, 2011.

In Matthew 24 we see that it is the angels who actually gather us to meet with Jesus. The significance here is that we are gathered to Him by the angels. This is not some secret rapture that no one will see. Many people will see the elect flying through the air. After all of the other events that they see with the first 6 trumpets, this will be cause for great despair, not only from those who are evil, but also from those who are not being raptured, i.e. those false Christians who refuse to follow Jesus in this life, who have refused to allow Him to be the Lord of their life.

Jesus said that we will be gathered from the four winds. If we are gathered from the four winds at a secret Rapture (as Pre-Trib teachers would have us believe) and if we are also gathered from the four winds when Jesus physically returns, then there is an inconsistency in the Bible. There is no point or rational explanation for being gathered twice. There is only one Rapture! Jesus is only coming back once! We are being raptured when Jesus comes back. It is so obvious; There exists no rational reason why many theologians refuse to understand this.

There are a couple things to note in this passage, the angels do the gathering, the people will be all over the world, there is the blast of a trumpet (i.e. the Last Trump), and those gathered are chosen. Why are they chosen? Because they have been following Jesus closely. Those who are not believers, fallen believers, rebellious believers and those in churches who preach doctrines that are opposed to Christ will not be gathered.

As you will see in the next section about the sheep and the goats, and the section on Armageddon, the entire world will have been gathered when Jesus sits on His throne. There seems to be two ways that the world will be gathered. The tares will be gathered, and the wheat will be gathered, both it appears by some sort of rapture; i.e. the gathering up from the angels.

Significance of the Ten Virgins, Talents and Sheep and the Goats

In Chapter 25 of Matthew, Jesus gives three parables that are all concerned with End Times events.

The first parable is concerning ten virgins. Five are wise and have their lamps ready for the bridegroom when He arrives, and five are foolish and haven't been prepared. The bridegroom arrived at midnight, in the dark of night.

The five who were prepared were ready and had their lamps burning, but the five foolish ran off to get more oil, and missed being brought into the wedding feast. It says that they were left outside of the wedding banquet, apparently left in the dark of night. I want to make a point in a second about being left in the dark, but I will wait on that for a minute until we've studied the other parable.

Many people point to this passage to say that we will be at the wedding banquet while the Tribulation is going on, however, this passage does not say that. In fact, it just mentions that there will be a wedding banquet. If we go to the corresponding passage in Revelation 19:9 that mentions the wedding banquet, you can easily see that it happens after the Tribulation. In fact, Revelation 19:9 places it after the bowls of wrath are poured out and after the destruction of Mystery Babylon but before the battle of Armageddon begins.

The second parable is about the three servants who were given talents. You probably know this story as well. One servant is given 10 talents, one 5 and the other only 1 talent. The one given 10 talents earns more; the one given 5 talents also earns more, while the one given 1 talent hid his talent and didn't get anything in return. Jesus says that the wicked servant who didn't make any profit was thrown into "outer darkness, where there will be weeping and gnashing of teeth." Notice these are His servants, not people who were not following Him.

Most people point to this passage and say that they are thrown into hell. I'm not entirely convinced that Hell is what Jesus is referring to here. There is something significant about Jesus' use of "outer darkness" here.

If you look at Revelation 8:12, Matthew 24:29, Joel 3:15 and Amos 5:18 and 20, you will see that they all mention the sun going dark on the Day of the Lord, the day that Jesus will return.

It seems that there is ample evidence to suggest that those who are left behind when the rapture does happen will be left in the darkness that follows the darkening of the sun in those Days.

If you give it some thought. In a world where Jesus is the light of the world, and the entire earth is in darkness, then wherever Jesus is will be the brightest place on the planet. Anywhere else on the planet will be dark. But like a candle, the darkness is gradual. So where Jesus is will be the brightest spot, and on the opposite side of the world would be the darkest spot. Now, I am not saying that this is literal. It did show up after all in a parable, which by it's very nature is figurative. But we saw in the 1 Corinthians passage mentioned earlier in this book, that Jesus must rule until all things are under his authority. Perhaps it is a spiritual darkness, and Christ's light gradually overtakes the entire earth during the Millennial reign. We do not have all of the answers for this, but it is food for thought.

Jesus follows these two parables up with another parable about the sheep and the goats. One of the points that I think is so crucial about the sheep and the goats parable that Jesus gives in Matthew 25:31-46 is that both sheep and goats are part of a flock. Shepherds often had both animals in their flocks. I think we often miss this when we study this story.

Jesus could have made a parable saying the sheep and the wolves, but He doesn't. He specifically picks out two animals that should be part of the same flock.

Don't be a goat. Those goats are told that they didn't help, didn't serve, didn't do the things that Jesus commanded them to do. They didn't show any faith by their works. They just came, warmed a pew and didn't serve Jesus or His body. Goats get sent off into eternal punishment.

This is why I feel so compelled to warn people to give it all for Jesus. It's all His anyway. Don't worry about whatever you have to lose or give up in order to follow Him. It's all worth it. Be a sheep; He says that sheep get to inherit the Kingdom that God the Father prepared from the creation.

Now as to the timing of these events, we can't be entirely sure, but Jesus may be giving us a clue by the sequence of the events. The parable of the Ten Virgins represents what will happen at the rapture. It is possible that the parable of the Talents is what could happen at the Wedding Feast. There is another parable Jesus gives in Matthew 22 where a man is at the wedding feast in improper attire, and the King has the man thrown out into "outer darkness where there will be weeping and gnashing of teeth."

I do not entirely understand how someone can get into the wedding feast, and still be thrown out, but apparently it could happen, because Jesus refers to it happening more than once. Because of this imagery, I believe the wedding feast will not be a spiritual event, and therefore, the "outer darkness" might not be a spiritualized situation either. We are being told here of something physical that we as Christians are looking forward to. The wedding feast is going to happen in Jerusalem, before the Battle of Armageddon, almost all Christians agree on this, and do not refer to it as something symbolic. So, perhaps there will be people who will walk up there seeking admittance to be turned away. Or perhaps there will be people who sneak in during all the excitement of the preparations.

Many people think that the sheep and the goats will happen with Jesus' second coming, however, it is also possible that this event happens at the Great White Throne of Judgment that takes place at the very end of the Millennium. I will explain more about that when we get to the section about the Millennium.

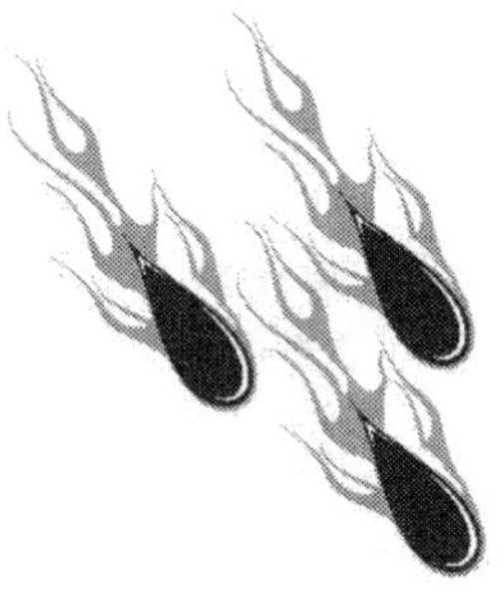

Signs

What's the point of a warning if we're not going to be here?

Good question. Why would God waste His time explaining in GREAT detail the events of the Last Days? Some would have us believe that sometime after the Rapture, someone is going to find a Bible and be saved by reading it. People have found Bibles, read them and gotten saved. The word of God is powerful and changes lives.

But the fact is God is a loving God. The overwhelming biblical evidence points to the fact that we *will* be here for the Tribulation. A loving God would want us to be prepared for the events that the church will have to endure during the Great Tribulation. Keep watch.

Paul in 1st Thessalonians 4 tells us to encourage each other about the fact that we will be raptured when it's all over. The truth is someday things will get very discouraging for those of us who are believers. We will see some people break ranks and follow after the Beast and Satan, just like some broke ranks when the Communists took over Russia, China, Romania and Viet Nam. They will not be willing to go through the hard things that are coming. So instead of standing strong they will cave in and do whatever the persecutors tell them. We are supposed to encourage each other because we will overcome if we stay true to Christ. Do not give in, do not fall away, do not back down, do not go against the leading of the Holy Spirit in your life, and you will come through. And then one day, you will stand before His throne and hear Him say, "Well done my good and faithful servant."

Stand firm. God gave us a warning for a reason.

What are the 4 Horsemen of the Apocalypse, and should I be looking out for them?

As I watched, the Lamb broke the first of the seven seals on the scroll. Then I heard one of the four living beings say with a voice like thunder, "Come!" I looked up and saw a white horse standing there. Its rider carried a bow, and a crown was placed on his head. He rode out to win many battles and gain the victory.

When the Lamb broke the second seal, I heard the second living being say, "Come!" Then another horse appeared, a red one. Its rider was given a mighty sword and the authority to take peace from the earth. And there was war and slaughter everywhere.

When the Lamb broke the third seal, I heard the third living being say, "Come!" I looked up and saw a black horse, and its rider was holding a pair of scales in his hand. And I heard a voice from among the four living beings say, "A loaf of wheat bread or three loaves of barley will cost a day's pay. And don't waste the olive oil and wine."

When the Lamb broke the fourth seal, I heard the fourth living being say, "Come!" I looked up and saw a horse whose color was pale green. Its rider was named Death, and his companion was the Grave. These two were given authority over one-fourth of the earth, to kill with the sword and famine and disease and wild animals. (Revelation 6:1-8, NLT)

Revelation 6 mentions four beings that ride on four horses of differing colors, that are commonly referred to the four horsemen of the Apocalypse. These four horsemen are the first part of the breaking of the 7 Seals of Revelation.

The first horse is the White. The rider on the White Horse carries a bow and wears a crown. He goes out to cause war and wins many battles. Some people have claimed that this first horse represents either Christ or the Antichrist. Muslims teach that this horse represents the Madhi, which is very similar to our Antichrist. Whether this is so or not, remains a mystery. I do not believe that this warrior king is Christ, because it is before the rider on the White Horse in Revelation 19:11 appears, which every Christian agrees is Jesus. I believe that the White Horse Rider in Revelation 6 is contrasted against the one in Revelation 19:11. The first Rider wears one crown, and conquers in war. The second White Horse Rider is called Faithful and True, and wears many crowns and wages a Righteous war. I believe that a strong case can be made that the first rider is the Antichrist and the second is Jesus.

However, I do not believe there is enough evidence to get dogmatic about either one. We do not know if the first White Horse rider is a physical person or a symbol or an angelic being, or a demonic being. It is simply too difficult to tell. And it is the same with the rest of the horsemen, for that matter.

The second horse is the Red Horse, and following him is war and destruction. Whether this means that spiritually this horse will cause people to rise up against each other, or if it represents an actual General in some demonic or angelic army is debatable, and hard to know for certain.

The third horse is the Black Horse and its rider has the power to cause calamity in the economic stability of the world. We know this is true because the price of bread sky-rockets to an entire days wage. It is interesting to note that Olives and Grapes will not be affected, apparently. Some people spiritualize the Olives and the Grapes to represent Israel and America, or some other symbols, but we do not have enough information. The fact is, it could simply mean that God in His kindness is going to allow at least these two crops to continue to be bountiful even in such a rough time as the Tribulation. It makes a lot of sense to me that our kind and loving heavenly Father would do such a good thing even in the midst of the most trying time on earth.

I find it interesting that many health experts tout the benefits of both olive oil and wine. Perhaps these will not only be useful as food during the End Times, but also as medicine as well. Grapes are known as the "queen of the fruits," and is know to treat many disorders including constipation and kidney disorders. According to some studies scientists claim that 1 or 2 glasses of wine a day are healthy and has the ability to reduce high blood pressure and fight heart disease and diabetes. Olive oil has long been known to be beneficial and is even reported to guard against heart attack and stroke. But we also know that since ancient times olive oil has been used as a fuel oil for lamps. So with just grapes and olives one could potentially survive for a while.

The final horseman is the Pale or Green or Grey horse. He is called Death and Hell *(or the Grave)* followed with him. He brings pestilence and death wherever he goes. Again this is probably not a literal person that we will recognize riding around on a greenish grey horse causing disaster, but it could be some type of angel or an evil spirit that is unleashed which we will not be able to see. But regardless of whether we can see the final horseman or not, we will be able to see the result of his passing, as diseases will run rampant.

When I was in Texas I had the honor of meeting a man who spent several years working on our behalf against disease for the Centers of Disease Control. This man told me that it isn't "if" an outbreak of disease happens, it's "when." He told me that we have been fighting an arms race against disease and bacteria for almost a hundred years, and the diseases we have been combating have become ever increasingly powerful, and that one day there *will* be an epidemic that we are unprepared to handle.

God's gracious hand has been on us, but we are already seeing outbreaks of Swine Flu, Bird Flu, Ebola, AIDS and many other diseases that can be devastating. I have read that the AIDS epidemic in Africa is so great that Africa is losing its population rapidly. It is impossible to say for certain that this rider has been unleashed, but it would seem that when he is unleashed for certain, the pestilence and plague that follows would be overwhelming.

Are the Animals that are dying off at alarming rates all over the world mentioned in the Bible, or are they just a sign that we are destroying the earth?

The prophet Hosea mentions massive die-offs of animals, and so does the book of Revelation, and Jesus talks about it in Matthew 24. Many of the prophets link animal deaths with judgment.

Regardless of the cause of their deaths, whether global warming, pollution, etc., the fact that they are dying off at this point in history is significant because it coincides with many other events that were prophesied in the Bible and should be taken into consideration in any study of this time period as being part of End Times scenarios.

Since 2010 there have been thousands upon thousands animals that have died all around the world, and in many cases with an unclear cause. Most of the animals that seem to regularly show up on the lists include birds and fish.

We are warned in Revelation 8:9 that a third of all life in the ocean will die at some point. We also see throughout the prophets that animals leaving, or dying is a sign of judgment against evil. (See Jeremiah 12:4, 33:10, 36:29, Ezekiel 14:19, Zephaniah 1:3 and Hosea 4:3) So these events, while not conclusively proof of the arrival of the time period commonly called the End Times, certainly are strange and might just be the events that coincide with the Biblical warnings and birth pangs.

I am including as an appendix to this book a list that I have compiled from several different websites that have been tracking this phenomenon over the past three years.

Also, included below is a chart I developed that shows the exponential progression over the course of time. As you can see July of 2012 so far as been the peak time for animal die-offs, but as of the date of publication for this book, the deaths continue.

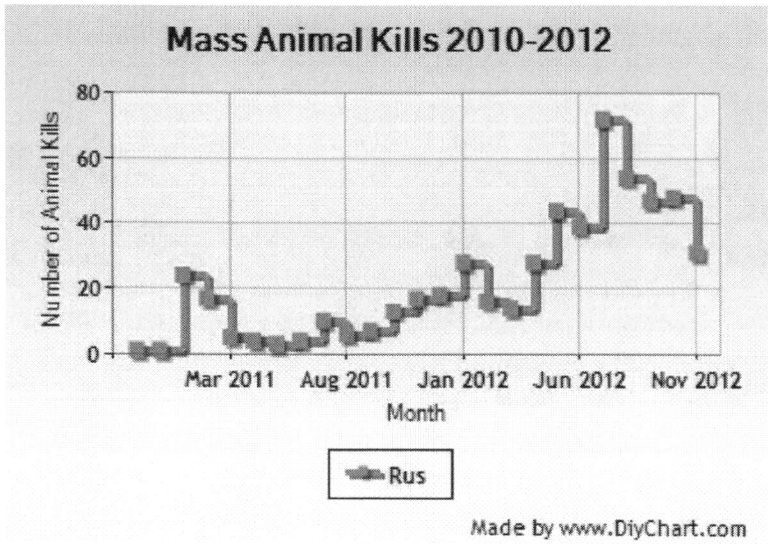

Jesus said that there would be earthquakes as a sign, but we've always had earthquakes. Is there any truth that earthquakes have been getting more frequent lately and is this a sign of the end as well?

You are referring to Jesus' words in Matthew, Mark and Luke that there will be earthquakes in diverse places.

For nation will rise against nation, and kingdom against kingdom, and in various places there will be famines and earthquakes. (Matthew 24:7, NASB)

For nation will rise up against nation, and kingdom against kingdom; there will be earthquakes in various places; there will also be famines. These things are merely the beginning of birth pangs. (Mark 13:8, NASB)

...and there will be great earthquakes, and in various places plagues and famines; and there will be terrors and great signs from heaven. (Luke 21:11, NASB)

Graph provided by DL Research: http://www.dlindquist.com

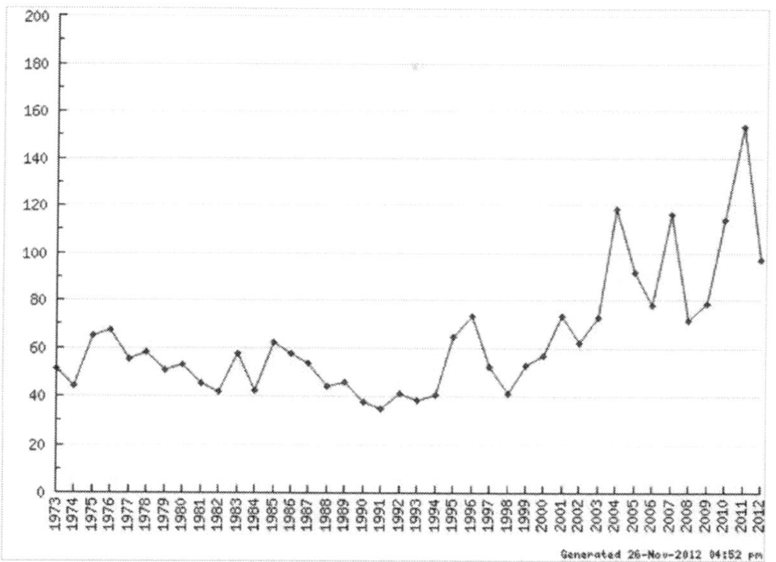

The above graph and the one below represent the growth in the magnitude of earthquakes from 1973 until 2012. As you can see, earthquakes in that time have grown in magnitude and frequency. The maps below show Earthquake Activity in 1973 and 2012.

According to the research at, http://www.earth.webecs.co.uk/, earthquakes in the past 100 years have increased in size from 12 to 164 in the time periods studied.

DATES FROM & TO	PERIOD	NO. EARTHQUAKES (Magnitude Greater Than 6.99)
1863 to 1900 incl	38 yrs	12
1901 to 1938 incl	38 yrs	53
1939 to 1976 incl	38 yrs	71
1977 to 2014 incl *	38 yrs	164 (to Mar. 2011)

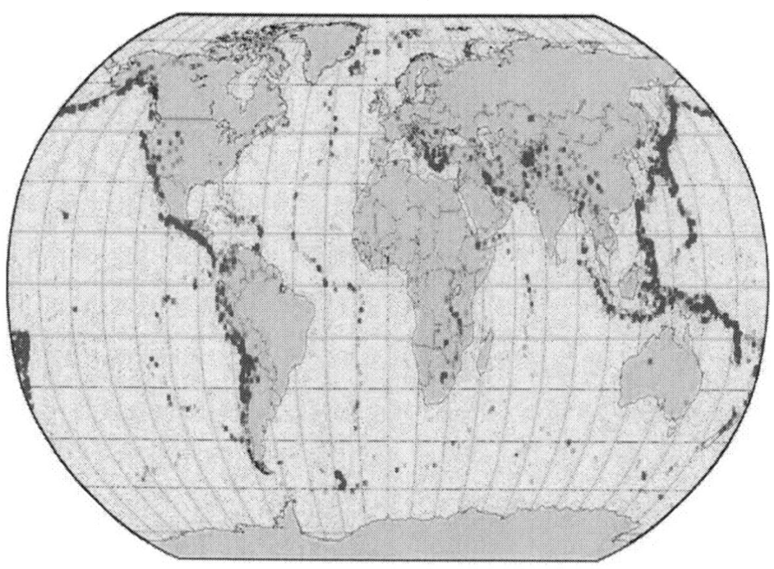

1973 – Global Earth Quake Activity

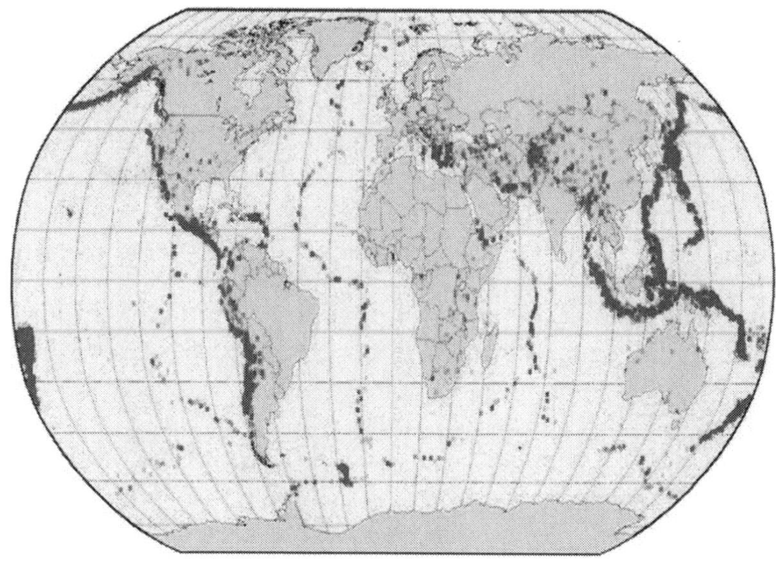

2011 – Global Earth Quake Activity

According to these maps from www.dlindquist.com, a research website that provides tools for you to generate maps for your own seismic research projects, we can see that in 1973, many of the areas of the world that have seismic activity today were active, but from the 2011 map, we can see that these areas are much greater in frequency and intensity.

Should I stock up on food to prepare for the End Times?

I can't tell you that you need to stock up on food and water for the End Times. But I can't see where it would hurt. You might not make it through the End Times. You might be martyred, or you might die before the End Times. Perhaps, by some miracle, you might live in a place that God will spare from much activity. But it never hurts to be prepared a little. You might have to go through a tornado, or an earthquake or a hurricane. And you never know who you might be able to help and share the gospel with in an extreme time of need.

I have friends that I suggested should get a few extra supplies in case something happened. Late in 2012, they had to go through Hurricane Sandy in New York. Because I had suggested that they stock up on extra supplies, they had plenty to carry them through the hurricane. So it is never a bad idea to be prepared.

If you are going to stock up on a few things that can be helpful, I would suggest storing up some water, and a few extra changes of clothes. I would store up some canned goods and some military MRE's which you can get online or from Army Surplus stores. It would be a good idea to have an emergency radio and a couple crank flashlights. It would also be a good idea to set aside some matches and lighters and candles, a few cooking utensils and perhaps something like a small camp cook stove. It would also probably be a good idea to put aside a decent medical and basic toiletry kit that has a lot of things that you might need in case of an injury. Antiseptic, alcohol, wipes, bandages and tape, along with any specific medicine you might need and some pain killers, like Aspirin or something similar is good to have as well. And then finally it would be a good idea to have some items like candles, a small game like dice or cards, a Bible and a couple books. This way, if you have these items at least you can get through a few days power outage at the minimum.

If you have some extra money it isn't a bad idea to get a couple extra backup power sources. A gas generator is a good idea, but you have to remember it might be hard to get gas, so if you can find a wind or solar generator or make one you'd be better off.

A few useful items to have would be a car battery, a solar charger and a power inverter. If you have these things you can make a portable power source that will allow you to recharge cell phones, etc.

One final thing that might be useful, if things get really bad, and you can't find food, you might want to have a few packets of seeds in reserve.

And if you have some extra room, you might think about putting in there a couple items that you might want to trade. Perhaps some hunting supplies, and a good knife or hatchet to cut some kindling for a fire if you need one to cook on.

Most of these items will not take up more space in your house or garage than a small storage bin. But wouldn't it be better to have a few of these things in case of an emergency than to have to do without?

Something very important to consider when pondering this question is that Revelation12 and a couple other passages mention that we will be directed by God where we can be safe during this time period. It is very important to be following closely to God and listening for

His voice. If you are listening to His voice, you will be able to get the directions that He has for you.

In the Matthew passage, Jesus tells us to flee very quickly. If you do want to plan ahead, as an effort to be a good steward, I would advise only taking a bug out bag with you, because you cannot keep all of your creature comforts with you. You have to decide are you going to trust God, or are you going to trust in your preparation, planning and supplies.

Whatever you have, it will not get you through a three and a half year period of hardship, but it might get you to the place God has been preparing for us to survive the End Times.

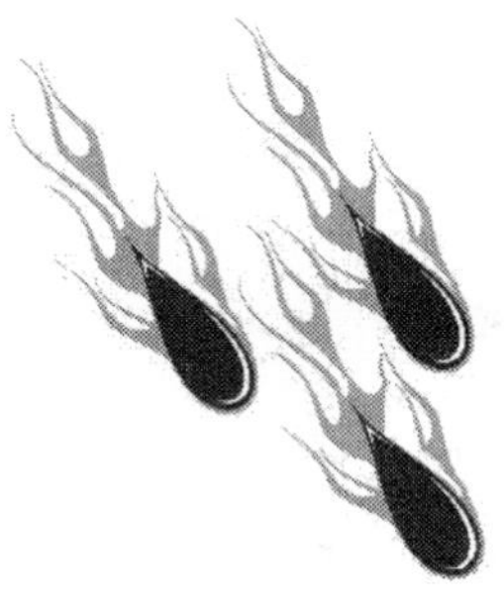

Armageddon

What is Armageddon?

There is a place in Israel called Megiddo. It is located south east of Haifa and overlooks the Jezreel Valley. It has long been associated with the final battle of the world known by the area's Greek name Armageddon. There have been several significant battles there in history as it is on a strategic location leading into the heart of Israel from the North. It was also an important stop along the trade routes from Egypt to Assyria.

Most of us who are prophecy buffs know that Armageddon is known as the site of the last battle when Jesus will return to vanquish the hordes of the Antichrist. However, most people do not know that Megiddo is also the first well documented battle recorded in ancient history. In 1478 BC there was a battle there between the Egyptian Pharaoh Thutmose III and the Canaanite King of Kadesh. This battle was the first battle that reported a body count, and it also boasts the first recorded use of the composite bow. A composite bow is a bow made of bone, and held together by leather and sinew. It was typically used in ancient times for mounted cavalry and may have been one of the deciding factors that lead to Egyptian victory. Most of the documentation about this battle is written in hieroglyphics on the walls of the Hall of Annals in the Temple of Amun-Re at the Karnak temple complex in Luxor Egypt, what was in ancient times called Thebes.

Megiddo is mentioned again in the Bible as the site of a battle between King Josiah and the Egyptian Pharaoh Neco. Josiah was slain in the battle. The battle is recorded in the Bible in 2 Kings 23:29-30 and in 2 Chronicles 35:20-35.

And then in modern times there was also an important series of battles there during WWI, between the British and the Ottoman Empire. The outcome of the battles led eventually to the capture of Damascus, and ultimately to the breakdown of the Ottoman Empire. Why is this important, you might ask? The Ottoman Empire was a vast Islamic Empire that rose out of the Eastern half of the Roman Empire. It lasted longer than the Roman Empire, longer than the Greek Empire, longer than the Babylonian Empire, and many End Times scholars believe that it refers to the last of Daniel's Empires represented by Nebuchadnezzar's dream recorded in Daniel 2. Technically, the Ottoman Empire was really in part a continuation of.the Roman Empire. After the Roman Empire splintered, it became the Holy Roman

Empire in the West, and the Byzantine Empire in the East.

When the Byzantine Empire fell apart in the 1200's AD, a charismatic Muslim leader named Osman I began to unite the splintered fragments. Eventually the Ottoman Empire would encompass most of the Middle East, spreading over Israel, Jordan and parts of Saudi Arabia and modern day Iraq, stopping at the Euphrates and extending up to the Caspian sea. It would encircle the Black Sea, parts of Russia, all of Turkey, Greece and Hungary in the North. Out in the Mediterranean it would include Cyprus. To the South it would extend all the way down the coast of the Red Sea on the Saudi Arabian side, it would spread along the Nile into Egypt, and extend to the east along Northern Africa from Egypt all the way to Algeria.

It is important to mention that all of these countries were once Christian countries.

There is a great movement in modern evangelical Christianity based on A.B. Simpson's remark that the Jesus would return when all of the world had heard the Gospel, which he made in response to a reporter asking him to set a date for Christ's return. Simpson pointed to Matthew 24:14 in response.

And the Good News about the Kingdom will be preached throughout the whole world, so that all nations will hear it; and then the end will come. (NLT)

Many Christians believe that if they can convert all of the countries of the world, it will cause Christ to return. They see the final piece to this puzzle as the band of Islamic nations that make up most of the Middle East, North Africa and many parts of India and Indonesia. This window of the world is now called the "10/40 Window" by some, and was formerly called the "Resistance Belt." This area comprises most of the Islamic countries and is one of the most resistant areas to the gospel.

The idea that these countries will convert to Christianity is faulty however, because all of the countries in this area are apostate countries (countries which used to be Christian, but when the Muslims took over, they renounced their Christian faith and converted to Islam), which explains why this area is so resistant. From studying the events that will lead to the End Times prophecies, I can be fairly certain that this area will never be evangelized again. Furthermore, it is absolutely impossible for these countries to ever convert entirely, because their conversion would make God's prophesies null and void, as will be explained shortly. But God's word is never void, and His prophesies will come true just as He said they would.

Not that it is a waste of time to reach people there, because there are Muslims who will come to know Jesus, and these areas seriously need Christian witness, but if we are trying to reach them because we think that by reaching them we will fulfill the mission and bring Jesus back, we are seriously flawed in our reasoning. A.B. Simpson may have been mistaken in his interpretation of what that passage meant, but more likely the people who came up with the 10/40 window theory are mistaken in their study of history.

When Simpson said that Jesus will come back when all the world has heard the Gospel, it did not mean that Jesus will come back immediately following the Gospel going into all the world. If that is what he thought, then he was mistaken. When Jesus made that statement, He was including it along with other signs that would show us when the end would come, not that it was THE marker to use as our measuring stick. Furthermore, if Simpson did mean this, then the Christian and Missionary Alliance, Assemblies of God and other denominations that sprung from his teachings, would have to abandon their belief in the imminent return of Jesus, because after Simpson made that statement, there were many countries that the Gospel had not gone into yet.

It is not logical to hold to a belief in the so-called imminent return of Christ simultaneously in the same doctrinal stance, with the belief in a need to evangelize the world in order to bring on that very same return of Christ. They are mutually exclusive. Sadly, some of the pastors of Churches who follow Simpson do in fact do just that, and then claim that they take these inconsistencies by faith. But the Word of God isn't inconsistent.

The fact is, at this point in history, the Gospel has gone into "all the world," due to Gospel broadcasts that can be heard in every part of the world thanks to television and radio signals, satellite signals, internet and cell phone availability, and the like. Are there still more people to reach? Certainly, but I would say we are on the very verge of that becoming a reality. Even many organizations that produce Bibles for various language groups show the rapid decrease in populations that need a Bible. And some report that unreached groups are requesting missionaries to come and preach to them. I believe all of the events needed to fulfill this prophecy are on the very brink of coming together.

The fact is almost every single language group and family has been reached. Sure there are some dialects that have not been reached, but in the study of language, dialectal differences are easily overcome. So we are much closer than a lot of evangelicals think. I just want to make it very clear, ***the conversion of the 10-40 window is not a sign that the end will come***. Some people have told me that they aren't even going to worry about Jesus' Second Coming until after they start seeing the Muslim countries evangelized, but they really need to think again and study the Bible and history.

For prophecy to be fulfilled as it is written, this area will have to remain predominately Muslim, and will rise up against Israel just as prophesied. If the area suddenly were to convert to Christianity, then all of the prophesied countries that rise up against Israel in the last days would not do so, and it would prove the Bible wrong. But God will not be proven wrong, and His word will stand, and these countries will rise up against Israel just as prophesied, as disheartening as this is to witness and observe.

There are several questions about the battle of Armageddon that would help clear up this misunderstanding. First it is important to understand who will be at the battle of Armageddon. The book of Revelation is rather vague about this; it merely states that all of the kings of the earth will be there. But it doesn't say which sides they will be fighting for, leaving most scholars to speculate that they will all be against Christ.

We first see the rumblings of what will become the battle of Armageddon mentioned in Revelation 17:11-14

"The scarlet beast that was, but is no longer, is the eight king. He is like the other seven, and he, too, is headed for destruction. The ten horns of the beast are ten kings who have not yet risen to power. They will be appointed to their kingdoms for one brief moment to reign with the beast. They will all agree to give him their power and authority. Together they will go to war against the Lamb, but the Lamb will defeat them because he is Lord of all lords and King of all kings. And his called and chosen and faithful ones will be with him." (NLT)

Notice a couple things here. This is talking about the battle that will come in Revelation 19. The people that this passage mentions will be primarily those who have aligned against the Jews. We can see in chapter 18 that God's People who have not been raptured in chapter 14 are told to come away from Mystery Babylon which is about to be destroyed. This might not make much sense to you, yet, until you read the part about survivors of the Tribulation mentioned in the Millennium section later on. Suffice it to say, the nations when they know that Jesus has arrived on the scene, will gather at Armageddon to fight Christ.

Are Tares snatched away to the battle of Armageddon?

Some Post-Trib people point to the wheat and the tares prophecy to show that it is the evil doers who are "raptured" to destruction, but I do not believe this is the case. I believe it is more likely that the kings of the world are the tares that Jesus speaks of in this parable.

Since when has any king in modern times ever gone into battle? The fact is most countries protect their leaders. The security precautions most countries place on their leaders would prevent this from happening. In fact we see in Revelation 6:15 that the rulers of the earth are hiding in caves trying to outlive the destruction that is being laid down from God. Now it could be that Satan has turned against his own people at this time, which would drive many of these leaders into caves to hide. But it also could be that because of the cataclysms that are wracking the planet, they go into their underground bases to hide from the destruction being poured out by God immediately before the return of Jesus.

It is interesting to note that currently there are places in Colorado, and several other places around the world that have been built as safety areas for our government officials. A great deal of information is available from the construction workers who helped build these structures and an afternoon worth of internet research will yield a bounty of information about these places that already exist!

So what do we make of the statement that the kings of the earth would be there? I think a potential scenario that I can piece together goes something like this. The world will go along just as it has been for most of this century. Global cataclysms will begin to manifest on the earth, as Jesus begins to open the seals mentioned in Revelation. Some event, perhaps something like the fiery mountain that is prophesied to fall on the world, or Wormwood, will drive the rulers of the world underground. When that happens all of the other events will happen in quick succession. (It is interesting to note that in Russian, Chernobyl is the same word as Wormwood, making some sort of connection between the fiery mountain and nuclear weapons.)

I think we can see in Revelation 13 that for the period of time of the Tribulation, that three and a half years of authority given to the Antichrist to rule, this chaos that precedes it will be what it takes to vault him into prominence. By the time the leaders of the world dig themselves out of their caves, the Antichrist will already be ruling the earth.

I do not know if the leaders of the world will give allegiance to him willingly, though it appears that they will for whatever reason, because it says in Revelation 13:7 that not only will he conquer God's holy people, but he will also rule over every tribe and people and nation and language. But we're also told that he only has a 10 country empire. So I am under the impression that during the period of chaos that happens when the seals and trumpets are enacted, the Antichrist will rise to power, conquer the world and subjugate the rest of the world with some kind of tyranny. Perhaps a viable method might be the use of nuclear arms. As suggested with the Wormwood Chernobyl connection, it is not unlikely that such arms would be used. So his empire will consist of 10 countries, but he will have authority over many more countries by use of threats, intimidation, bribery and other such means.

At any rate, when the battle of Armageddon happens, there are two things that I think could bring the kings of the world there for battle. Perhaps, the Antichrist threatens, cajoles or encourages by whatever power he wields over the world leaders to get them there, or perhaps this is where the parable of the tares comes in, and Jesus sends His angels out to gather the kings of the world to the battle. We know that some of the armies are not gathered there in this fashion, because they have to drive to get there. We see this in Revelation 16. The sixth bowl of God's wrath is poured upon the Euphrates River so that the kings of the east can march their armies to the battle of Armageddon. This would suggest that the Kings of the East are at least coming along with their armies, and might argue against a literal fulfillment of the Wheat and the Tares parable. I could imagine armies being driven along by angels.

I do not know if the Wheat and the Tares needs to be taken literally, as some argue, because it was a parable. The Rapture portion obviously is literal, because Jesus, Paul and John all re-affirm this in other places. But this is the only place mentioned where the tares are gathered by the angels. Perhaps God uses angels to convince the kings to gather. I believe there may be some support for this, as verse 16 of Revelation chapter 16 says the demonic spirits are the ones who gather all of the rulers. So apparently under the guidance of demonic spirits, who are technically fallen angels, the kings come to Armageddon of their own accord.

Regardless of how they get there and why, the leaders will be there and will be among the dead after the battle, because in Revelation 19 the angel standing in the sun tells the vultures to feast on kings, generals, strong warriors, horses and riders, etc.

One possible idea could be that the kings of the world are invited for some event, possibly some sort of celebration that the “Great Satan” of the world, Israel, is finally defeated. Maybe the kings gather thinking that finally the Jewish people they hate so much will finally be destroyed.

It seems funny right now to think that most of the world will hate the Jews, but we can see in the media at the time of this writing that a very successful campaign against Israel is being waged in the American and British media, and even in the UN which was instrumental originally in Israel coming into the Land, in an effort to sway people from sympathizing with the Jewish state. Oddly enough, it is the Germans who seem to be Israel's best friend in their current conflict against Hamas.

Is The Gog/Magog War the Same as The Psalm 83 War?

Many people claim that the Psalm 83 war has never happened. And as far as we can tell, there has never been a time in the history of Israel when the countries listed there all attacked Jerusalem when the Jews lived there. One could argue that when the Ottoman Empire took over the area during the time around the Crusades, it could have been a fulfillment of this prophecy, but technically that was during the time of the Diaspora, and therefore not part of the time when Israel belonged to the Jews, or the descendants of Jacob. The key verse here in this Psalm is 83:4 where it reads: *They have said, "Come, and let us wipe them out as a nation, that the name of Israel be remembered no more." (NASB)*

The countries listed in the Psalm 83 war include: Edom and the Ishmaelites, Moab and the Hagrites; Gebal and Ammon and Amalek, Philistia with the inhabitants of Tyre; Assyria. Of course, other countries are mentioned in this passage, but they are mentioned as countries that God has already dealt with and destroyed. The modern day versions of these countries include mainly Jordan,

Lebanon and Syria, though a case could be made that areas including Iran, Egypt, Iraq, Turkey and Saudi Arabia could be included as well depending on the extent of the Assyrian Empire at the time of the penning of this Psalm. I am not convinced that the Gog Magog War is the same as the Psalm 83 war, but it is possible that they could be related. The Psalm 83 war countries are encompassed by the Gog/Magog countries, and it seems very likely that such a war as the Psalm 83 war could indeed lead to a larger Gog/Magog type war, or it could be that the Gog/Magog war does not happen until after the Millennium as mentioned in Revelation chapter 20.

Currently, we see many of the countries that are mentioned in the Psalm 83 war either in Civil War or in confrontation with Israel. The Palestinian's have been attacking Israel. Israel has fired shots into Syria, and vice versa as the Syrian civil war escalates. The UN and US are trying to decide if they should intervene. It seems that Jordan is in a very tense position at the moment, and the tension between Israel and Lebanon has always been high as well.

Also, although Egypt and Turkey have long been strong allies for Israel, they are quickly showing signs of anti-Semitism and violent rhetoric against Israel due to the rise in what is being called "radical," but in reality is just "traditional," Islam.

So while I do not think the Psalm 83 war is the same as the Gog/Magog War, we could see that a War with the same countries could lead to a much larger scale war, which could grow to encompass much of the world powers, and which could give rise to the Antichrist. Furthermore, since many of the countries from the Psalm 83 War are not mentioned in the Gog/Magog War, it is possible that these countries could be destroyed by the former war which would give rise to the latter war.

What is the Gog/Magog War and Is Armageddon the same as the Gog-Magog War?

Some of the countries mentioned in Ezekiel 38 are explained by Josephus and other ancient writers. Put is now essentially modern day Libya. Cush or Kush was comprised of parts of Southern Egypt, Sudan and northern Ethiopia. And the Persia of Ezekiel's day included most of the Middle East from Iran up to Libya, north to Turkey and parts of Greece and parts of Iraq and Saudi Arabia, and stretched all the way over to the Indus River.

The Gog/Magog War is mentioned in Ezekiel 38 and 39, and again in Revelation chapter 20. Some previous Bible scholars believed that the land of Magog, which has areas called Meshech and Tubal are actually Russia, based on their study of the Table of Nations, mentioned in Genesis, which details where the descendants of the sons of Noah migrated to.

There is a problem with using the Table of Nations to determine this, as the Table is based mainly on speculation, but not on hard facts. The fact is most scholars point out that Meshech and Tubal were actual places during Ezekiel's time, and refer to places that are part of modern day Turkey. If one considers that these areas are parts of Turkey and the surrounding regions, and if you include the ancient Persian Empire, instead of just the limited modern day country of Iran, and also include the entire region of Put, which some scholars believe also included Algeria and Tunisia, as well as Cush which includes Sudan and parts of Egypt, then what we are looking at is very similar to the Ottoman Empire.

If the revived Ottoman empire is the Antichrist's empire, then it could possibly qualify the Gog/Magog war as the same as Armageddon. Also since in Ezekiel chapter 39 verse 29 it says that after this war, God will never again turn away from Israel.

However there are two things that make me question the validity of this claim. First the Battle of Armageddon is known to start when the "Kings of the East" bring their armies across the Euphrates River. This is shown in Revelation 16:12.

And Gog/Magog seems to start when the armies to the North come down against Israel. We see this in Ezekiel 38:15. So there must be something that distinguishes Gog and Magog from the Battle of Armageddon. We do know that both of these battles include the Antichrist, because most scholars agree that Gog is another term for the Antichrist. What is confusing here is that Revelation places Gog/Magog after the Millennium, while

Gomer Togarma
Meshech Tubal
? Magog
Persian
Empire
circa 600 BC
PUT?
CUSH
? Could be slightly further north
? Could be slightly larger or smaller
The Gog Magog War

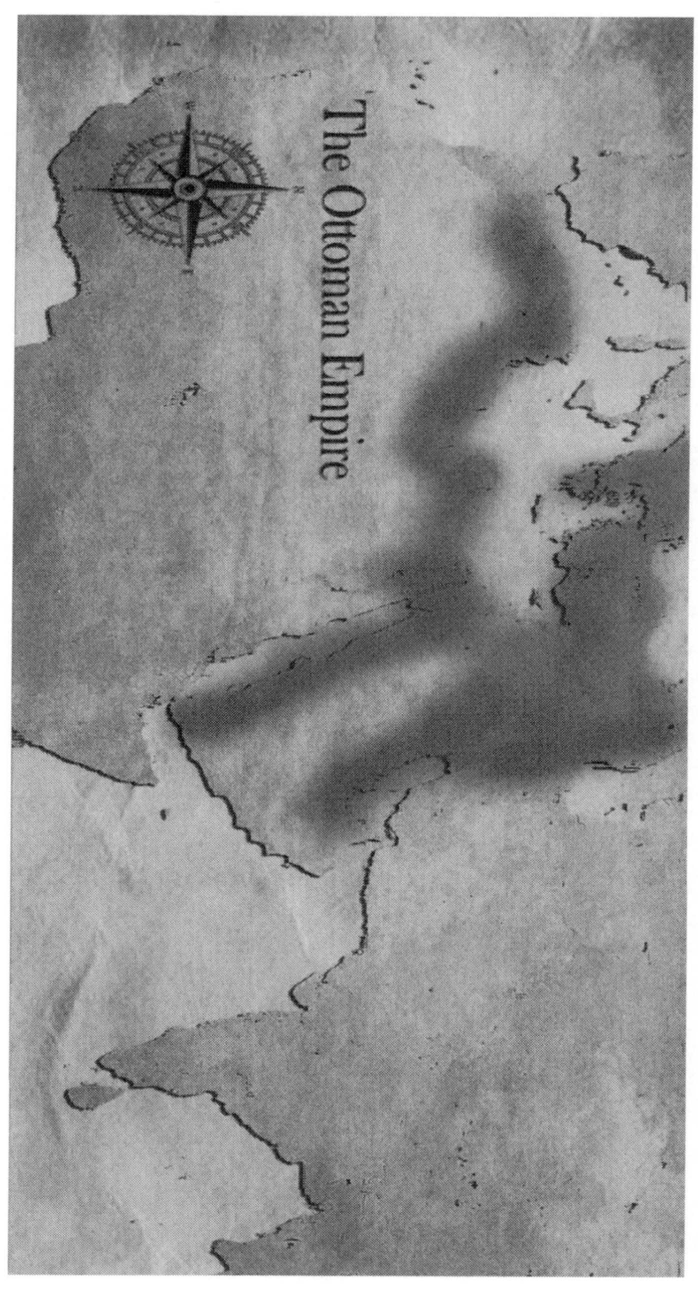
The Ottoman Empire

the time of Ezekiel's Gog/Magog seems to be before the Millennium.

There are some who think that Gog/Magog is not referring to the Antichrist at all, and is an entirely separate war. This seems to me to be the most logical explanation because if we believe that the Bible is the inspired word of God, then our ultimate goal is to harmonize the scripture, and resolve apparent contradictions in it. The war that is mentioned at the end of Revelation when Satan deceives the kings of the earth to attack Jesus right before the Great White Throne of Judgment, is called the Gog/Magog war, and so I believe a very strong case can be made that Gog/Magog is not the same as Armageddon. There is no mention in Revelation chapter 16 that Armageddon is the last battle *ever*. And we see that there is another war yet to come at the end of the Millennium.

The biggest problem that I have with my own theory is that Revelation 17-18 is an almost direct quote from Ezekiel 39:17-19. I believe this is what gets most bible scholars scratching their heads. It is hard to harmonize this, unless it happens twice.

There are some dispensational theologians, most notably J. Dwight Pentecost, who argue that the Battle of Armageddon is actually an entire war that is fought for a good portion of the Tribulation. This would make sense of some of the more obscure prophetic battles that are mentioned in Scripture. It would also go along with the Antichrist's role as a conqueror.

If this is true, then one could argue that the war is actually the Gog/Magog war. And the last battle of the war will be Armageddon. This war will follow a three and a half year period of peace that will be ended when the Antichrist stabs Israel in the back, conquers the land, and begins the worst three and a half years of Israel's long and tumultuous history. This 3.5 year period will conclude with Jesus returning to fight Armageddon against the Antichrist and his minions.

In such a scenario, the Gog/Magog war very well could be the event that reveals the Antichrist to us. It is very possible that such a war (whether Gog/Magog or not) is on the very brink of happening at the time of this writing, and if the outcome is a seven year peace treaty with Israel, then we will know for sure.

So while it might not be exactly clear what the Gog/Magog war is, it is very likely a war including many of the same players will be the event that sets up the 3.5 year time period of peace. The aftermath (or potential continued devastation) of this war is what would give the Antichrist the platform to present Israel with the peace treaty that Daniel speaks of.

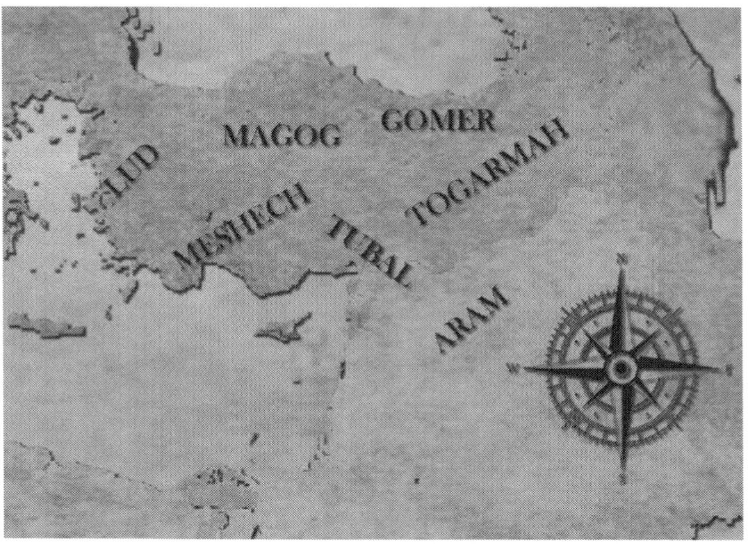

Detail of a map based on a similar map from the Zondervan Atlas of the Bible, which shows that Magog, Meshech, Gomer, Tubal and Togarmah, are all within the confines of modern-day Turkey. Other Bible atlas books including the IVP Atlas of Bible History, The New Moody Atlas of the Bible, and many others include these areas in very similar locations. A more complete list including many maps can be found at Joel Richardson's website: www.joelstrumpet.com.

Recovering from War…

In 38:8, Ezekiel states that in the far future *after* the people of Israel return from many nations and are living securely as they recover from a war, or literally "from the Sword," then Gog will be called into action to move against Israel.

Currently, Israel is living in a time following a period where they were recovering from a devastating war, WWII. I think this is significant because the settlement of Israel by the Jews was a direct result of the Holocaust that took place in WWII. And the Jews came back from "many nations" where they were scattered. I do not think that it is referring to a war yet in the future, because that would mean that there needs to be another Diaspora. Furthermore, this is most likely not a war still to come because many of the nations mentioned as being allied with Magog are already coming against Israel at the time of this writing.

A group of nations is listed as fighting along with Magog, Persia which is modern day Iran, Ethopia, which included Sudan back in the days Ezekiel was writing this and Libya, one of the nations affected by the "Arab Spring," "with all of their weapons." (NLT) It also mentions Gomer and all of its armies along with the armies of Beth-togarmah from the distant north. According to Josephus Gomer is Anatolia, which is in modern day Turkey as well, again a part of the Ottoman empire. Anatolia was the western two thirds of what is now modern day Turkey. Beth-togarmah was supposed to be somewhere north of Carchemish in what was Syria, which would place it possibly in Turkey, Georgia or southern Russia.

Today all of these nations are Muslim nations, and they are all bent on destroying Israel. I think this should wake Christians up to the fact that we are seriously close to the times mentioned in these prophesies. This convinces me that writers such as Walid Shoebat and Joel

Richardson are correct in their assessment that the Antichrist will be the next and last Islamic Caliph, also called the 12th Imam or the Mahdi, their Messiah.

Syria…

An interesting side note, since we mentioned Syria in the previous section, it could be brought into this discussion. In Isaiah 17 Damascus is prophesied as being utterly wiped out along with an area called Aroer. Many scholars claim that Aroer is a place known to archaeologists as Gad-Aroer, and is now in modern day Jordan. However, when comparing and overlaying ancient maps with modern ones, the town Aroer is incredibly close to the modern day Syrian city of Daraa.

This town Daraa was bombarded on April 25, 2011, and was almost completely destroyed during the Syrian civil war that is still raging at the time of this writing. The fighting there became a significant part of the Syrian civil war, as it lead to the closing of the border with Jordan. Furthermore, at the time of this writing, the fighting in Daraa is still on-going. This Syrian civil war is bringing Unites States as well as UN troops into the area, along with Russians. The Iranians are eyeing this conflagration, and we hear in the news that “war games” are being held by many different groups in the region. I highly doubt that the “war games” are really games, but are probably being called that to keep the public from being aware of just how volatile the situation really is.

What war is ended at Christ's Return?

It is fairly safe to say that the war, or at least the battle, ended by Christ's return is the Battle of Armageddon. At this battle the Antichrist and the False Prophet will both be captured and thrown into the "lake of fire." However the fighting does not stop. We can see in Joel 1:15, and chapter 2 and following, that this begins the Day of the Lord, where Jesus also liberates Egypt and Assyria, among other battles that Jesus fights.

Isaiah backs this up when he says that Egypt and Assyria will both one day be filled with God's people, and will freely worship God. We find the prophecy for Egypt and Assyria in Isaiah chapter 19.

Is there a difference between what happens to the people who are brought to Armageddon, and the foolish Christians/Virgins who aren't raptured when the rapture actually happens?

Later that same day Jesus left the house and sat beside the lake. A large crowd soon gathered around him, so he got into a boat. Then he sat there and taught as the people stood on the shore. He told many stories in the form of parables, such as this one:

"Listen! A farmer went out to plant some seeds. As he scattered them across his field, some seeds fell on a footpath, and the birds came and ate them. Other seeds fell on shallow soil with underlying rock. The seeds sprouted quickly because the soil was shallow. But the

plants soon wilted under the hot sun, and since they didn't have deep roots, they died. Other seeds fell among thorns that grew up and choked out the tender plants. Still other seeds fell on fertile soil, and they produced a crop that was thirty, sixty, and even a hundred times as much as had been planted! Anyone with ears to hear should listen and understand."

His disciples came and asked him, "Why do you use parables when you talk to the people?"

He replied, "You are permitted to understand the secrets of the Kingdom of Heaven, but others are not. To those who listen to my teaching, more understanding will be given, and they will have an abundance of knowledge. But for those who are not listening, even what little understanding they have will be taken away from them. That is why I use these parables,

For they look, but they don't really see. They hear, but they don't really listen or understand. This fulfills the prophecy of Isaiah that says,

'When you hear what I say, you will not understand. When you see what I do, you will not comprehend. For the hearts of these people are hardened, and their ears cannot hear, and they have closed their eyes— so their eyes cannot see, and their ears cannot hear, and their hearts cannot understand, and they cannot turn to me and let me heal them.'

"But blessed are your eyes, because they see; and your ears, because they hear. I tell you the truth, many prophets and righteous people longed to see what you see, but they didn't see it. And they longed to hear what you hear, but they didn't hear it.

"Now listen to the explanation of the parable about the farmer planting seeds: The seed that fell on the footpath represents those who hear the message about the Kingdom and don't understand it. Then the evil one comes and snatches away the seed that was planted in their hearts. The seed on the rocky soil represents those who hear the message and immediately receive it with joy. But since they don't have deep roots, they don't last long. They fall away as soon as they have problems or are persecuted for believing God's word. The seed that fell among the thorns represents those who hear God's word, but all too quickly the message is crowded out by the worries of this life and the lure of wealth, so no fruit is produced. The seed that fell on good soil represents those who truly hear and understand God's word and produce a harvest of thirty, sixty, or even a hundred times as much as had been planted!" Matthew 13:13- (NLT)

Jesus taught about five types of seed. Good seed of course grows and produces a crop. One seed falls on sandy soil, one gets eaten by birds, and one is choked out by the cares of the world. But there is a fifth type of seed He mentions in another parable, and that is the tares, which are weeds sown into the garden.

There is a difference between true believers and lukewarm believers, shown over and over in the gospel. The parable of the sheep and the goats, the parable of the talents, the parable of the forgiven servant who wouldn't forgive others, and the parable of the 10 virgins were all about the difference between the two types of people in the church. So there are really three types of people, people who follow Christ, people who are drawn to Christ for some reason or another but who don't make a lasting commitment, and people who are opposed to Christ.

When Jesus returns, the tares will be snatched away to Armageddon, the believers will be snatched away to be with Jesus. From what we read in the Biblical accounts, those people who are undecided will have to be left where they are. This sounds entirely opposed to everything we've been taught in church, but this is the only logical way of understanding the most famous phrase in Christianity, "those who call upon the name of the Lord will be saved."

We use this phrase a lot in evangelism, but what we don't realize is that in the context, Joel is talking about Jesus second coming, when He is waging war against the nations who are opposed to Him. This verse if found in the midst of Christ's slaughter of people who oppose Him, and any one who calls upon His name at that moment will be saved from His destruction as He takes over their countries.

We know this is true, because Joel and Zechariah both show us that there will be survivors. That's a very particular word to use. Why call the people who survive the battle of Armageddon survivors if no one survives? Why call the people who survive this Ultimate Holy War "survivors," if everyone is either raptured or destroyed? Where do these people come from? It is obvious that some people are neither raptured nor destroyed. Zechariah tells us in 14:17 that these survivors will have to come up to Israel every single year, during the 1,000 year reign of Christ to pay tribute to Him, or else they will not receive rain for their crops. Who are these people?

They are made up of people who are not raptured and changed in a twinkling of an eye, but who also were not at the final battle to wage war against Jesus.

A further point to back this up is one that many people miss. At the very end of the millennium, Satan is released from his prison. He goes about the world deceiving the nations to rebel against Jesus. Now, if we are all raptured, and are not having kids based on Jesus' saying that in the Resurrection they will neither marry nor be given in marriage *(Matthew 22:30),* then who are the people that rebel against God at the end of the millennium?

If everyone is changed in the twinkling of an eye to live forever with Christ, and everyone else is thrown into Hell at the point of Christ's return, then who would be around to rebel against God? Surely not the believers who have given up everything to follow Him? There must be other people who survived the Second Coming, who have lived on after Armageddon, and have repopulated the earth after the great destruction of the Tribulation and other End Times events. We know that many of these people will be Jews, because they will finally inherit the Land God promised to Abraham, and will continue to have children. But according to Joel, *anyone* who calls on the name of the Lord, when He is in the middle of waging war against the infidels, will be saved. A couple things about this passage the Hebrew word for anyone, can also mean “everyone,” or “whosoever.”

I see two things here. Some people survive the outpouring of God’s wrath. We know that some do because many soldiers and kings converge on the battle of Armageddon. If many soldiers and kings survive only to be slain by Jesus at the Armageddon, then it is quite conceivable that many others throughout the earth would survive as well, to repopulate the earth during the Millennium, and that these would be the ones who are required to pay tribute to Jesus in order to receive rain.

List of Countries Mentioned In Various Prophetic Wars and Current Dominant Religion:

PSALM 83 WAR	GOG/MAGOG WAR	ARMEGEDDON
Key Verse: *4 They have said, "Come, and let us wipe them out as a nation, that the name of Israel be remembered no more."* *Edom* = Area controlled by modern day Jordan; modern day religion is Islam *Ishmaelites* = Area controlled by modern day Saudi Arabia; religion Islam *Moab* = Also an area controlled	Key Verse: Ezekiel 38:2 *"Son of man, turn and face Gog of the land of Magog, the prince who rules over the nations of Meshech and Tubal, and prophesy against him."* Meshech = Area in modern day Turkey; religion Islam Tubal = Area in modern day Turkey; religion Islam Paras = Another name for Persia, or Modern Day Iran; religion Islam	Key Verse: Revelation 20 Gog/Magog War All the Nations = this is in dispute. It could either mean all of the nations that are in the region of Israel, or it could mean every single nation of the earth. If it means all of the nations near Israel, then that would include only Islamic

by modern day Jordan; again modern day religion is Islam Hagrites = They lived east of Gilead in what is modern day Jordan; Religion Islam Gebal = This city was located in what is now modern day Lebanon; religion Islam Ammon = Area contolled by modern day Jordan; actually capital of Jordan derives name from Ammon; religion Islam Philistia = Area controlled by	Cush = Area that includes modern day Sudan, South Sudan, Ethiopia and Somalia; religions Islam and Coptic Christianity. Put = Modern Day Libya; religion Islam. Allies on the Coast = Not sure, but could be Libya, could refer to the nations already mentioned. Sheba = Modern day Yemen; religion Islam. Dedan = Located in modern day Saudi Arabia; religion Islam Tarshish = Not sure, three of Amalek = It is unclear where these people live in modern time, as they were supposed to be exterminated	countries. If it means all of the nations of the world, then that would infer that the Great Falling Away will turn formerly Christian nations against Israel. Currently, "All the nations of the world" are represented by the United Nations, an organization that has recently leveled sanctions against Israel in an effort to force a peace of some sort in the escalating conflict that is presently going

modern day Palestians; religion Islam Tyre = Controlled by modern day Lebanon; religion Islam Assyria = Lesser Assyria includes area controlled modern day Syria, Iraq and parts of Turkey; Greater Assyria also includes Saudi Arabia, Egypt and parts of Iran; religion Islam.	though it might refer to Palestinians, interesting that these people were reported to be Nephilim; religion unknown, but if Palestinian – Islam. The most popular guesses are Spain, Turkey and Carthage; 2 of which are Islamic Valley of Travelers East of Dead Sea = It is unclear where this valley is located, but it could be the valley between the mountains on the western edge of Jordan which connected the Nabetean kingdom with the Tran-Jordan area; religion Islam Ezekiel 39: 17-19 very similar in language to Revelation 19:17-18.	on in the Middle East. More information seems to come out daily on the UN's incursion into land that belongs to Israel, and it seems very likely that as the time progresses we will see a greater push from the UN to side with Palestinian terrorists against Israel.

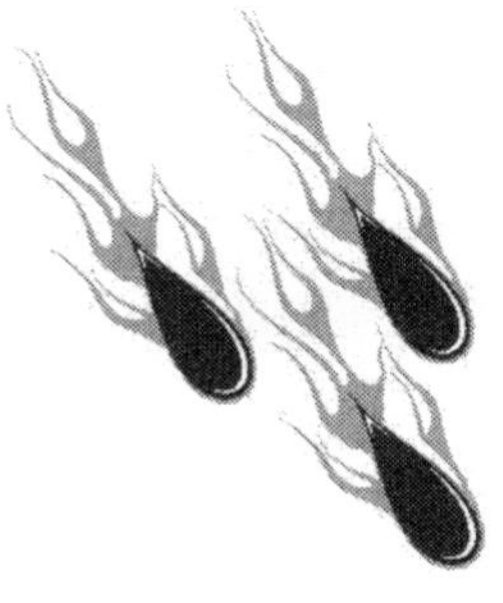

Millennium

What is the Millennium?

The Millennium is the 1,000 year time period referred to in Revelation chapter 20:6, where it says that people who are part of the first resurrection will reign with Christ for 1,000 years, while Satan is bound in chains. Amillennialists claim that there will be no literal thousand year reign, and that this portion of Revelation is allegorical. However, it is very clear that at some point Satan will be bound. If this were not true, then what is the point of including his binding and his releasing in the verses that follow this passage? It is hard to understand why Satan is released to Gog and Magog if the Gog and Magog war is the same as the Antichrist's war, unless even after 1,000 years without Satan's influence, the people of those lands would still hold a bitter grudge against Jesus for the Antichrist's defeat, though as shown in a picture earlier, those lands are part of the area promised originally to Israel.

We are told in Isaiah 65:20 that during the Millennial reign if anyone dies under the age of 100 they will be considered young. So perhaps some of the survivors from the war will still be around, or maybe the first or second generation of their children would be around to be deceived by Satan.

There is really no solid reason to believe that this passage isn't literal. If one believes that Satan is real, and that God has the power to chain him, then it only makes sense that this passage is literal as well.

Certainly, with all of the evil, hurt, misery and pain that happen on the earth on a daily basis, Satan is active and well, though if the full extent of his influence is present currently we do not know. Our hope is that one day we will live in a Kingdom that is ruled by Christ. But if we believe that we are going to live in that Kingdom based upon what is written in chapter 20 and 21 of Revelation, then it does not make sense to say that it is an allegory. Either we have hope of a Kingdom of Christ on earth, or we do not.

Another question that is related and also important is:

Who Will Be In The Millennium?

The first answer and the most obvious is: "Believers." People who believe in Jesus will be in the Millennium. We also see in Revelation 20 that the people who sit on the thrones will be there. We see in Matthew 19:28 that these thrones are for the 12 apostles (though with presumably Mathias or possibly St. Paul to replace Judas who betrayed Jesus), who will judge the 12 tribes of Israel. So that shows us that members of the 12 tribes of Israel will be there. Many people think that only means the 144,000 mentioned in Revelation 14, but that seems highly unlikely, as that would mean that out of all of the descendants of Abraham who ever lived on the face of the earth, only 144,000 of them made it in. But this cannot be, because the passage specifically states that these 144,000 are virgin males from the tribes of Israel, which rules out the Jehovah's Witnesses claim that it refers to them, as Jehovah's Witnesses are often married, and are not of Hebrew descent.

We also see in Revelation chapter 20:4 that Tribulation Martyrs are part of the first Resurrection. We know this is true because it specifically refers to them as the ones who were "beheaded because of the testimony of Jesus and because of the word of God, and those who had not worshiped the beast or his image, and had not received the mark upon their forehead and upon their hand…" It is obvious that these believers were murdered during the Tribulation as it refers back to Revelation chapter 13.

Again this is solid proof that the Pre-Trib rapture theory is not valid. These believers would not be present in a Pre-Trib rapture scenario, because they would have missed the Resurrection of the Dead that would have happened in a Secret Rapture. These people can only be included in the number of believers in the Millennium if the Rapture happens at the ***END*** of the Tribulation.

Finally, of the people who will be present during the Millennium, perhaps the least understood and written about are those survivors that are mentioned in the books of Joel and Isaiah.

After so many years of teaching on this subject, many believers must think that all evil is destroyed at Christ's second coming. From the conversations I've had with them, most amillennialists certainly believe this way. However, it does not account for the fact that Revelation chapter 20 speaks of Satan being released "to deceive the nations… and to gather them together for the war."

Now Isaiah 1:18 shows us that God wants us to use our reason to understand salvation, and the message that He has given us. So let us reason this matter out. If the only people who are left on the earth during the Millennium are believers who have been Resurrected and transformed into Resurrection bodies, who on earth would follow Satan, as it is described in Revelation 20, to wage war against Christ? This would be absolute lunacy, especially after 1,000 years of living in fellowship with Jesus!

Furthermore, Revelation 19:15 shows us that Jesus will rule the nations with a "rod of iron," a reference to a strict disciplinary rule. Why would Jesus have to rule the nations with a "rod of iron" if the world is populated with people who were transformed in the Resurrection? The people who will be transformed will be people who deeply love and follow Him. So there would be no need for an iron rod.

"The Complete Idiot's Guides to the Last Days," by Richard H. Perry is the first and only book that I have ever read on the subject that addresses the topic of survivors into the millennium, but Perry doesn't seem to have come to many conclusions beyond mentioning that survivors seem to exist.

But when one reads the passages critically, it is obvious there will be survivors. The first instance we see of this is in Isaiah. In 10:20, 15:9 and 37:32 we are told of various types of survivors. Some of these possibly are referring to survivors from some of the various attacks on the people of Israel in the past, but a very solid case can be made that 37:32 is speaking of End Times events.

We see more about survivors in Joel 2:32 where it says, *"But everyone who calls on the name of the LORD will be saved, for some on Mount Zion in Jerusalem will escape, just as the LORD has said. These will be among the survivors whom the LORD has called." (NLT)* This is a famous passage used in evangelism, but we can see in the context that it is referring to people who survive after Christ returns to conquer.

"I have wiped out many nations, devastating their fortress walls and towers. Their streets are now deserted; their cities lie in silent ruin. There are no survivors— none at all. Zephaniah 3:6 (NLT) One might use this passage in Zephaniah as a proof text that there will be no Survivors into the Millennium, however, this passage merely states that the people of "many nations" have been destroyed, not "every nation." In fact since it

doesn't say "every nation," we can see that there must be some nations with people who survive.

Will All Believers Be Raptured?

Then again, there is the possibility that there might be people who claimed to be believers, who did not get raptured, but who nevertheless survived the time period of the Antichrist.

Only those who are actively following Christ will be raptured. Wishy-Washy believers will not be raptured. This fact actually agrees with Margaret MacDonald's vision. She claimed that only believers filled with the Holy Spirit would be raptured, although her idea of being filled with the Holy Spirit might be different from many other believers idea of what that means. Nevertheless, those who are not fully following Christ will be left behind, to either be destroyed, or if they survive, to repopulate the earth during the millennium.

There is the possibly brief period of time between Christ's return and the end of what many consider Tribulation. We know there has to be a time period between the harvest of the church and the pouring out of the bowls of wrath. We do not know how long this time period is going to be. But there are several events that happen after Christ returns, and before the millennial reign begins. This time period is referred to as the Day of the Lord, but we do not know how long the Day of the Lord will be. We do know that the sun and the moon will be darkened, and that Christ's light will be the glorious light that people see.

We also see that during that Day, people who call upon the name of the Lord can be saved. So if wishy-washy Christians miss out on the Rapture and are left behind it would be in the "outer darkness," where the light of Christ isn't shining, where Jesus said there will be weeping and gnashing of teeth. So when Jesus tells in many parables that people will be thrown out into the "outer darkness," we can see that this correlates to the Day of the Lord, when Jesus is establishing His Kingdom on earth. During this time Christ is seen waging war against the forces of evil.

There are 3 types of people. True Believers, People with what John refers to as an antichrist spirit, and Everyone else. The True Believers are those who get raptured and transformed, the people with an antichrist spirit are the tares who are taken to the Battle of Armageddon to be slaughtered, and Everyone else is all the other people, both wishy-washy Christians and Unbelievers who were not filled with an antichrist spirit, and Jews who were being attacked by the Antichrist.

John tells us that there are many antichrist's. But we know there will be one, final Antichrist designed to reign during the Great and Final Tribulation.

After Christ puts everything under His rule, people of the world will be subject to Christians who were raptured and transformed. The leaders of the world will have to come up to Jerusalem once a year to pay tribute to Christ and affirm His rule over their land so that they will receive rain.

Any nation in the world that refuses to come to Jerusalem to worship the King, the LORD of Heaven's Armies, will have no rain. (Zechariah 14:17, NLT)

Some would like to say that Christ's rule on earth is not physical, and that passages such as the Zechariah passage are allegorical, but we know that Jesus' reign is physical because Zephaniah tells us it is.

(Zephaniah 3:15, NLT) For the Lord will remove his hand of judgment and will disperse the armies of your enemy. And the Lord himself, the King of Israel, will live among you! At last your troubles will be over, and you will never again fear disaster.

His first advent was physical, and His second one will be too.

If there are Survivors into the Millennium, why do they get a second chance, but the people who died before Jesus comes again go to Hell?

The people who survive into the Millennium are not being given a "second chance." They will survive only by submitting to Christ while the bowls of wrath are being poured out, and faith has now become sight. Before in order to be right with God, you needed to believe by faith in Christ and submit to His rule in your life and in your heart. Once Christ returns, Faith is now Sight.

So, in the Millennium, faith has now passed away, and only sight remains, and so for those who are not transformed, it is now a matter of obedience and submission to His physical rule.

At this present time, people who are believers are submitting to His rule by faith. The only chance of survival outlined in the book of Joel to allow one to survive the Tribulation and the Day of the Lord is by submitting to His rule when He comes to bring justice by the sword. This is what Joel means when he says, “any who call upon the name of the Lord in that Day will be saved.” The day of the Lord is the dividing point between the Great Tribulation and the Millennium.

But everyone who calls on the name of the LORD will be saved, for some on Mount Zion in Jerusalem will escape, just as the LORD has said. These will be among the survivors whom the LORD has called. (Joel 2:32, NLT)

Who will rebel against Christ at the end of the Millennium?

It appears that Satan deceives many people from other nations throughout the world. Because in Revelation 20 it says that Satan will go to the kings of the nations, deceive them and they will wage war against Christ. But of course, Christ will win and Satan will be tossed into the lake of fire along with the Antichrist and the False Prophet.

What Will Believers Do In the Millennium?

Rule over those who are survivors. We see this principle being taught in Matthew 25 in the parable of the talents, and in Luke 19. We also see the promise of authority in Revelation 2.

To all who are victorious, who obey me to the very end, to them I will give authority over all the nations. They will rule the nations with an iron rod and smash them like clay pots. They will have the same authority I received from my Father, and I will also give them the morning star! (Revelation 2:26-28, NLT)

Now this is to me the greatest proof that there has to be survivors into the Millennium, because if there are no survivors, who do we rule over? Each other? Why would we smash them like clay pots, if they are also believers who were transformed at the Rapture too? It makes no sense. Jesus obviously meant that there would be a period of time when life on earth would be similar, if not exactly the same, as it was before He returns. This time period would need to be populated by people in order for someone to rule over them.

What is Heaven and how is it different from the Millennium?

This is an important question to answer, as I believe we have seen so many differing views espoused in the media that it pollutes sound doctrinal thinking. The best book I ever read on the subject is called “Resurrection,” by Hank Hanegraaff. I mentioned Hank earlier in the book, and I totally disagree with his Amillennial stance, which he terms “Partial-Preterism.” However, that being said, “Resurrection,” is a wonderful treatise on what we can expect when the Resurrection happens.

We have seen so many erroneous views of what we commonly call Heaven. Some false ideas include things like we will be floating around on clouds playing harps; we will meet St. Peter at the Pearly Gates and be judged according to our deeds, and not on the Blood of Christ. And so on and so forth.

One thing that is different between Heaven and the Millennium is that what we commonly refer to as Heaven is simply being present with Christ when we are dead. When we die, we go to be with Jesus. Wherever that is, that is what we believe is Heaven. But when Jesus comes to rule on earth it will not be the same as Heaven. The Millennium is actually the first part of what Hank describes as the Resurrection. The Resurrection is when all of the things of this earth are reborn, remade and renewed. What Hank is referring to in that book is what I would explain to be the period of time after the

Millennium, but the Millennium will be the path towards what is described in Hank's book.

But there is an order to this resurrection: Christ was raised as the first of the harvest; then all who belong to Christ will be raised when he comes back. After that the end will come, when he will turn the Kingdom over to God the Father, having destroyed every ruler and authority and power. For Christ must reign until he humbles all his enemies beneath his feet. (I Corinthians 15:23-25, NLT)

We see here that there is an implied period of time between the first Resurrection when "all who belong to Christ will be raised," and the time when Christ "humbles all his enemies beneath his feet."

After this period of time, and after the final defeat of Satan, then we see in the concluding chapters of Revelation that the New Jerusalem will descend and the entire universe will be recreated.

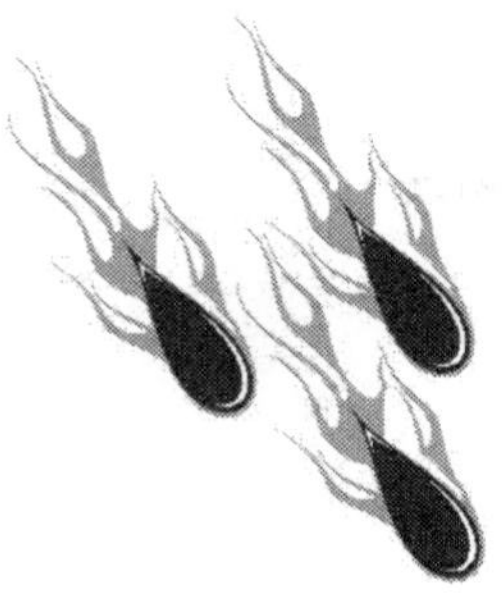

Islam

Are Islamic Views of the End Times Important for Christians?

Why does it appear that Islamic prophecy coming true? Islam is a false religion, so why would their prophesies be accurate?

I do not think that Islamic prophecy is accurate. I do, however, believe that Islamic prophecy is based on Biblical prophecy, and is a twisted perversion of it. Many things that we see as being an aspect of the Antichrist, they see as being an aspect of their Mahdi, or their version of the Messiah. Also we have a False Prophet that we are warned about, and they have a false Jesus who will come and convert the Christians to Islam.

Our False Prophet and the Antichrist are called Beasts. The biblical False Prophet is called the “Beast of the Earth,” and Muslims have a “Beast of the Earth,” literally “Dabbat al ard.” Their beast will give people a mark with the staff of Moses on the face of all true believers causing their faces to glow. Muslims are looking forward to the "mark of the beast."

The Bible does warn against divination. There is a good book by Christian magician André Kole called *"Mind Games,"* where he demonstrates that a great deal of divination is fake. He claims that all divination is fake, but I disagree with him on a few points. Satan may not be able to tell the future, but he is wise and practically immortal compared to our puny life spans. He's been around a long time and as any good general can, he is able to guess the moves that God is going to make, especially since God is bold enough to lay out His moves well ahead of time in prophecy.

Satan has had a *long* time to study prophecy, but where we only have a short time and might debate some of these things, he not only has had a greater time to study it, he sees things in the spiritual realm and has access to information that we do not.

It does not take a great leap of imagination to see that Satan has information that he could reveal to his followers that would be very detailed and accurate in comparison to the guessing games theologians often make.

So I believe that some divination obviously is fake, as pointed out in *"Mind Games,"* but some is real. Also, consider the ability of some mediums to understand details of certain people's lives. A few years ago there was a television show with a supposed medium entitled

"Crossing Over." In the show the host supposedly spoke to the departed loved ones of the guests, however, investigative reporters proved that he was faking it. But consider that some mediums do seem to have this ability, but they are in contact with a demon. The demon would be able to watch a person and collect all sorts of information from them without them ever knowing they were being spied upon. So, though I would agree with Kole that most are probably fake, it is not too hard for me to believe that some divination must be real, and is satanic and demonic in origin.

In addition to divination, there are other forms of prophecy such as the prophesies of St. Malachy and of the 12th century Jewish Rabbi Judah Ben Samuel, which seem incredibly accurate. I do not know how these men got most of their prophetic information. It seems in the Rabbi's case his predictions came from calculations made from the Torah, which in my opinion makes it similar to any other Biblical scholar's predictions, interesting, and possibly correct, but nothing we should stake everything on, but at the same time nothing sinister, as it appears to be based on Bible study methods many Christians use as well.

And so sometimes it is interesting, and maybe even helpful to read some of what the Muslims and others have written about prophecy, *but like everything*, it has to come back to Scripture to be weighed. If it goes against the Bible, it is not true.

Of course there are some things that the Bible does not say. For instance, the Muslims are looking for a prophecy to be fulfilled about a king in Saudi Arabia named Abdullah. They believe that when such a king reigns and then dies the Mahdi's coming will not be far off.

Currently the king of Saudi Arabia *is* named Abdullah, they have not had a king named Abdullah in over 100 years. This is fascinating, and incredibly interesting. The Bible is silent on this matter, so we have no way of knowing whether this is a true prophecy or not. But if it happens, then it obviously is part of the information that Satan imparted to Mohammed in the guise of the Angel Gabriel, or else it could be information gleaned from some other demonic source from some other Muslim after Mohammed.

Joel Richardson has done a great deal of research on these things, and his book "The Islamic Antichrist" is highly recommended for anyone who wants to know more information about the Islamic point of view. Also, Walid Shoebat's incredible book "Why I Left Jihad" is great as well. I advise you to read both of them.

Is the Dome of the Rock the Abomination that Causes Desolation?

Possibly. But if it is, it doesn't follow the rest of the description related to the Abomination that Causes Desolation. However the Dome of the Rock is a very blasphemous object. It rises above the place where the Temple stood, some say at the very location where the Holy of Holies stood, and declares that there is no god but Allah, who many scholars agree is not Yahweh, but the Arabic moon-god Sin, and that Mohammed is his messenger. Mohammed may truly be Sin's messenger, but he was most certainly not Yahweh's messenger. And as Christians we follow Yahweh, who sent His Son Jesus to die on a cross for our sins.

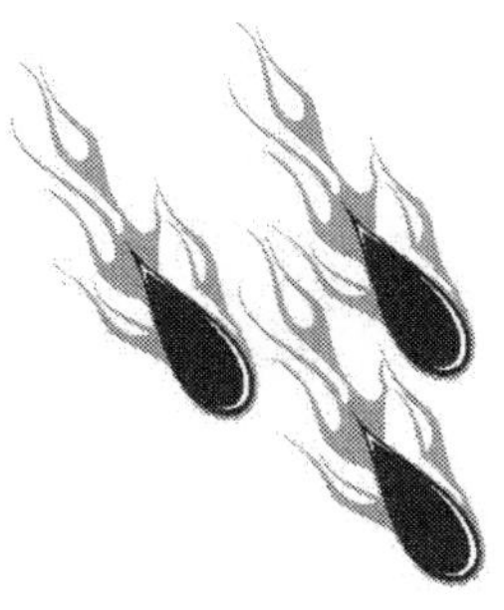

Other Questions

What is Preterism and is it False Teaching?

The Problem with Full Preterism

Full Preterists believe that since Jesus said He was coming soon, then He must have returned in 70 AD, and that there will be a third coming (though they refuse to call it a 3rd coming, calling it instead a fulfilled 2nd Coming).

There is another stance, represented most famously by *"the Bible Answer Man"* Hank Hanegraaff, which he calls partial-Preterism. While Preterists are right that some prophetic events were fulfilled with the fall of Jerusalem in 70 AD, they are gravely mistaken about most, if not all of the prophecy in the book of Revelation. The bulk of all scholarship shows that the book of Revelation was not written until after the fall of Jerusalem in 70 AD. The very earliest date that could be given for the book of Revelation is 68-69 AD, hardly enough time for a copy of this book to make it to Jerusalem to warn anyone.

Furthermore, the book is not addressed to the Jerusalem church, so John obviously had no intention of warning the Jerusalem church of any such tribulation coming to them. Nor were any of the letters addressed to any church in Israel, so it would make sense that by the time Revelation was written, the church had already been driven from Israel.

There is also what I am terming the "Global Problem." In Matthew 24 Jesus said there will be Great Distress unequaled from the beginning of the world until now and never to be equaled again. If those days were not cut short no one would survive. Again in Revelation 3:10 Jesus says that the coming trial will be for the "whole world." 70 AD was a horrible time for the Jews living in Jerusalem, but it was most definitely not the worst time in human history. WWI, WWII and even the 1960's were all periods of global unrest far greater than the destruction of Palestine in 70AD, which hardly registered a blip on the radar screen of vast destruction and oppression caused by the Roman Empire in their long history.

Some other information that contradicts partial and full Preterism include:

Nero was not the Antichrist: He ruled for 16 years, not 3 and a half years as Daniel states the Antichrist will rule.

Vespasian was not the Anti-Christ: He ruled for 10 years, again not the 3 and a half years as Daniel states

Rome's rule over Israel was far longer than the prophesied 7 or 3 and a half years. Rome simply does not fulfill the prophesies that Daniel made, and by trying to force these events on the prophesies it undermines the prophecies and makes it seem that prophecy is not accurate. But when compared to how accurate the prophecies of the first advent of the Messiah were, we should expect the prophecies of the second advent to be just as specific and accurate.

Antiochus Epiphanes did not fulfill all prophecy that some would like to believe he did. Many point to Daniel 11 as being fulfilled by Antiochus Epiphanes before Jesus was born.

It is true that the first part of Daniel 11 is dealing with the Kingdom of the North (modern day Turkey, Syrian, Iraq, Iran alliance) which was the Seleucid Dynasty. They were at war with the Southern Alliance – (modern day Egypt, Libya, Sudan) which was an African alliance under Ptolemy.

But we can easily see that after Daniel 11:36, the information shifts and starts speaking about the Antichrist. It talks about specific things that Antiochus never did. And it says in the “Last Days” these things will take place.

It is abundantly obvious that the “Last Days” were not in the time immediately following Jesus’ ascension because Jesus didn’t return then. It is more likely that there will be some form of reformation of these two powers. It could be that there will be a war between these two powers, and perhaps mirroring the history of the Seleucid/Ptolemy war. Some scholars speculate that there will be a reformed Caliphate, and that it may have a civil war at some point, or perhaps some other Southern Muslim countries will not want to give allegiance to the reformed Caliphate which will cause a war. The northern portion of the Caliphate will defeat the southern Muslim Alliance, and then on the way back, just like Antiochus, they will attack Jerusalem. We will have to wait and see if the scholars who believe this will prove to be accurate, but with the current political climate of the Middle East, it isn't too far of a stretch to see it as a possibility.

Importance Of Prophecy

How do fulfilled prophecies compare with prophesies that still need to be fulfilled? How accurate/detailed will prophesies be that we are looking for?

Dr. Hugh Ross on his website reasons.org includes some mathematical figures that demonstrate the reliability of prophesies of the Bible.

Unique among all books ever written, the Bible accurately foretells specific events-in detail-many years, sometimes centuries, before they occur. Approximately 2500 prophecies appear in the pages of the Bible, about 2000 of which already have been fulfilled to the letter—no errors.

(The remaining 500 or so reach into the future and may be seen unfolding as days go by.) Since the probability for any one of these prophecies having been fulfilled by chance averages less than one in ten (figured very

conservatively) and since the prophecies are for the most part independent of one another, the odds for all these prophecies having been fulfilled by chance without error is less than one in 102,000 (that is 1 with 2000 zeros written after it)!

My opinion is that if God was so incredibly accurate with the previous round of prophecy, then we can expect as much for the next round.

Why Is This Topic Important Today?

As Christians, it is always important to investigate every doctrine espoused by preachers to see if they match up with Scripture. I also think that God does not waste space, or His time. He added to the Bible a great deal of prophecy, prophecy that seems to be coming true today. Where Amillennialists will stress that the prophecy is important to know what God did in the past, and the Pre-Trib teachers will stress that prophecy is our hope for the future, I believe that both of these things are true. I also believe that God used prophecy as a warning in the past, and unfulfilled prophecies (and there are far more than Amillennialists want to admit) serve as a warning not only to the sinners of the world, but also to the church.

So it is important to understand both the prophecies that have already been fulfilled, and those that are still to come, and to understand our role as a church in these prophecies. It is also highly important to understand what is false teaching and what isn't. If something is false teaching, then we as the church should shun it. False teaching has only one purpose, no matter which part of doctrine it addresses: to confuse God's people so they will be unproductive. We are told in many places in the Bible that God does not want us to be ignorant. And we are also commanded to study to show ourselves approved. So we need to address false teaching when we find it.

We are also warned not to fall away, and not to be led astray by false teaching which can cause us to fall away. 2 Peter 3 gives us a clear warning, as does John 15 and 16:1.

So it is very important not to allow false teaching to take root, and where it is deeply rooted, to uproot it and cultivate sound doctrine. When it comes to doctrines such as the Pre-Trib fallacy, tracing the rise of this false teaching, as well as many other false doctrines, is as easy as tracing the popularity of sales of the study Bibles that Darby and Scofield published. Where Darby or Scofield Bibles reached popularity so did the false doctrines that are taught in their commentaries. In MacPherson's book, *"The Incredible Cover-Up,"* the author gives a very detailed and well-researched account of the origins of the Pre-Trib doctrine, and I highly recommend his work for serious students of eschatology.

Even if you are hold a Pre-Trib slant, and haven't been convinced by my arguments, you really should do your self a favor and at least read where your doctrine came from, because you might find that it flies in direct contradiction to some other doctrines of your church. I find it very strange today that many of the so-called "Cessationist" churches hold strongly to a Pre-Trib doctrine which came directly from a *charismatic vision*, which they claim ceased with the first Century believers. This is what baffles me the most about Dallas Theological Seminary's stance on this doctrine. They are perhaps the number one seminary for Cessationist teaching, yet they are also one of the greatest proponents of the Pre-Trib Rapture doctrine. Logically, these two doctrines are mutually exclusive, and you cannot be a Cessationist and a Pre-Trib person at the same time.

I believe Cessationism is a false teaching as well, but that is perhaps for another book. However, our doctrines should at least be logical. Everything else about the Bible follows a powerful Divine logic, and so too should Eschatological doctrines.

Throughout the 1970's the Pre-Trib doctrine gained a boost with the writings of Hal Lindsey, and then again in the late 1990's with the popularity of the "Left Behind" books by Tim LaHaye and Jerry Jenkins. *(I find it interesting to note that on Joel Richardson's site, one in which he talks about how the church should prepare for martyrdom, he has a quote from Tim LaHaye highly recommending his book "Islamic Antichrist." Maybe Dr. LaHaye is beginning to see the light! We can only hope.)* These books set sales records not only for Christian books, but for the publishing industry in general. A movie was made and several children's spin-offs followed in the wake of popularity.

If you watch the news every day, it is easy to see many things that we read about in Scripture coming to pass, in ways that have NEVER happened in history before. Some teachers would like to condemn Christians for reading their Bible in one hand and the newspaper in the other, and maybe there was a time when this was true, but certainly as we approach the time of Jesus' return, and the fulfillment of very detailed and specific prophecies begin to transpire, the newspaper will become a much more relevant tool for Bible study. There are events happening that are on a Global scale like never before, and they fall right in line with the so-called allegorical descriptions mentioned by the prophets. The more I see, the less allegorical the descriptions of the prophets appear. Just because the prophet didn't have the technical name for the equipment we now have, does not mean that the description is not an accurate representation of modern technology.

But all of that aside, there are several key teachings that Pre-Trib people use. We have discussed many of these in this book. Some of these arguments are genuine points of debate that could be taken either way, and some are serious stretches that one really must twist the Scriptures to make them stick. Where possible, I have tried to give concession if these points are genuine points of debate, though most are not the points of debate that many preachers would have you believe.

As I mentioned, there are many Christians who feel that studying these things is not of primary importance. I feel that this attitude is highly immature, especially in light of the fact that non-Christians are noticing many things happening in the world that they have heard are prophesied about. They are filled with fear, and seeking answers. Now more than ever, non-Christians are asking Christians what the Bible says about these events. Christian scholars are being asked to come on news channels such as CNN and MSNBC, of all places, to discuss these events. Sadly, most of those invited hold to the unbiblical teaching of the Pre-Trib doctrine, so they are not giving the full truth to these hungry people. Instead they are preaching that if "you'd only come to Jesus, you'll be spared these horrible events."

From my perspective, I see this only as setting up the apostasy that was prophesied. Many people will make a nominal commitment to Christ, only to betray and turn in true Christians, when the heat is on, just as has happened in Communist countries such as China, Russia, Romania and Viet Nam.

Sadly, a cavalier attitude has become pervasive in the church today with regards to the Tribulation; and not only the Great Tribulation, but trials in general.

Many Christians are lukewarm, chasing after the things of the world, spending at least as much time (if not more) pursuing leisure activities, as they pursue God. When asked if they have given any thought to the idea that they might have to endure tribulation, they respond with statements like, "I read the Left Behind series, and I'm not going to be here for that." But when asked to provide Scriptural support for why they believe this, they usually have nothing to offer. Some have a lot of theories, false doctrine and speculation, but very little actual Biblical support to back up what they believe. Those who do have Biblical support often quote passages completely out of context and severely mishandle the text.

Those of us who disagree with the Pre-Trib doctrine often point to Scripture after Scripture in an effort to change their hearts, and hopefully wake them up from their foolish pursuit of the comforts of the world, but often to little avail. There seems to be a demonic stubbornness with many people who refuse to even entertain the idea that they might have to endure some discomfort in their lives. I hope and pray that isn't you.

And yet there is growing in our time a secondary doctrine, that represents the pendulum swinging to the other end, back towards a more historical view of the End Times, yet also very unbiblical. This doctrine, known as Amillennialism, teaches that there will be no literal millennium, and all prophecy in the Bible except the Return of Jesus has been fulfilled. This is a great mistake as well, because obviously not all prophecy has been fulfilled. There are clearly difficult things ahead for the church that surpasses even what Third-World countries have experienced up until this time.

I believe it is of utmost importance to study this topic primarily because Satan is setting up the church for the "Great Deception" that Jesus warned about. This deception is so great that Jesus said in Matthew 24 that it would lead to the "Great Falling Away."

"But Christians can't fall away," you might say. Perhaps we can debate the validity of whether a true Christian can fall away, but I do not think any of us would debate that our churches today are filled with a great deal of non-believers, semi-believers and lukewarm charlatans and wolves in sheep's clothing. In fact, many of our pulpits are filled today with non-believers! So perhaps, *you* can't fall away. Perhaps your Pre-Trib preacher might not fall away, and is merely confused or mistaken about doctrine, but that doesn't mean all of the people who are sitting around you in church are truly following Christ. There is a good chance that they are in danger of falling away. And when the Tribulation finally does arrive, these are people you have grown accustomed to leaning on, who might not be able to be trusted in the difficult situation that the Tribulation will be.

It appears that the real reason that many people are so opposed to a Post-Trib point of view is due to fear, and not "fear of God," but just plain old fashioned fear. And they use any twisted form of bad exegesis to keep from dealing with a subject, that Malachi calls the Great and Terrible Day of the Lord. It can be a frightening thing to think about, but Hell is a frightening thing to think about too, but it is certainly a topic that is important. It seems that the Pre-Trib and the Amillennial stances are both rooted in fear, and are both guilty of dodging the real issue, that the church will have to be strong and endure persecution.

Many Christians do not want to use the term "false teaching," when it comes to these doctrines, instead they use phrases such as "We should stick to the basics and not get caught up in foolish debate over non-essentials." However, they only bring these phrases out when faced with the hard core Biblical truth that defeats their arguments. I have come to believe that as the End Times scenario plays out, we will need to be strong, and not confused. These other doctrines will bring confusion, and thus a weakened faith when people realize that things are not going the way they were taught, and they will believe they either missed the Rapture, or God has rejected them and they are not loved by Him anymore.

But if Christians would just face the truth, that like their brothers and sisters who are being martyred right now all over the world, they may one day too be called to face that hard situation, they can begin to pray and prepare their hearts to be strong in that time.

When we study the Bible we want to be careful to take everything in context. And yes, there are things in the Bible that are not totally literal, such as parables and proverbs. But we should examine each passage to see if it can fit a literal view first, before we immediately dismiss it and claim that it is figurative. Sometimes even if a literal view is somewhat harsh, it might be the correct view. We often forget that we live in a very comfortable society, but Jesus' society was much harsher. When He said, for example, that it would be better to cut off your hand or pluck out your eye instead of going to Hell, he was being very *literal.* If we would just spend one minute thinking about the horrendous reality of Hell, we would say, "Yes, I can see that it would be better to lose a hand or an eye than to go to Hell."

So yes, many things that might appear to be allegorical, or that we have been taught to see as allegorical, may in fact be literal. And some things that appear literal, may be the prophet's best way of trying to describe something he saw that he couldn't understand, because the technology was far too advanced for him to comprehend. It is our jobs as faithful students of the Word to examine each passage to discern if it is indeed literal or figurative. If it is unclear, then we need to be humble enough to say that the particular passage is complex and unclear, and not use it to build cases for our particular slant. I find that when Pre-Trib teachers will honestly remove all of the unclear passages (and passages that are only tangentially related) that they use as proof for their viewpoint, they have no Scripture at all to back up their points of view. Likewise for most Amillennial proof texts.

There are many unsound methods of Bible study, which a lot of people fall victim to. When we must chop up Scripture or use obscure translation methods or adopt an attitude that the average layman cannot understand these events or teachings, we fall into the same sin that the Catholic Church fell into before the Reformation that led to so many of the abuses it was guilty of during the Middle Ages. (We see it today with many church building programs, where unsound Bible study is used to convince people to increase their tithing to raise funds.) When pastors use these faulty methods, they are setting themselves up as priests and interpreters for the "uneducated masses who cannot possibly understand" this information.

This is evil, plain and simple. Pastors are not some special class of people who can read the Bible "for all it's worth" and understand it, where their congregants cannot. The same Holy Spirit that indwells the pastor, can also educate and guide the congregation. If the pastor must jump all around the Bible, taking Scripture out of context to create some "ear-tickling" theology that makes congregants feel good, or else create some dry and completely "non-sensational" doctrine that also isn't true, then something is terribly wrong. Many times, these pastors are more concerned with the money that will be donated than they are the truth.

Questions we have to ask include: Are pastors teaching faulty End Times theology because they are convinced it is Biblical? Or are they teaching it because they are actually afraid of the alternative? Are they afraid that preaching an unpopular doctrine will cause them to lose their livelihoods? So instead of preaching the Truth are they willing to water It down to protect their jobs? Are pastors abandoning the Pre-Trib theology in favor of Hanegraaff's "partial Preterist/Amillennial" views because they believe it is truly biblical, and have studied the history to see if what he is teaching is actually true? Or are they latching onto this new fad in End Times theology because they are too afraid to preach the truth that the end will be a time of great trial, just as the Bible has said all along? Is it distasteful to them to think they might have to face hardship? Are they afraid they won't be able to hold up to the tortures their brothers and sisters endure even now in many countries in the world?

To hammer this in, and to perhaps reveal why I feel so passionate about this subject, I had a conversation with a pastor about world missions a few weeks before I started writing this book. He said that he cared so much about world missions because we needed to reach this world for Christ in order for Jesus to return. And the last places we needed to reach were the Muslim countries. I pointed out to him that all of the Islamic countries are actually apostate Christian countries; actually the very first Christian countries. And that in order for the events prophesied in the Bible to actually play out as prophesied, they *can not* convert to Christianity, but must remain Islamic countries. He told me, "Even if that were true, I would never preach it because then people would *stop giving money."*

We live in an evil time where pastors refuse to preach the truth simply because collecting money is more important than preaching *TRUTH*! And since we can't necessarily trust what our preachers are teaching us we need to investigate these things for ourselves and examine the Scriptures thoroughly to find out what it does teach. But if we are going to study it, we need to understand how to study it. So how do we study and understand prophecy?

Some steps that I use are as follows:

1. What is the preliminary idea the Bible is teaching me?

The first thing I ask myself after I read something in the Bible, is what is this saying to me, what is the main idea that I am getting from what I just read? Some passages are kind of confusing, and need to be researched, some are very straight-forward and easy to understand. But some seem straight forward, but cannot mean what they seem to imply.

For instance, in Acts 2:38 Peter says that believers must, "repent and be baptized in the name of Jesus Christ for the forgiveness of your sins, and you will receive the gift of the Holy Spirit." Some people have taken this to mean that if we are baptized, then we will be saved. In other words, baptism is what saves us. Both Catholics and Oneness Pentecostals (two groups who are largely diametrically opposed) both espouse this doctrine. But this doctrine is in direct contradiction to Romans chapter 3 which teaches that we are saved by faith in Jesus Christ alone. Since we believe that if God is wise (i.e. logical and truthful) then God does not contradict Himself. And if we further believe that the Bible is His Word, then we cannot accept both of these doctrines at the same time. Either faith saves us, or baptism saves us. Either one or the other is wrong. If we say that Romans 3 is wrong then we are saying that Paul's writings are not God's word for us as well, and therefore must throw out most of the New Testament. However, if we logically conclude that Peter is describing a progression that happens after we believe in Jesus in faith, then we see that there is no contradiction at all.

So sometimes a verse that appears straight forward isn't enough to build a doctrine on. We must test that verse in light of other Scripture to see how it fits together. In order to do that we need to ask questions of the text:

1. What is the verse saying?

Every single verse of the Bible is saying something. Even the passages that repeat other parts of the Bible are saying something to us usually about a deeper truth of which the original prophet may not have understood the full context.

For instance, Peter quotes Isaiah about the fact that Jesus' stripes (i.e. the beatings He took for us) provide healing for us. Isaiah was pointing forward to something that God was telling the people of Israel to watch for, but Peter was explaining that Jesus fulfilled that prophecy, and we could cling to its truth in our time of need.

But when we read a verse we need to ask ourselves what it is saying to us. In step one, we often will come to a verse with some kind of preconceived notion about that particular verse. But sometimes we need to divorce our previous opinion and look at the very simple facts that are being presented in the verse.

To do this well requires us to examine some of the historical background and the grammatical background of the words being used. Sometimes it's even important to understand the literary genre being used, so we can know what stylistic devices are being used. And we always want to keep in mind how it fits in with the doctrine we know.

3. How does this verse fit in with the context of the passage in which it's found?

Once we know the very basics of what is being communicated in the verse, we need to look around at the other verses that surround it to get the fullness of the passage.

It is very easy to build a faulty theology or doctrine based on portions of passages. Whole cults have been developed around this technique of Bible study. But we do not want to have a cult mindset, we want to walk in the light of the Word, and understand what the Bible teaches us. So we need to examine the full context to make sure that we have an understanding of the entire teaching of the verse or passage we are studying.

4. How does the passage fit in with the chapter it is in?

After examining the passage in context, we want to move further out to the chapter and make sure that we are understanding the passage completely. One thing to keep in mind, the Bible was not originally written with chapters and verses, so sometimes it is easy for us to think that information in one chapter isn't related to information in the previous or following chapter, but very often they are related, which leads to the next question.

5. How does this chapter fit in with the overall section that it's in?

We have to also examine the passage to see if it makes sense in light of the entire section that contains the teaching on whatever topic is in question.

6. How does the section fit in with the book that it's in?

And then we go on to see how it relates to the section of the book if applicable. Some books are very short and do not have separate sections, but others have several ideas that are being discussed within each book.

7. How does the book fit in with other books/passages that are from similar categories or genres?

I believe this is an often neglected portion that is sometimes missed. We need to be careful to cross-reference what we are reading in one book with other books that deal with related subjects, or the same subject to see if we understand the doctrine that is being formed in our mind as we study the concepts being brought by the original verse in question.

This is important so that we do not build contradictory doctrines, such as adopting a Pre-Trib view, based on a Vision from a Scottish Woman in 1830, and then claiming that charismatic visions ceased with the first century church. This not only is foolish, but causes intelligent unbelievers to shoot holes in our teaching, make fools of us, and draw away people who otherwise would have learned how to grow in Christ.

8. How does the genre and category, and all of the preceding information fit in with the Bible as a whole?

This final step of what I consider the textual study is often overlooked. We need to examine our passage to see how the information fits with other parts of the Bible. Sometimes we need to see if the passage speaks of something historical that we missed, or if it speaks of something that hasn't happened yet.

9. How does this teaching fit in with the story of Salvation?

Once we have a fairly complete understanding of the text, we need to ask ourselves how the information we gained fits in with our understanding of the gospel message. Does the information contradict anything we know about how we are saved? If it does, is our understanding of salvation faulty, or is our understanding of the text faulty? Sometimes people preach a different method of salvation than the Apostles preached. Sometimes people want to make God less harsh and more palatable to people we are teaching, but the text is harsher than we are. And sometimes people make God out to be harsher than He is, and make salvation seem unobtainable, when it is clearly there for us all to have if we believe. Bottom line, we have to remain true to the text.

10. How does this teaching fit in with what we know about God's nature and principles?

This is similar to the previous question. We have to make sure that the information we are learning about is consistent with what the Bible teaches about God's nature. If it contradicts God's nature as revealed in the rest of Scripture, then we probably have misunderstood the text.

11. Is this teaching logical in what we know about the rest of our knowledge of the truth?

Furthermore, it is important to make sure that the information is logical. God is very logical, and has established very detailed rules for the governance of His universe. If we have a theory that doesn't follow a logical progression and thought process, then we might have misunderstood the text.

12. The Simplicity test – Does my information adhere to a simplicity test?

Finally, in light of the previous information, and in the words of the words of Isaiah 35:8 about the way of holiness being plain, and in the spirit of Proverbs 15:19 (The way of the slothful man is as an hedge of thorns: but the way of the righteous is made plain.), I propose a simplicity test. Is the doctrine that we are getting from the text simple, or is it so convoluted and complex that it can't be boiled down for a child to understand? Sure some doctrines are difficult to explain, such as the doctrine of the Trinity, but in actuality even that doctrine is simple to explain.

God reveals Himself in three ways: Father, Son and Holy Spirit. The Son came to die on a Cross for our sins, and was rejected by the Father. In order for there to be forgiveness of sins, there has to at least be a Duality to God. How can one reject Himself, unless there is at least two parts? And finally once we are saved by faith in the Son, we can have the Holy Spirit to change us and make us like the Son. How can God live in our heart, but still be in eternity controlling the universe? So again we see another duality. When you connect the duality of the Father with the Son, and with the Father and the Spirit, you get the triangular connection that ancient scholars labeled the “Trinity,” or in other words, “Tri-unity.”

This simple paragraph demonstrates how even a difficult to understand doctrine can be boiled down to simplicity. So the simplicity test should be the last question we ask ourselves when we are studying and formulating a doctrine. Is this doctrine simple?

Finally, I use a little phrase that helps me when I study. *“I am looking for the Truth, not trying to find support for my own idea.”* I’ll repeat that in a different way. We go to the Bible to find Truth, not to promote an agenda, or find support for our own ideas. Truth is always paramount. We always must put Truth first, and if it teaches us something different from what we were originally taught, we have to be willing to abandon our original teaching to cling solely to the Truth, no matter how strange or frightening it may seem to us at first.

Scholars use what they call “the 4 hermeneutical principles” to “exegete” a text. Which simply means that there are four steps to understand a text. They are Context, History, Grammatical, Theological. I have expanded them to 8 steps as follows:

8 Steps to Good Exegesis

1. Pray for guidance

2. What is the text telling me?

3. How does this passage fit in with what I know about the context?

4. Is there something I am missing from the original language?

5. Is there something about the history surrounding this text that will help me understand it better?

6. Are there any theological implications about this passage that need to be weighed in light of basic doctrine, or is there something that strengthens or weakens certain doctrines.

7. Logically consider what you have learned & pray for more guidance. Be willing to admit and accept it if you just don't have an answer.

8. Does it fit in with a simplicity test.

Our ultimate goal, if we believe the Bible is God's inspired word, is to harmonize the passages so that they make sense.

We go to the Bible to find truth, not support a man made idea or theory.

Why Is It Important for Christians to Care about This Discussion Now?

We just asked the question why is this topic important today. And we explored that from a theological stance. I'd like to reconsider the question again here at the end of the book.

There are many events that are happening in the world right now that are "tipping believers off" that something is happening in the world, and that the return of our Lord cannot be that far off.

So many times the Bible tells us to be watching and prepared. There are many events that have happened in the past few years that have been very difficult things to live through. Hurricane Katrina, 911, the Japan Tsunami, the New Zealand Earthquake, the oil spills, the volcano in Iceland that shut down air travel for weeks, Hurricane Sandy, on and on the list goes and grows. Currently, we are looking at a possible future conflict in the Middle East that seems to escalate each day. We live in a time in America where our constitutional rights are being attacked and destroyed on a daily basis due to "Executive orders" from our US president and his administration.

Since approximately January of 2010 animals have been dying off at an alarming rate. It seems to have started with Honey Bees. After the Honey Bees started dying in what came to be termed "Hive Collapse Disorder," Black Birds started dying off in the droves. Then fish from many parts of the world began washing up on beaches, followed by Cattle from many parts of the world, some in Vietnam, some in the Mid West of America. The list goes on and on: Crabs in California, Dolphins, Whales, Eagles, Penguins in the Southern hemisphere. Seals, peacocks, etc. At the time of this writing 780,000 chickens suddenly died. The common denominator: No one knows why these animals are dying. Oh sure, the articles will give some theories, but then when you read further, the scientists are just giving speculation, but no real hard facts as to why the animals are dying.

Then there are strange events that no one seems to be able to explain such as “red rain” that is falling in India. It seems to be some sort of microorganism, but no one is giving a really good reason as to where it comes from. And this is reminiscent of the “red tides” that have been growing off the coast of Florida, again with no apparent reason.

Then of course there is the growth of FEMA camps across the country in the event of natural disasters. Yes, I know that there are many conspiracy theories abounding out there about these things, and you can investigate these things on your own and formulate your own opinion. But there appears to be currently over 800 FEMA camps across the United States, fully staffed, fully operational, but also totally empty. We don’t know why they are there, but the government obviously feels that they are needed in the event of some future catastrophe.

And there are many underground safety shelters such as the one under the Denver International Airport. Again, I’m not trying to provide conspiracies, or trying to suggest why these things are there, but the fact that they are there raises some questions as to the extent of what our government thinks could happen in a national crisis.

Clearly the United States is not beloved around the entire globe. We have Islamic extremists calling daily for our demise. We are on very uneasy terms with Iran and North Korea, and we seem to be losing our influence in many areas of the world. Perhaps the government knows that there could be a real state of emergency in the near future should one of our enemies decide to conduct terrorist activities against us.

But knowing what I know about Bible prophecy and the future Antichrist, I could foresee a possible event where these places built for our safety could be turned against us and used against believers. The Bible states that there will be a great deal of persecution. It is very important that we fix in our minds that we will cling to Jesus and not give in to the persecution and walk away from God.

Panic Shock & Trauma

By the time you get to this part of the book, you might think, "There's no way I can prepare for what is going to come. What can I possibly do?"

The first thing that you have to keep in mind is that it is very important not to panic in a life threatening situation. You have to prepare your mind that you will keep a clear head. You can have a clear head by being prepared. You need to prepare your heart, your mind and your spirit for hardship that might come.

First of all, you want to pray continually as the Bible advises. Pray that God will speak clearly to you. Pray that God will direct you to safety, and that He will direct you as you help others.

Secondly, it doesn't hurt to be prepared. Sure you can't stave off the Tribulation, or be prepared for every contingency, but there are some things you can do to get ready for it. The first thing that helps is to study what will and what will not happen. And it also doesn't hurt to have a few things together in case you have to leave in a hurry.

In the aftermath of Hurricane Katrina, I was in Austin, TX and we had to help with a lot of the refugees that came in to Texas from Louisiana. Some of those poor people had been without toiletries, water and food for a great while after the event. It would have been helpful if the people had prepared bug-out bags ahead of time.

No one really wants to have to leave their home, but if a disaster happens, it doesn't hurt to be prepared.

Obviously volumes have been written on this subject, and I can't include much here, but I hope that you would give it some consideration. I believe in the midst of hardship, those of us who know the Lord have the greatest opportunities to witness for Him.

Finally, prepare your heart. Worse comes to worse, you might die. I hate to be the one to break it to you, but the body you are living in isn't immortal. The good news is if you love Jesus, are following Him and prepared, then death isn't a bad thing. The bad news is if the Antichrist's minions are anything like the communists that overran places like Romania, then you might get tortured. I suggest reading Richard Wurmbrand's amazing book *"Tortured for Christ."* Or Corrie Ten Boom's books. These dear saints endured much at the hands of demonic people, but God brought them through. Trust Him no matter what, and He will bring you through too.

Appendix - How Do I Witness To My Pre-Trib Friends?

1. First realize that Pre-Trib doctrine is false teaching, and needs to be addressed in the church. Prepare yourself for a great battle, because Satan doesn't want this pet doctrine to go away, because it will be used to set up the Apostasy that will precede the Lord's Return.
2. Understand that if your friends are holding tightly to the Pre-Trib Doctrine, and refuse to have a reasonable discussion with you about the truth, they are most likely blinded by Satan, and cling to the doctrine for one of three reasons:
    a. They are clinging to Pre-Trib Doctrine because of Fear
    b. They are clinging to the Pre-Trib Doctrine because of Tradition; (I do not honestly believe any Pre-Trib thinker of reasonable intelligence, after studying the facts, continues to cling to it because they are convinced it is the truth.) Furthermore, people often cling to tradition because of fear as well. They are often afraid that if they go against their traditions, they might be wrong, and it is safer to cling to the tradition than to actually think through the issue for themselves.
    c. They are being paid to cling to the Pre-Trib doctrine. I come down pretty

hard on some Pre-Trib teachers, but in all fairness, in many cases their entire livelihoods are dependent on the Pre-Trib doctrine. If you are a member of the Assemblies of God, Calvary Chapel or even some of the Southern Baptist Churches, if you are a pastor who genuinely is searching for the truth and become convinced that the Pre-Trib fantasy is a lie, then you will automatically lose your job. Sadly, oftentimes ministers are more afraid of being out of work than following wholeheartedly the God who will judge them more harshly for passing on false teaching.

3. Pray before sharing the truth with them. Most people who are greatly enmeshed in Pre-Trib doctrine got that way because they were afraid of the horrors that were coming at the end, and started studying it to give themselves some comfort that they wouldn't have to endure it. You have to remember that most of the teaching of Pre-Trib theology came along with sermons, movies and books that describe how utterly awful and hopeless the Tribulation period would be, and used it as an evangelistic tool to win converts. If people were converted out of fear, instead of because of a love for God, then this is an incredibly solid building block of their faith. And so they cling to Pre-Trib theology as their only source of hope. They don't understand that God can protect them and walk with them through it, just like He did for Noah and Lot.

4. Share the truths that you learned in this book, and any other truth that God has taught you about this topic.
5. Continue to pray for them, pray against their blindness, pray that God will open their eyes, pray that the Scripture that you share with them will do its work, and pray that they will realize that they are trying to combat your Scripture with theories and rhetoric, but not with truth. Remember the Word of the Lord will accomplish what it sets out to accomplish. Just remember also that sometimes it might accomplish driving a wedge between a heretic and a true believer. But where two true believers are together there will be no wedge, only freedom from false doctrine.
6. Don't give up, but realize that they are imbedded in deception, and it sometimes takes time to break these ideologies.
7. Continue to be there for them when things get bad, because only God's love and mercy will tear down the walls they put up. Try to refrain from saying "I told you so," when the Tribulation actually hits!

Appendix - Getting Ready

Understanding the stages of Catastrophe

In every catastrophe there are certain stages leading up to it. I am sure that organizations dealing with catastrophe have better and more complete information about this topic, but for this appendix, I have simplified some of the more common emotions that are part of any catastrophic event. The Tribulation will bring about some of the most disastrous catastrophes in the history of the world, and I believe it will help to have some understanding of the process that we will be called to endure.

1. Anticipation and Buildup – Not every catastrophe begins with a buildup, but when we see it coming, there is often a time period of anticipation that brings with it a flood of emotions that range anywhere from panic to acceptance.
2. Impact – When the catastrophe hits, this is considered the moment of impact. When the catastrophe becomes real for you the victim, then you have been impacted by it.
3. Disorientation/Shock – Often immediately after the event, there is a period of time that can range from mere moments to something more long term, in which the catastrophe victim is either disorientated or in a state of shock. Sometimes

this can play out in physical ways, such as vomiting or nausea, or emotional ways, such as denial in the face of the evidence, etc.

4. Realization of Gravity of Situation – After the shock wears off realization of the gravity of the situation sets in and allows us to react to the catastrophe. The shorter the time period of phase number 3, the better are your chances of survival in a catastrophic situation. Those who are well prepared for the catastrophe, often suffer less from the disorientation and shock when it hits.
5. Shelter – After any catastrophe, whether it is physical or mental, some type of shelter needs to be sought. In a physical catastrophe such as a hurricane or explosion, a safe place needs to be found. In an emotional catastrophe such as a death in the family, or some other form of emotional trauma, a safe place in your mind needs to be found. First and foremost we need to cultivate a safe place in our minds and hearts where we meet with God. If we do not have that safe place in a time of peace it will be difficult to find it in a time of panic. I think this is why Jesus told us to practice getting alone in our prayer closet to talk to God. If we can talk to Him there, we can talk to Him anywhere.
6. Waiting – Waiting can be the hardest part of dealing with a catastrophe. Sometimes we have to wait for many different factors. Some of the following include:
    a. Grief over Loss – sometimes it takes a great deal of time to heal. Most psychologists say that it takes at least 2 years to deal with the loss of someone or something we love. I have also heard that many psychologists say it takes at least 3

years to form new neuro-pathways to learn a new behavior or erase an old addiction. Don't feel surprised if you find yourself dealing with grief until we see our Lord who will wipe away all grief forever. Paul told us in I Thessalonians to encourage each other with the FACT that we will be reunited with our loved ones with Jesus forever if we continue to endure.

b. Waiting for Aid and Supplies – Sometimes in a physical catastrophe we might have to wait for aid and supplies to come. Do what you can to survive and to help others survive. Share your hope with them.
c. Rioting and Looting – Sometimes in a physical catastrophe we might need to deal with rioting and looting, and the aftermath that comes from that, which can cause the cleanup to be delayed. If possible, try to set an example, because you can often sway others who are rioting and looting as a response to their own fear, and use the catastrophe to give them hope, peace and strength in spite of their weakness.

7. Anger – Often times when we are in a traumatic event, after the shock wears off, and we are beginning to heal, we experience anger that results from losing the comfort we once possessed, the loved one we cared for, or whatever it is that has changed. If we know that the anger is coming, it will help us deal with it in a godly manner, because even Jesus was angry at times, but even in that He never sinned. We are told to be angry but not to sin. So it is possible,

and recognizing that it will come to us will help us get through it. Try to keep this in mind when dealing with others, and in dealing with their anger, because anger in a catastrophe can often lead to death, or to doing things that you will regret forever.

8. Clean Up – Finally, after everything has settled down, we get to experience the clean up stage, and this can be the hardest part as everything we once knew is piled up on the rubbish heap. But this too can be dealt with if we can see it coming.
9. Moving On – And then if we survive the catastrophe we will eventually have to move on. Life goes on, and so must we. If we are to survive the Tribulation, then the moving on part will be glorious as it will mean we are "moving on" to be with our Lord in the air when He appears to end the Tribulation and to pour out His wrath on evil doers of the world. Remember this is only a momentary affliction.

There are several books out there detailing the stories of people who have gone through disasters and survived. One tactic that I notice from Scripture is evidenced in the life of the Apostle Paul. He frequently reminded people to be looking forward to the great day of the return of our Lord and the resurrection.

Often if we hold so tightly to the things and people around us as our means of comfort and security, when they are taken away we are devastated. But if we spend our time thinking about the Resurrection, thinking about what we will do with our loved ones, then we are constantly investing our hearts into the Kingdom to come, and not clinging too tightly to the things of this world.

People who invest in the Kingdom to come are not as traumatized as people who only live for the present. We have so much more to benefit from when Jesus comes back, that our hope should always be in what's to come, and not what's behind or what is with us now. Sure we can enjoy the things we have now, and we can cherish the memories of the past, but what's to come is far greater than anything we've ever experienced. That is our blessed hope. That is what Paul is talking about when he tells us in Thessalonians to encourage each other about the Second Coming.

Below are a few topics that would be good for you to investigate on your own. A lot of information about the Underground Church, Torture and how not to deny Christ can be found at www.persecution.com. Other topics such as food storage, emergency preparedness how to survive can be found at many different sites on the internet.

Some Useful Topics to Research and Consider…

Emergency Prep
Food Storage
Under Ground Church
Torture
Denying Christ
Martyrdom
The Communist Takeover of Russia, China and Korea

Appendix – Animal Die-Offs 2010-2012

Listed by Date, Animal Type and Region.

List of Mass Animal Deaths 2010

November 2010
November 2, 2010 – 1,000+ Birds, Tasmania, Australia

December 2010
December 20, 2010 – 1,000+ Birds, Esperance, Western Australia

List of Mass Animal Deaths 2011

January 2011
January 1, 2011 - 200,000+ Fish, Arkansas River, Arkansas
January 1, 2011 - 5,000+ Birds, Beebe, Arkansas
January 3, 2011 - 2,000,000 Fish, Chesapeake Bay, Maryland & Virginia
January 4, 2011 - 100 Tons Fish, Parana Region shores, Brazil
January 4, 2011 - 3,000+ Blackbirds, Louisville, Kentucky
January 4, 2011 - 500 Birds, Louisiana
January 4, 2011 – 1000+ Fish, Volusia County, Florida
January 5, 2011 – 100+ Snapper (with no eyes), Coromandel, New Zealand
January 5, 2011 - 40,000+ Crabs, Kent, England
January 6, 2011 – 100+ Grackles, Sparrows & Pigeons, Upshur County, Texas
January 7, 2011 - 8,000 Turtle Doves, Faenza, Italy
January 14, 2011 – Fish, Baku, Azerbaijan

January 14, 2011 - 300 Blackbirds, Athens, Alabama
January 15, 2011 - 200 Cows, Portage County, Wisconsin
January 17, 2011 - 10,000 Buffalos and Cows, Vietnam
January 17, 2011 – 100+ Seals, Labrador, Canada
January 18, 2011 – 1000+ Octopus, Vila Nova de Gaia, Portugal
January 20, 2011 - 55 Buffalo, Cayuga County, New York
January 21, 2011 – 1000+ Fish, Detroit River, Michigan
January 22, 2011 – 1000+ Herring, Vancouver Island, Canada
January 23, 2011 – 100+ Fish, Dublin, Ireland
January 27, 2011 - 200 Pelicans, Topsail Beach, North Carolina
January 27, 2011 - 2000 Fish, Bogota, Columbia
January 31, 2011 – 100,000+ Mussel Shells, Waiheke Island, New Zealand

February 2011
February 2, 2011 – 100+ Pigeons, Geneva, Switzerland
February 4, 2011 – 1000+ Fish, Amazon River, Brazil and Florida, US
February 5, 2011 - 14 Whales, New Zealand
February 8, 2011 – 100+ Sparrows, Rotorua, New Zealand
February 9, 2011 – 1,000+ Fish, Florida
February 11, 2011 - 20,000 Bees, Ontario, Canada
February 11, 2011 – 100+ Birds, Lake Charles, Louisiana
February 16, 2011 - 5 Million Fish, Mara River, Kenya
February 16, 2011 - Thousands of Fish and Ducks, Ontario, Canada
February 16, 2011 – Fish, Black Sea Region, Turkey
February 19, 2011 – Blackbirds, Ukraine
February 20, 2011 - 100 Whales, Mason Bay, New Zealand
February 20, 2011 - 120 Cows, Banting, Malaysia
February 21, 2011 – 100,000+ Fish, Texas
February 21, 2011 - 16 Swans Stratford-on-Avon, UK
February 23, 2011 - 28 Dolphins, Alabama and Mississippi

February 25, 2011 – 100+ Chickens, North Sumatra, Indonesia

March 2011

March 3, 2011 - 80 Dolphins Gulf Region, TX and FL
March 8, 2011 – Millions of Fish King Harbor Marina, CA
March 26, 2011 – 100+ Fish Gulf Shores, AL
March 28, 2011 – 1 Whale, Virginia
March 29, 2011 – 1300+ Ducks Houston, Minnesota

April 2011

April 18, 2011 – 100+ Fish Ventura Harbor, CA
April 20, 2011 - 6 Tons of Sardines Ventura Harbor, CA
April 20, 2011 – 100+ Dead Abalone Cape Town, Australia
April 22, 2011 - Leopard Sharks, San Francisco Bay, CA

May 2011

May 13, 2011 - Dozens of Sharks, California
May 13, 2011 – 1,000+ Fish, Lake Erie, Ohio
May 1, 2011 - 2 Whales Waiinu Beach, New Zealand

June 2011

June 4, 2011 - 800 Tons of Fish Taal Volcano, Philippines
June 5, 2011 – 1,000+ Earthworms, Ohio
June 17, 2011 – 750+ Fish, River Des Peres, Missouri
June 29, 2011 – 100+ Fish, Georgia

July 2011

July 1, 2011 - Turtles Queensland, Australia
July 14, 2011 – Fish, Oklahoma
July 15, 2011 – 100,000+ Birds, New Zealand
July 19, 2011 – 1000+ F Cape York River, Australia
July 21, 2011 – Fish, Louisiana
July 22, 2011 – Fish, Haihe River, China
July 22, 2011 - Fish North Falmouth, MA

July 22, 2011 - Sea Turtles Queensland, Australia
July 23, 2011 - 15 Whales, Scotland
July 26, 2011 - Chickens and Ducks, Marshall Islands

August 2011
August 1, 2011 – 100+ Fish Rio Grande River, New Mexico
August 1, 2011 – 1000+ Fish San Angelo State Park, Texas
August 14, 2011 – 100+ Fish and Turtles Pearl River, LA
August 19, 2011 - Dolphins and Seals Oxnard Beach, CA
August 19, 2011 - Fish Fuhe River, China
August 22, 2011 – 100+ Salmon and Trout Bandon River, Ireland

September 2011
September 3, 2011 - Black Dolphins Bulgaria
September 6, 2011 - 10 Million Fish Minjiang River, China
September 17, 2011 – 400+ Squid San Diego, CA
September 20, 2011 – 1,000+ White Bass Arkansas
September 22, 2011 – 100+ Giant Squid Orange County, CA
September 27, 2011 - 10 Tons of Fish Butre Lagoon, Ghana
September 30, 2011 – 1,000,000+ Bees Florida

October 2011
October 3, 2011 - 17 Dolphins Ujung Kulon, Java
October 4, 2011 – 100+ Harbor Seals New England, US
October 8, 2011 - Fish West Lake, Vietnam
October 13, 2011 - 15 Horses Queensland, Australia
October 21, 2011 – Fish Briar Creek, Georgia
October 22, 2011 - Birds Georgian Bay, Canada
October 24, 2011 - Fish Little Wabash River, Illinois
October 25, 2011 - 300 Fish Canada
October 28, 2011 - 3 Dolphins Mississippi
October 29, 2011 - Thousands of Fish India
October 31, 2011 - 500 Songbirds West Virginia
October 31, 2011 - 3000 Fish London, England

October 31, 2011 – Oysters Pensacola, FL

November 2011

November 2, 2011 - Millions of Fish Texas Coast
November 4, 2011 - Thousands of tiny sea creatures Lyall Bay, New Zealand
November 5, 2011 - Birds and Fish, Guyana
November 8, 2011 - Hundreds of Fish Changbanggang River, China
November 11, 2011 – Fish Lake Poway, California
November 12, 2011 - Fish Dubai
November 13, 2011 - 22 Sperm Whales Australia
November 14, 2011 - Thousands of Fish Zhangjiang, China
November 17, 2011 - Fish Kill Western Iowa
November 17, 2011 - 91 Whales in course of a week Australia & New Zealand
November 23, 2011 - 77 Elephants over 3 month span, Zimbabwe
November 26, 2011 - Massive Fish Kill Estero Bay Florida
November 27, 2011 - Five Dolphins Mississippi
November 27, 2011 - 1000 Fish Beachmere, Australia
November 28, 2011 - Fish, Frogs and Snakes India
November 30, 2011 - 100 birds North Carolina
November 30, 2011 – 1000+ Crows India

December 2011

December 3, 2011 - Thousands of Fish Germany
December 5, 2011 - 30 TONS of Fish dead in India
December 6, 2011 - 75 Seal Pups England
December 9, 2011 - 300 Seals Cape Town in South Africa
December 10, 2011 - 10 Whales Corfu, Greece
December 12, 2011 - 300 Crows India
December 15, 2011 - 1000 Chickens Nepal
December 15, 2011 - Thousands of Birds Utah
December 17, 2011 - 4,000 Crows India

December 18, 2011 - Massive Fish Death Australia
December 19, 2011 - 25 Ponies New South Wales in Australia
December 20, 2011 - 17,000 Chickens Hong Kong
December 20, 2011 - 400 Birds Davis County USA
December 20, 2011 - Dozens (Possibly Hundreds) Crows New Mexico USA
December 20, 2011 - Mass death Herring West Iceland
December 25, 2011 - 50 Birds Mount Sterling, KY
December 27, 2011 - "Red Tide" Florida
December 27, 2011 - Huge amounts of fish Bavla Pond, India

List of Mass Animal Deaths 2012

January 2012
January 1, 2012 - 200 Blackbirds, Arkansas
January 2, 2012 – 20 Tons Fish, Norway
January 4, 2012 – Birds, Scotland
January 5, 2012 - 3000 Fish, Ghana
January 7, 2012 – 1000+ Fish, Gholani River, India
January 7, 2012 - 7 Whales, New Zealand
January 7, 2012 – 1000+ Fish, California
January 8, 2012 – 1000+ Deer, Billings, Montana
January 9, 2012 – 100+ Wildlife Animals, Zimbabwe
January 9, 2012 – Dozens of Turtles, Florida
January 10, 2012 - 2000 Chickens, India
January 10, 2012 – Fish, China
January 11, 2012 – 100+ Fish, The Bahamas
January 14, 2012 - 20 Dolphins, Cape Cod, MA
January 16, 2012 - 53 Fur Seals, Australia
January 19, 2012 - 20,000 Birds, New Zealand
January 19, 2012 - 3 Tons Fish, Somalia
January 21, 2012 - 4 Whales, New Zealand
January 22, 2012 – 100+ Birds, India
January 24, 2012 - 5,000 Fish, Perth's River, Australia
January 24, 2012 - 61 Dolphins, Cape Cod, MA

January 24, 2012 - 82 Whales, New Zealand
January 27, 2012 - 64 Dolphins and Porpoises, Atlantic Coast
January 27, 2012 - 10,000 Fish, Japan
January 27, 2012 - 12 Dolphins, Louisiana
January 27, 2012 - 10,000 Ducks, Australia
January 31, 2012 - 800 Star Fish, Japan
January 31, 2012 – Fish, Philippines

February 2012
February 3, 2012 – 1,000+ Fish, Nigeria
February 3, 2012 - 100 Pigeons, South Dakota
February 3, 2012 - 1,000 Fish, Virginia
February 6, 2012 – 10,000+ Birds, Nepal and India
February 7, 2012 - Dozens of Birds, Florida
February 9, 2012 - 200 Dolphins, Peru
February 9, 2012 - 800 Birds, Christchurch, New Zealand
February 14, 2012 - 124 Dolphins, Cape Cod, MA
February 15, 2012 - 100 Birds, Maryland
February 16, 2012 - Tons of Fish, Somalia
February 18, 2012 – 1000+ Lambs, England
February 21, 2012 - 3,000 Tuna Fish, Dubai
February 21, 2012 – 25 Turtles, Bangladesh
February 25, 2012 - 60 Gulls, New Zealand
February 27, 2012 – 1000+ Fish, England
February 28, 2012 - 20,000+ Chickens, Dharke, Nepal

March 2012
March 1, 2012 - 800kg Of Dead Fish, Cyprus
March 2, 2012 – 1000+ Jellyfish, Texas
March 3, 2012 – Penguins, Perth, Australia
March 4, 2012 - 400 Grey Seals, Cape Breton, Australia
March 8, 2012 - 34 Dolphins, Texas
March 9, 2012 - Dozens of Birds, Florida
March 12, 2012 - 170 Chickens, South Africa

March 13, 2012 – 10,000+ Salmon, Marlborough, New Zealand
March 13, 2012 - 5,000 Fish, Malaysia
March 17, 2012 - 4 Whales, China
March 20, 2012 – 1000+ Fish, Singapore
March 20, 2012 – 1000+ Fish, Minnesota
March 29, 2012 - 10,000 Geese and Waterfowl Redding, Oregon
March 30, 2012 – 100+Birds, Texas

April 2012
April 1, 2012 - 9,000 Livestock, Egypt
April 1, 2012 - 3,000 Dolphins, Peru
April 3, 2012 – 1000+ Dolphins, Gulf of Mexico
April 4, 2012 - 615 Dolphins, Peru
April 4, 2012 - 100 Catfish, Boyne River, Australia
April 5, 2012 – 1000+ Fish, Ganga River, India
April 6, 2012 - 50 Turtles, India
April 6, 2012 – 1000+ Fish, Malaysia
April 9, 2012 – 1000+ Fish, India
April 9, 2012 - 3 Whales, India
April 11, 2012 - 300 Dolphins, Peru
April 11, 2012 - 14,000 Fish, Missouri
April 13, 2012 – Bees, Canyon Country, CA
April 13, 2012 – 100+ Fish, Durban, South Africa
April 16, 2012 – Livestock, Kyrgyzstan
April 17, 2012 – 1000+ Fish, Tennessee
April 17, 2012 – 1000+ Fish, Zandvlei Estuary, South Africa
April 17, 2012 – 1000+ Fish, India
April 19, 2012 – 1000+ Fish, also Cows and Dogs, Pakistan
April 22, 2012 – 1000+ Fish, Pakistan
April 25, 2012 - 11,000 Fish, Kettering, OH
April 25, 2012 - 28,000 Fish, Strongsville, OH
April 25, 2012 – Porpoises, China
April 25, 2012 - 4 Dolphins, Bandra Bandstand, India

April 26, 2012 – 1,000+ Storks in Thailand
April 27, 2012 – Fish, Lake Elsinore, California
April 28, 2012 - 1200 Pelicans, Peru
April 30, 2012 – 100+ Bull Red Fish, Alabama

May 2012
May 2, 2012 – Fish, China
May 2, 2012 – Fish, Turkey
May 3, 2012 – Fish, Lake Houston, TX
May 4, 2012 – Fish, Spain
May 4, 2012 - 2 Tons Fish, Jinzhou, China
May 4, 2012 – Fish, Muttar River, India
May 5, 2012 - 50,000 Fish, Shenzhen, China
May 5, 2012 – Bird, Finland
May 6, 2012 – Fish, Heritage Park Pond, Massachusetts
May 7, 2012 – Fish, Kuwait Bay, Kuwait
May 8, 2012 - 12 Tons of Fish, Chengdu, Sichuan, China
May 8, 2012 – 100+ Fish, Harris Brake Lake, Arkansas
May 10, 2012 – Fish, South Negril River, Jamaica
May 10, 2012 - 5,000 Birds, Peru
May 10, 2012 - 550 Tons of dead Salmon, Norway
May 10, 2012 – 1000+ Fish, Lake Simcoe, Canada
May 12, 2012 - 500 Fish, Eichbaum Lake, Germany
May 12, 2012 - 2,300 Birds, Chile
May 13, 2012 – Fish, River Periyar, India
May 14, 2012 – Fish, Lake Bito, MacArthur Town, Philippines
May 14, 2012 – 1000+ Fish, Nanjundapuram, India
May 15, 2012 - 10,000+ Fish, Guanzhou, China
May 16, 2012 – Fish, Arcadia Lake, Oklahoma
May 17, 2012 – Bees, Minnesota, Nebraska and Ohio
May 17, 2012 - 34 Deer, Greater Qiu Islet, Taiwan
May 17, 2012 - Over 8 TONS of Fish, Guiyang China
May 19, 2012 - 500,000 Salmon, Vancouver, Canada
May 20, 2012 – 100+ Fish, Minnesota
May 20, 2012 – Fish, Sanya Egret Park, China

May 21, 2012 – 1,000+ Fish, Mula-Mutha River, India
May 23, 2012 - 60,000 - 100,000 Fish, Maryland
May 24, 2012 – 1000+ Fish, Sichuan, China
May 24, 2012 – 100+ Fish, Briar Creek, North Carolina
May 25, 2012 - 10 Tons of dead Fish, Laguna de Bay, Philippines
May 25, 2012 - 300 Dolphins, Black Sea, Russia
May 25, 2012 – 1000+ Shellfish, Peru
May 25, 2012 - 540 Antelopes, Kasakhstan
May 27, 2012 - Entire Fish Farm stock to be killed, Washington
May 29, 2012 - 13,000 Fish, Ohatchee, Alabama
May 30, 2012 – Fish, Chacahua, Mexico
May 30, 2012 - 500 Fish, England
May 30, 2012 – 1000+ Fish, Maryland
May 30, 2012 - 55 Million Abalone, China
May 31, 2012 – 1000+ Fish, Burma

June 2012

June 5, 2012 – Reindeer, St Paul Island, Alaska
June 5, 2012 – 1000+ Fish, Imperial Lakes, Florida
June 5, 2012 - 2500 Fish, Swan River, Australia
June 6, 2012 - 100,000+ Fish, China
June 6, 2012 – Fish, Coevorden, Netherlands
June 6, 2012 - 10,000+ Blue Springs Lake, Missouri
June 6, 2012 - 5,000 Fish, England
June 7, 2012 - 200 Tons Sardines, Ohara, Japan
June 7, 2012 – 100+ Birds, East Melbourne, Australia
June 8, 2012 – Fish, East Lake Park, China
June 9, 2012 - 40 Tons Fish, Guangzhou, China
June 11, 2012 – Fish, Chovva Canal, India
June 14, 2012 - 130 Sea Birds, Australia
June 15, 2012 – Fish, Lake Manitoba, Canada
June 15, 2012 – 10,000 Sardines, Kanagawa, Japan
June 16, 2012 – Fish, Big Birch Lake, Todd County, Minnesota
June 19, 2012 - 17 Seals, Parnu, Estonia

June 19, 2012 – 100+ Fish, Red Hill Creek, Canada
June 19, 2012 – Fish, Buffalo Pound Lake, Canada
June 19, 2012 - 4,000+ Fish, River Nene, England
June 20, 2012 - 750 Bee Hives, New South Wales, Australia
June 20, 2012 – 100,000+ Fish, Sutherland Reservoir, Nebraska
June 21, 2012 – Turtles, Delaware and New Jersey
June 21, 2012 - 150 Birds, Florida
June 22, 2012 - Horses and Cattle, Kiev, Ukraine
June 22, 2012 – Fish, Lake Odessa in Louisa County, Iowa
June 23, 2012 – Cattle, Elgin, Texas
June 23, 2012 - 67 Birds, Kanaha Pond Wildlife Sanctuary, Hawaii
June 25, 2012 – 1000+ Fish, Georgia
June 25, 2012 – 1000+ Fish, Gomti River, India
June 26, 2012 - 200,000 Bird, Mexico
June 26, 2012 - 75,000+ Goats, Congo
June 26, 2012 – 1000+ Sardines, Taboga Island, Panama
June 26, 2012 – Fish, Wisconsin
June 28, 2012 – Fish, Platte River, Nebraska
June 28, 2012 – Fish, River Vartry, Wicklow, Ireland
June 29, 2012 – 100+ Fish, Ontario, Canada
June 29, 2012 - 73 Turtles, Australia
June 30, 2012 - 1,000,000 Birds, Mexico

July 2012
July 1, 2012 - Mass Fish deaths, Fujian Jinjiang Cizao Reservoir, China
July 2, 2012 – 1000+ Fish, Havana, Cuba
July 2, 2012 – 1000+ Chickens, Xinjiang, China
July 2, 2012 - 10,000 Fish, Knoxville, Tennessee
July 2, 2012 - 18 mass Fish kills, Periyar River, India
July 3, 2012 - 14 Tons of Fish, ChangshouReservoir, China
July 3, 2012 – 100,000+ Fish, Lake Wichita, Texas
July 3, 2012 – 100+ Fish, Upstate Lake, South Carolina

July 3, 2012 – Catfish, Fort Meade, Florida
July 3, 2012 - 2,300 Fish, Butts County, Georgia
July 4, 2012 – 1000+ Fish, Dexter City Lake, Missouri
July 5, 2012 – Fish, Canary Islands
July 5, 2012 – Fish, Century Village Lakes, Florida
July 5, 2012 – Fish, Roy Lake, South Dakota
July 5, 2012 – 1000+ Fish, Lamoure, North Dakota
July 5, 2012 - 20 Egrets, Rockport, Texas
July 6, 2012 - 128 Bison, Fort Providence, Canada
July 6, 2012 - 560 Wild Animals, Kaziranga, India
July 6, 2012 – 1000+ Fish, Silver Lake, Delaware
July 6, 2012 – Fish, Salt River, Arizona
July 6, 2012 – Fish, Trout River, Prince Edward Island, Canada
July 6, 2012 – Fish, Patoka River, Indiana
July 6, 2012 – Oysters, 60 Million, Quang Ninh, Vietnam
July 7, 2012 – 1000+ Fish, Godavari River, India
July 7, 2012 - 50 Ducks and Geese, Ohio
July 8, 2012 – Salmon, Marlborough Farm, New Zealand
July 8, 2012 – 1000+ Fish, Arugam Bay, Sri Lanka
July 9, 2012 - 28 Seals, Netherlands
July 9, 2012 - 450,000 Salmon, Newfoundland, Canada
July 9, 2012 – 200 Pike, Fountain Lake, Minnesota
July 10, 2012 - 23 Bison, Canada
July 10, 2012 - Dozens of Birds, Illinois
July 10, 2012 – Lobster, Connecticut
July 11, 2012 - 58,000 Fish, Des Moines River, Iowa
July 11, 2012 – Fish, Xindong, China
July 11, 2012 - 2.5 Million Birds, Mexico
July 11, 2012 - 19,000 Fish, Lake Odessa, Iowa
July 11, 2012 – 1000+ Fish, Ireland
July 12, 2012 – 10,000+ Fish, Horicon Marsh, Wisconsin
July 12, 2012 – 1000+ Fish, Namibia, Africa
July 12, 2012 - 6,500 Fish, North Carolina
July 12, 2012 – 1000+ Fish, Vermilion River, Illinois

July 13, 2012 - 450,000 Salmon, Newfoundland, Canada
July 14, 2012 - 512 Penguins, Rio Grande do Sul, Brazil
July 16, 2012 - 100,000 Fish, Nakhon Ratchasima Province, Thailand
July 16, 2012 – Fish, Wuhan, China
July 17, 2012 – Millions of Crab-like creatures, Hawaii
July 17, 2012 - 17 Seal Pups, Bay of Firth, Scotland
July 17, 2012 - 200 Tons of Fish, Egypt
July 17, 2012 - 10,000 Fish, Liu Yueqing City, China
July 19, 2012 – 100+ Frogs, Chesterfield Lake, Missouri
July 19, 2012 - 3.8 Million Birds, Mexico
July 20, 2012 - 300 Birds, Agate Beach, Oregon
July 20, 2012 - 1300 Animals, Kenya
July 20, 2012 – 1000+ Fish, Piney Point, Maryland
July 20, 2012 – Fish, Shangqiu City Lake, China
July 21, 2012 - 1,700 Cattle and 105,000 Turkeys, South Dakota & Minnesota
July 21, 2012 – 1000+ Fish, Lake Elsinore, California
July 22,2012 – Fish, Lake Erie, Ohio
July 23, 2012 - 50 Peacocks, Pakistan
July 23, 2012 – Fish, Big Sandy Lake, Minnesota
July 23, 2012 – 1000+ Fish, Alberta, Canada
July 23, 2012 – 1000+ Fish, Daytona, FL
July 24, 2012 - 100 Turtles, Uraguay
July 25, 2012 - 30 Turtles, Pavana, India
July 26, 2012 – Fish, Plantation, Florida
July 27, 2012 - 2,500 Fish, Bradford, England
July 29, 2012 – 1000+ Fish, Colorado River
July 30, 2012 - 100 Peacocks, Pakistan
July 30, 2012 - 5 Million Birds, Mexico
July 30, 2012 - 4,000 Fish, Ascot Waters Marina, Australia
July 31, 2012 - Dozens of Turtles, Cayman Brac, Cayman Islands
July 31, 2012 - 20 Deer, Stone Mountain, GA

August 2012

August 3, 2012 - 340 Bison, Fort Providence, Canada
August 3, 2012 - 3,000 Fish, Petit Jean River, Arkansas
August 3, 2012 – Bird, Bandon, Oregon
August 3, 2012 - 150 Sheep and Goats, Pakistan
August 4, 2012 - 66,800 Birds, Vietnam
August 5, 2012 - 40,000 Sturgeon & 1000+ other Fish, Iowa
August 6, 2012 - 167 Peacocks, Pakistan
August 6, 2012 – 1000+ Fish, Srinagar, India
August 6, 2012 – Fish, Dunleer River, Ireland
August 7, 2012 - 900 Birds, Minnesota
August 7, 2012 – Fish, Neuse River, North Carolina
August 8, 2012 - 786,000 Chickens, 41,000 Ducks, 300+ Pigs, South Korea
August 9, 2012 – 100+ Crabs, Tiana and Shinnecock Bay, NY
August 9, 2012 – Shrimp, Vietnam
August 9, 2012 - 20,000 Fish, Lake Contrary, Missouri
August 10, 2012 - 200 Tons of Fish, Zi River, China
August 10, 2012 - 500 Tons of Salmon, Vancouver, Canada
August 10, 2012 – Fish, Japan
August 10, 2012 - 3,000 Fish, Scarborough, England
August 11, 2012 – 1000+ Earthworms, Komatsu city Ishikawa, Japan
August 13, 2012 - Elk & Wild Birds, Sweden
August 13, 2012 – 100,000+ Fish, Galveston, Texas
August 13, 2012 – Fish, Pago Bay, Guam
August 14, 2012 - 431 Bison, Fort Providence, Canada
August 14, 2012 – 1000+ Fish, Kiltha River, Ireland
August 14, 2012 - 68 Cattle, Pakistan
August 15, 2012 - 5,000 Fish, Sugar Creek, Ohio
August 15, 2012 - Dozens of Birds, New Jersey
August 16, 2012 - 900 Deer, Michigan
August 16, 2012 – 100+ Fish, Widnes, England
August 16, 2012 - 100 Cattle, Colorado and Texas
August 16, 2012 – Fish, Wolf Creek, Iowa

August 17, 2012 - 1 Million Fish, Texas
August 17, 2012 - Fish and Stingrays, Myrtle Beach, South Carolina
August 17, 2012 – Fish, Tunisia
August 18, 2012 – 10,000+ Birds, Vietnam
August 20, 2012 – Fish, Anson Lake, Texas
August 20, 2012 – 1000+ Fish, Neuse River, North Carolina
August 20, 2012 – Fish, Highland Park, Texas
August 20, 2012 - 20,000 Fish, Contraband Bayou, Louisiana
August 20, 2012 – 1000+ Fish, Montreal, Canada
August 21, 2012 – 1000+ Fish, Cheshire, England
August 22, 2012 – 1000+ Fish, Cuyahoga River, Ohio
August 23, 2012 - 2,700 Pheasants, Wyoming
August 28, 2012 - 1,000 Ton Fish, Baiyangdian Lake, China
August 28, 2012 - 45,000 Sea Turtles, El Salvador
August 28, 2012 - 100 Deer, Chicago, IL
August 28, 2012 - 30 Antelopes, Kruger National Park, South Africa
August 29, 2012 – Salmon, Osoyoos Lake, Canada
August 29, 2012 – Rats, Jaipur, India
August 29, 2012 - 24 Sea Turtles, Oaxaca, Mexico
August 30, 2012 – White-fish, Idaho
August 30, 2012 – Fish, New Philadelphia, OH
August 30, 2012 - 50,000 Chickens, Parganas, India

September, 2012

September 1, 2012 - 200 Deer, Chicago, IL
September 1, 2012 - 58,000 Ducks and Chickens, Quang Ngai, Vietnam
September 2, 2012 - Dozens of Birds, Pakki Tibbi, India
September 2, 2012 - 16 Whales, Fife, Scotland
September 2, 2012 - 17 Whales, Florida
September 4, 2012 – 1000+ Fish, Bayou Lafourche, Louisiana
September 4, 2012 – Fish, Bayou Casotte, Jackson County, Mississippi

September 4, 2012 – 1000+ Fish, Broadkill River, Delaware
September 5, 2012 - 400 Deer, Caldwell County, North Carolina
September 5, 2012 – Fish, Louisiana
September 5, 2012 – 181,000 Ducks and Chickens, Vietnam
September 5, 2012 – 10,000+ Rats, Mississippi
September 6, 2012 – 10,000+ Fish and Birds, Lake Erie, Canada
September 7, 2012 – 100+ Cattle, Plaquemines Parish, LA
September 7, 2012 - 30 Dolphins, Bulgaria
September 7, 2012 – Moose, Sweden
September 8, 2012 – Fish, San Carlos Lake, Arizona
September 10, 2012 – 100+ Fish, New Orleans, LA
September 12, 2012 – Fish, New Smyrna Beach, Florida
September 12, 2012 - 362 Cattle, Manzini, Swaziland
September 12, 2012 – 1000+ Fish, Arrowhead Lakes, Arizona
September 12, 2012 – 1,000,000+ Fish, Salton Sea, California
September 13, 2012 – 100,000+ Jellyfish, Cable Beach, Australia
September 14, 2012 - 22.3 Million Birds, Mexico
September 14, 2012 - 131,000 Fish, New York
September 14, 2012 – 100+ Fish Arlington, TX
September 14, 2012 – Fish, Mangalore Coast, India
September 14, 2012 - 2,200 Deer, Nebraska
September 17, 2012 - Dozens of Pigeons, Birkenhead, Australia
September 17, 2012 – Fish, Corpus Christi, TX
September 18, 2012 – 100+ Prairie Dogs, Arizona
September 18, 2012 – 10,000+ Fish, Cha Va River, Vietnam
September 19, 2012 – Fish, Lake Auburn, Maine
September 19, 2012 - 588 Cattle, Mpumalanga, South Africa
September 19, 2012 - 6,300 Ducks, Guangdong, China
September 21, 2012 – Rabbits, St Louis, Missouri
September 21, 2012 - 13,000 Sheep, Iceland
September 21, 2012 - 15 Beluga Whales, Quebec, Canada

September 22, 2012 - 8000 Cattle, Swaziland
September 23, 2012 - 20 Ducks, Arden Park, Arizona
September 24, 2012 – Fish, North Sterling Reservoir, Colorado
September 24, 2012 – 1000+ Sheep, Uzbek, Kyrgyzstan
September 25, 2012 – 100+ Fish, Neuse River, North Carolina
September 26, 2012 - Deer, Wyoming
September 26, 2012 - 2000+ Birds, Oregon
September 28, 2012 – Fish, Harvey's Run River, Pennsylvania
September 28, 2012 – Fish, Roosevelt Lake, Arizona

October 2012
October 1, 2012 - 100 Starlings, Austria
October 1, 2012 – 1000+ Fish, Katherine River, Australia
October 2, 2012 - 43 Pilot Whales, Indonesia
October 4, 2012 – Honeybees, Massachusetts
October 4, 2012 - 2,043 Deer, Illinois
October 4, 2012 - 15,000 Fish, Coquitlam River, Canada
October 4, 2012 – Fish, Sarasota, Florida
October 5, 2012 - 1000+ Fish, Vancouver, Canada
October 7, 2012 - Fish, Muktagachha, Bangladesh
October 8, 2012 – 1000+ Deer, North Carolina
October 8, 2012 – 100+ Animals, Manicaland, Zimbabwe
October 9, 2012 – Fish, Florida
October 9, 2012 - 400 Cows and Goats, Kamrup Rural District, India
October 11, 2012 – 10,000+ Fish, Dagupan City, Philippines
October 11, 2012 - 70 Sea Turtles, Lake Bardawil, Egypt
October 12, 2012 – 1000+ Fish, Anson Bay, Australia
October 12, 2012 - Hammerhead Sharks, Hawaii
October 12, 2012 - Silver Carp Fish, Jimo Reservoirs, China
October 13, 2012 – 100+ Tons of Salmon, Scotland
October 15, 2012 - 8,000 Catfish, Brisbane River, Australia
October 15, 2012 – 1000+ Deer, Indiana
October 15, 2012 - 2,000 Chickens, Bode, Nepal

October 16, 2012 - 343 Cows and Buffaloes, Sualkuchi, India
October 16, 2012 – Fish, Dalton Creek, Georgia
October 17, 2012 – 1,000,000+ Fish, Neuse River, North Carolina
October 17, 2012 - 7,000 Cattle, Pakistan
October 17, 2012 – 1000+ Bass, Dickinson County, Iowa
October 19, 2012 - 45+ Flamingos and Avocets, Walvis Lagoon, Namibia
October 19, 2012 - Doves all across the Permian Basin, Texas
October 19, 2012 - 1,000 Livestock, Dien Bien, Vietnam
October 21, 2012 - 28,600 Sheep, Pakistan
October 22, 2012 – 1000+ Fish, Collier Beach, Florida
October 22, 2012 – 10,000+ Gizzard Shad Fish, Oneida Lake, New York
October 23, 2012 – Scallops, Long Island, NY
October 23, 2012 - 40,000 lbs Fish, Foshan, China
October 23, 2012 – Fish, Ningbo, China
October 23, 2012 – Fish, Sri Lanka
October 24, 2012 - 3,600 Turkeys, Bangalore, India
October 24, 2012 - 5,000+ Deer, Missouri
October 25, 2012 - 900+ Birds, Sleeping Bear Dunes, Michigan
October 26, 2012 – Fish, Blairstown, Iowa
October 26, 2012 - 40 Whales, Andaman Island, India
October 31, 2012 - 125,000 Chickens, Fermanagh, Northern Ireland
October 31, 2012 - 25 Bee Hives containing 1 MILLION Bees, New York
October 31, 2012 – Fish, Chizhou City, China
October 31, 2012 – 1,000,000+ Fish, Mackay, Australia
October 31, 2012 - 9,000 Fish, Xiamen, China
October 31, 2012 - 15,000+ Fish, Lake Madeline, Texas

November 2012

November 1, 2012 - 84 Sea Turtles, Egypt

November 3, 2012 - 4,000+ Birds, Gazipur, Bangladesh
November 4, 2012 - 700 Water Birds, Lake Michigan
November 4, 2012 – 1000+ Cattle, Zimbabwe
November 4, 2012 - 80 Whales and Dolphins, King Island, Tasmania
November 5, 2012 - 500+ Pigeons, Bihar's Bhagalpur, India
November 6, 2012 – Fish, Nanchang, China
November 7, 2012 – Antelopes and 30 Hippos, Kruger Park, South Africa
November 7, 2012 – Fish, Shenzhen River, China
November 7, 2012 – Fish, Bradford Branch, Ohio
November 7, 2012 – Seagulls, Lake Neangar, Australia
November 8, 2012 – Salmon, Seattle, WA
November 8, 2012 - 13,000+ Deer, Michigan
November 9, 2012 – 100+ Fish, St Peters Billabong, Australia
November 10, 2012 - 185,000 Hens, Northern Ireland
November 10, 2012 – Fish, Guangdong, China
November 12, 2012 - 100+ Cattle, Lamwo, Uganda
November 12, 2012 – Seagulls, Morocco
November 13, 2012 – Fish, Shimen Lake, China
November 14, 2012 – 1000+ Birds, England
November 14, 2012 - 6,000 Deer, Nebraska, America
November 15, 2012 - 40,000 Fish Quanzhou, China
November 15, 2012 - 28 Whales, Golden Bay, New Zealand
November 16, 2012 – Salmon, Ireland
November 16, 2012 - 40 Tons Red Tilapias Fish, Thanh Binh, Vietnam
November 16, 2012 – 1000+ Fish, Lake Erie, New York
November 17, 2012 - 50,000 Chickens, New South Wales, Australia
November 19, 2012 – Fish, Philippines
November 20, 2012 - 100 Starlings, Missouri
November 20, 2012 – 100+ Fish, Phuket, Thailand
November 21, 2012 - 4,000+ Birds Dhaka, Bangladesh
November 22, 2012 – Fish, Liwan Lake, China

November 24, 2012 - 26 Turtles, West Virginia
November 30, 2012 - 10 Tons of Fish, China
November 30, 2012 - 4,000 Ducks, Krasnodar, Russia

December 2012

December 1, 2012 – Catfish, Marco Island, Florida
December 2, 2012 - 50 Birds, Collin County, Texas
December 3, 2012 – 100+ Carp, Pinto Lake, California
December 4, 2012 – Fish, Yaojiang River, Ningbo, China
December 6, 2012 - 19 Horses, Canon City, Colorado
December 6, 2012 – 1,000+ Fish, Kiawah Island, South Carolina
December 6, 2012 - 36+ Buffalo, Kanchanpur, Nepal
December 7, 2012 – 100+ Chickens, Penghu Island, Taiwan
December 7, 2012 - 25,000 Fish, Guangdong, China
December 7, 2012 – Fish, Pudong, China
December 10, 2012 - 1,600 Sheep, Nigeria
December 10, 2012 – Squid, Santa Cruz, CA
December 11, 2012 - 300,000 Ducks, Java Island, Indonesia
December 11, 2012 – 1000+ Squid, California
December 11, 2012 – Fish, Louisiana
December 12, 2012 - 6 Dolphins, Gavelston, Texas
December 13, 2012 – Fish, Lanxi, China
December 13, 2012 – 100+ Fish, Crabs and eels, Tern Island, Australia
December 14, 2012 – 10,000+ Sardines, Japan
December 14, 2012 - Fish, 3 or 4 different places in China
December 14, 2012 – 1000+ Jellyfish, Oreti Beach, New Zealand
December 17, 2012 – 1000+ Herring, Iceland
December 17, 2012 – 1000+ Turtles, Paradip Sea Beach, India
December 18, 2012 – Songbirds, Sonoma County, California
December 20, 2012 – 1000+ Fish, Queensland, Australia
December 20, 2012 - 3,000 Fowl, Nepal
December 21, 2012 – 1000+ Chickens, Muarojambi, Indonesia
December 22, 2012 - 1,500 Hens and Geese, Germany

December 25, 2012 - 230 Tons of Fish, Xinjiang, China
December 25, 2012 – 1000+ Trout, Bandipora, India
December 26, 2012 - 8,000 Fish, Foshan, China
December 26, 2012 - 150,000 Birds, Bangladesh
December 27, 2012 - Fish kills, Pangasinan, Philippines
December 27, 2012 – Fish kills, Charlotte, NC
December 28, 2012 - Birds, Kafr El-Sheikh, Egypt
December 31, 2012 - 300 Birds, Tennessee
December 31, 2012 – 1000+ Fish, Tallow Beach, Australia

I've stopped the list at 2012, but as of 2013 the mass animal deaths continue to occur, and appear to be growing more frequent. For a complete up to date list including links to articles see below.

In addition to other news articles, one of the main sources for this section came from the following website. For a well documented list complete with photos and links to original articles check out - http://www.end-times-prophecy.org/animal-deaths-birds-fish-end-times.html WARNING: I do not endorse their opinions or end times theories. It appears that the webmaster may somehow be related to the 7th Day Adventists, and I do not agree with their positions. That being said, their Animal Mass Death List is the most complete and well documented I've seen, and is listed as free to distribute with the caveat that in doing so their site will be credited.

Appendix

Does Enoch Support A Pre-Trib Rapture?

In short, no, it doesn't. We'll get to that in a minute. First some background information would be helpful, because some readers might be wondering why we are talking about Enoch in the first place.

I have included this as an appendix to the book, because Enoch is not a book included in our Bibles, and it is also not something that we can point to with the same type of authority as we do the books of the Bible. The oldest surviving complete copy of what we call Enoch 1 is in Ethiopian Coptic, and we do not have complete original sources for this book in Hebrew, or if it really stretches all the way back to Genesis, Proto-Hebrew. It is true that a book called Enoch was quite popular in the first century, and many church fathers quoted from it. Even the Bible quotes from Enoch as well. But does it quote from the Enoch we have or was it another Enoch? We use the book we have as an incredible source of background info for the Bible, but we don't have enough source material to lend it the credibility as we do Scripture.

The Enoch that we do have is a very important book that scholars sometimes use to shed some light on early apocalyptic literature. But it is one of several books that bear the title Book of Enoch. The book that we often call Enoch 1 is the most likely candidate of the books we have as being closest to the authentic Enoch. Enoch 1 claims that it was written by Enoch himself, the one that Genesis 5 tells us was translated or raptured by God for walking with Him. Many scholars claim that Enoch was not written by the real Enoch, but by someone in the 3rd or 4th century BC using Enoch's name to tell a moral story, or parable. However, we do know that Jude said, in 1:14, that Enoch was written by the very same Enoch, so if Jude was wrong and this same Enoch was not the Enoch of Genesis then Jude is fallible and should not be included in the Bible. So we know that *some* version of Enoch read by Jude was a reputable copy of something that predated our Ethiopic version.

I think it is also important to point out, that if Enoch was taken away by God, it is not impossible to surmise that perhaps he was returned at some point. It is not entirely far fetched to believe that he could have been returned in the years preceding the Messiah to prepare the way for his coming, as Jesus described that John the Baptist, in some way, embodied the spirit of Elijah. What that meant exactly is unclear, but perhaps whoever wrote Enoch, wrote it in the same manner that John encapsulated Elijah's spirit.

So what we see is Enoch seems to have been an important book to the early church, some claim that it was even seen as Scripture, though we do not have that book, and we cannot be sure that our Enoch is exactly the same Enoch, and not subject to corruption. We do have some partial copies of Enoch from the Dead Sea scrolls that show that our copy is very close to the fragments that exist there. However, as I stress, there is not enough info to hang everything on Enoch, or even to use it to build foundational doctrines on.

All that being said, Enoch is useful for historical study, and for understanding the though process of the Christian and Jewish apocalyptic writers. Some Pre-Trib writers, such as J.R. Church and Gary Steerman of *Prophecy in the News,* television program claim that Enoch does point to a Pre-Trib rapture. So the big question as concerns this book is as we started this appendix: Does Enoch point to a Pre-Trib rapture of the church? And the answer is clearly, no. I do not disagree with Church and Steerman's belief that Enoch is important, nor that it might definitely reflect information that might indeed date back to Genesis, but I do disagree entirely that it points to a Pre-Trib doctrine.

To investigate this further, let's take a look at the opening portion of Enoch 1. The translation that I will be using comes from Joseph B. Lumpkin's book "The Lost Books of the Bible," from Fifth Estate press, published in 2009. It is a very readable version, but adheres very closely to both the Richard Laurence and the R.H. Charles manuscripts, which were the first two editions in English, but without the thees and thous found in their versions.

The Book of Enoch chapter 1

1 The words of the blessing of Enoch, with which he blessed the elect and righteous who will be living in the day of tribulation, when all the wicked and godless are to be removed.

2 And he began his story saying: Enoch a righteous man, whose eyes were opened by God, saw the vision of the Holy One in heaven, which the angels showed me, and I heard everything from them, and I saw and understood, but it was not for this generation, but for a remote one which is to come.

3 Concerning the elect I said, as I began my story concerning them: The Holy Great One will come out from His dwelling,

4 And the eternal God will tread on the earth, (even) on Mount Sinai, and appear in the strength of His might from heaven.

5 And all shall be afraid, And the Watchers shall shake, And great fear and trembling shall seize them to the ends of the earth.

6 And the high mountains shall be shaken, and the high hills shall be laid low, and shall melt like wax in the flame.

7 And the earth shall be wholly torn apart, and all that is on the earth shall be destroyed, And there shall be a judgment on all.

8 But with the righteous He will make peace; and will protect the elect and mercy shall be on them. And they shall all belong to God, and they shall prosper, and they shall be blessed. And the Light of God shall shine on them.

9 And behold! He comes with ten thousand of His holy ones (saints) to execute judgment on all, and to destroy all the ungodly (wicked); and to convict all flesh of all the works of their ungodliness, which they have ungodly committed, and of all the hard things which ungodly sinners have spoken against Him.

Jude 1:14 And Enoch also, the seventh from Adam, prophesied of these, saying, Behold, the Lord cometh with ten thousands of his saints, 15 to execute judgment upon all, and to convince all that are ungodly among them of all their ungodly deeds which they have ungodly committed, and of all their hard speeches which ungodly sinners have spoken against him.

First of all let's examine verse 1. We see here that Enoch says the wicked are to be removed in the Tribulation. This matches up with those who use Jesus' parable of the Tare's to point to a Post-Trib rapture, though I do not know if using a parable is the best example to build doctrine. But this passage in Enoch appears to agree with the idea that the evil ones will be gathered and removed from earth.

We also see that the purpose of writing is for the Elect, who are going through the Tribulation. They were not raptured, and they are in the midst of the Tribulation, clearly not a Pre-Trib point of view. Also we see that Enoch is blessing the Elect by writing this, in other words, it will be something that encourages the Elect during those days, which obviously will be discouraging.

Enoch gives us some clues as to what else is happening during this "tribulation."

In verses 2 through 4 we see that the time period these Elect live in will also be the time when Jesus is physically on the earth. Since it didn't take place during His first visit, it must therefore take place, if Enoch is to be believed, during His second visit.

Verses 5 and 6 show us that Jesus' coming to the earth results in a great earthquake unlike anything that has ever happened, and this lines up with Jesus' description of His return in Matthew 24, which as we have shown earlier in this book, lines up with a Post-Trib rapture theory.

Verse 7 speaks of the earth being destroyed, which lines up with the description of what the earth looks like after the bowls of wrath are poured out in Revelation, and also it lines up with what Peter says about the earth being destroyed at the end of the world. This also points to a Post-Trib rapture, because obviously Jesus is returning at the end of all of this, or as it appears here, His return causes all of this.

Verse 8 shows us that the righteous are on the earth, and His return causes peace and mercy to abound. Again, this couldn't be the case with a Pre-Trib rapture, because they would already be at peace and dwelling in Christ's mercy.

And finally in verse 9, He comes with his Holy Ones to execute judgment on all and to destroy ungodly. This is the biggest passage that some people use to point to a pre-trib doctrine in Enoch, however, it doesn't say that the Holy Ones here are glorified resurrected saints. In fact, it doesn't tell us who the Holy Ones are. But even if the Holy Ones are the saints, and I believe Lumpkin's point of adding the Jude passage is to show that the Greek word is often used for "saints," it doesn't mean that they have received their glorified bodies at that particular moment. It could mean that the Holy Ones are the spirits of those who have already died, and are coming to get their resurrected bodies, which is what everyone teaches, not just Pre-Trib teachers. This just isn't a strong enough passage to base a claim for a pre-trib slant to Enoch.

I think in order to make sense of this we need to look at the Greek. The word used by Jude, translated here and in Enoch as "saints," is "αγιαις," transliterated as "agiais," and the word used for angels in the other passages is "αγγελων," transliterated as "aggelon." What is most confusing about this passage in Enoch, as well as the Jude passage, is that everywhere else, the fact that Jesus returns with His *holy angels* is what is typically stressed. In Matthew 16:27 we see this, as well as 25:31, Mark 8:38 and Luke 9:26. We also see this in 2 Thessalonians 1:7-8. I believe that though the spirits of the departed will be with Him as well, it is His powerful angels that seem to be the main focus of passages like these, because His angels play a vital role in the second coming, and have many duties from the minute Jesus returns until the millennial reign begins. They separate the wheat from the chaff, they bring the wicked to destruction and bring us to Jesus, they bind the Antichrist and False Prophet, and they pour out God's wrath on the evil ones. Though the word "saints" is used, it stems from the same root word which gives us the word "angels," literally "holy ones." So it is not an absolute certainty that Jude and Enoch are referring to the souls of the departed in these passages.

The one thing to keep in mind, whether in a Pre-Trib, Mid-Trib, Post-Trib, Amillennial or Post Millennial or even Preterist, we all believe that when Jesus actually does return, He will bring with Him the spirits of those who have died who were believers. So anytime you read a passage that points to this truth, it doesn't automatically prove any particular doctrine, it just confirms what we all agree on anyway.

Appendix – Bug Out Bag

Check List for at least 72 Hours

Disaster Plan
- Including Maps, Passwords, Emergency Numbers, etc.

Food and Water for 72 Hours
- Could be 3 or 4 MRE's per person, and 3 gallons of water

Water Purification Supplies
- Could be water purification tablets
- Or a Water Filter Bottle

Cooking Supplies
- Pot
- Spoon
- Fork
- Cooking Cup

Jacket
- Probably won't fit in the bag, but should be kept near the bag, even in summer could be useful to have available for the night time.

Change of Clothes
2-3 Pairs of Socks
2-3 Pairs of Underwear
2-4 Water Bottles, or a couple Canteens
Folding Knife or Fixed Bladed Knife
A couple snack foods (Low Sodium so as to preserve water)
Candy (can be used to trade)
Toilet Paper
Tooth Paste
Deodorant

Tampons/Panty Liners/Pads (for women, but pads are good for medical kit too)
50' of Para-cord
Extra Money
- Both Cash
- And Bag of Quarters, in case an operable vending machine is found

Sliver or Gold Coins or Jewelry (to trade)
Two Leatherman type tools
- (Need 2 because some things need two wrenches to open)

Crank or Solar Flashlight with built in radio
Fire Starting Equipment
- Lighter
- Fire Starting Kit with waterproof matches and tinder
- Magnesium fire starter

Small Medical Kit (some things to include:)
- Extra pain killers
- Bandages
- Cloth Scissors
- Medical Tape
- Antibiotic ointment
- Burn Cream
- Iodine
- Alcohol swabs, or small container of Alcohol

Survival/solar blanket
Duct Tape
Rain Parka
Small Fishing kit
Small sewing kit
Compass
Glow Sticks
Spool of String
Extra Medicine if you take prescriptions
Extra pair of glasses if you need them

Small Bible
Small Survival Manual
Sunglasses
Pictures of people you love
Road Flares or a Flare Gun
Small bag of Edible Seeds to Plant in case of a longer emergency, or to eat if needed.
Deck of Cards or Dice or something to play especially if Children are present.
Medical Papers if Needed
ID – Driver's License, Passport, Birth Certificate, etc.
If you have room, any item you might wish to trade for other things
Large Plastic Tarp for water collection or shelter
Sling Shot, Pellet Gun or Blow Gun for small game
Wire for building traps
Plastic Zip Lock Bags to keep perishable items in
Sleeping Bag and Blanket, small pillow
Heavy Duty Backpack

Optional
Flare Gun with Flares
Axe or Machete (if you have room)
Gun and Ammo (Pick one best suited for your situation)
Whatever extra food, water and medical supplies you can carry
Car battery, Auto Power Inverter, Solar Charger – To charge cell phone, emergency medical equipment, etc.
Tent – If Space Permits

Appendix – Other Arguments

As I was working on the completion of this book, someone directed me to several Pre-Trib videos and articles. Below are listed some of the main arguments, and some problems with the Post-Trib stance. I took notes as I watched the videos, and I will address several topics that I may not have addressed in this book.

Are the Rapture and the 2nd Coming 2 Events?

I have covered this somewhat in this book already, but I will give a more detailed discussion here. Some people claim that Rapture and the 2nd Coming are two different events. It is true that they are, but they happen on the same day. Here are some of the arguments listed:

Rapture	***2nd Coming***
Translation of believers	*No translation involved*
Translated saints go to heaven	*Translated saints return to earth*
Earth not judged	*Earth judged*
Imminent signless	*Follows definite predicted signs*
Not in the Old Testament	*Predicted in the Old Testament*

Believers Only	*Affects all men on the earth*
Before the day of wrath	*Concludes the day of wrath*
No reference to Satan	*Satan bound*
He comes for His own	*He comes with His own*
He comes in the air	*He comes to the earth*
He claims His Bride	*He comes with His bride*
Only His own see Him	*Every eye shall see Him*

Alleged Problems With Post-Trib View

In addition to these apparent differences between the Rapture and the 2nd Coming, one of the videos goes on to bring to light several things that they think are problems with a Post-Trib viewpoint. Which are given mainly in the form of questions. I will address the apparent differences first, point by point. Then I will explain all of the following matters as well:

Post Trib Denies Doctrine of Immanency

Requires Church to be on Earth During Daniel's 70th Week

Who Will Populate the Millennium?

How can the Bride Come With Him?

Who Are The Sheep And The Goats?

Church Experiences God's Wrath

How Can Virgins Buy Oil In Matthew 25 without the Mark of the Beast?

Contradiction with Daniel 9:28 – Israel and the Church Are Mutually Exclusive

Rebuttal

Number 1 – In answer to the idea that the Rapture and 2nd Coming are two different events separated by a 7 year time period, the Bible as well as all the early church fathers, for at least 400 to 600 years (but more likely 1800 years), taught that the rapture and the 2nd coming were two events that happened on the Day of the Lord. In other words the very first event of the Day of the Lord would be the Rapture, and then the conclusion of the Day of the Lord would be the Descent of Jesus from the clouds (the 2nd Coming). Even if Pseudo-Ephram was the earliest teacher of the Pre-Trib doctrine, which he wasn't, but for the sake of argument let us assume for a moment that he was, 600 years after Revelation and the gospels were written is not a very convincing argument for its validity.

Number 2 – Translation of Believers vs. No Translation – There needs to be no translation of believers at the Second Coming, because it does happen at the Rapture. The historical Post-Trib view doesn't argue against this. As mentioned in the discussion on *harpazo,* the entire Rapture picture is one of greeting our coming King and returning to earth with Him. Just because Pre-Tribers recognize the distinction that there are two things that happen in this one event, does not make it a two staged event 7 years apart as they claim. Jesus returns in the sky, we are raptured, we return to earth with Him, He begins to establish His kingdom, we celebrate, etc. These are all events that happen on the same Day.

Number 3 – Earth not judged vs. the Earth is Judged – There is no biblical support for the idea that the earth is not judged at the time of the Rapture. The earth is judged during the Tribulation. This is evident when one studies the bowls of wrath, which begin to be poured out either right before we are raptured (and we are protected from them), right after we are Raptured, or simultaneously at the same time as we are Raptured. In addition to the bowls of wrath, the trumpets and seals represent forms of judgment as well. As mentioned elsewhere in this book, the bowls have to happen in a very short time span, and could very well happen simultaneously as the Rapture. But remember, the Tribulation is called the Tribulation because of the distress caused to the church as Satan pours his wrath on her. The Tribulation is not God's wrath on the earth. That comes with the Bowls of Warth.

Number 4 – Imminent Sign-less vs. Signs pointing to 2nd Coming– This is simply not true. And the idea that Immanency is a "doctrine" of the church is erroneous. Some churches do have Immanency as a Doctrine, Calvary Chapel and the Assemblies of God to name a couple. But it should never be considered a doctrine for several reasons. Primarily, it is not pertinent for Salvation. But secondarily, it is highly suspect and dependent on faulty Bible study methods. Jesus told us to be watching for His coming numerous times. How can we watch if there are no signs? And why does He give signs every single time He tells us to watch for His coming and our rapture if there are no signs? I'm sorry to any genuinely confused but descent Pre-Trib people out there, but it is lies such as this that lead me to believe that the Pre-Trib argument is evil and directly from Satan to mislead believers.

Number 5 – The 5th argument mentioned above is that the Rapture is not mentioned in the Old Testament. This is ridiculous. Of course it's in the Old Testament. It talks again and again about Christ's second coming, and the Resurrection of the dead. Jesus even challenged the Sadducees and the Pharisees about searching the scriptures in regards to the Resurrection. John 5:39. If Jesus pointed to the Old Testament as teaching on the Resurrection, and in the NT we see that the rapture is when we are Resurrected (Pre, Mid and Post all agree on this point) then of course the Resurrection/Rapture is taught in the OT.

Number 6 – Rapture is an event for believers to see only. This is not valid either, because if millions of people suddenly disappeared it would have a great impact on the entire world. Economies would be plunged into chaos, people would have car crashes all over the world, some we can assume would be fatal, the news would wonder where everyone went. It's unbelievable to think that no one else would be affected. In fact, it's so ridiculous in fact that a couple of non-Christians wrote a tongue in cheek book entitled *"How to Profit off the*

Coming Rapture: Getting Ahead When You're Left Behind." Everyone will be affected by the Rapture when it happens no matter if it's Pre, Mid or Post Trib. And thus everyone will know that it happened. The only difference is when it really does happen they won't have time to react to it.

Number 7 - Before the day of wrath/Concludes the day of wrath – Again just because Pre-Tribbers recognize that there are two events happening, does not mean that they do not happen on the exact same day. The Rapture could be the very first thing to happen on the Day of Wrath, much like the Resurrection of Jesus was the first thing that happened that day, but later He talked with Mary and others on the same day, etc. There can be several events that make up the one main Event.

Number 8 – No reference to Satan/Satan bound – This is not accurate at all. The binding of Satan for 1,000 years happens after the Tribulation, whether you are Pre, Mid or Post. This is a millennial stance, so anyone who is millennial believes in the binding of Satan, and it has nothing to do with the Rapture or the Second Coming. It is one of the millennial events. This is irrelevant, and I believe Pre-Tribbers throw this into arguments as a distraction as it has absolutely nothing to do with the debate between Post and Pre Trib. Using things we all agree on to point to some sort of drastic divergence is a common Pre-Trib tactic, and not very ethical in my opinion.

Number 9 – He comes for His own vs. He comes with His own. Of course He comes for His own and with His own. We're raptured up to meet Him in the air, and then we descend as His gathered saints back to the Earth. Again, just because Pre-Trib people recognize there are two events as part of the same Event does not mean they do not happen in close proximity to each other.

Number 10 and 11 – He comes in the air/He comes to earth and He claims His bride/He comes with His bride. Again this follows the same broken logic I addressed in point 9 and 7. There is not one single verse anywhere in the Bible that tells that these events do not happen on the same day, at the same Event, the 2nd Coming of Christ.

Number 12 – Only His own see Him vs. Every eye shall see Him – Again there is no Biblical support for this argument. Nowhere, in the totality of the Bible does it claim that the Rapture is a secret event that no one will see. Pre-Trib people will point to parables where Jesus is clearly using hyperbole and metaphor to get His point across, as a way to bolster their argument. But they are also often the same ones who will say we shouldn't take the parables literally when Jesus tells us to make ourselves eunuchs for God, or to cut off our hand that offends us. You can't have it both ways. If you're going to properly exegete the text, you have to follow the same rules all the time. You can't pick and choose how and when you want to follow the rules. The truth is, the Bible says that when He returns every eye will see Him, and we know from elsewhere in this book that His Return and our Rapture happen at the exact same time: 2 events for the 1 Event.

Then there are the supposed problems with the Post-Trib view that I included after the list of differences between the Pre and Post Trib views:

Post Trib Denies Immanency

Some Pre-Trib teachers claim that a Post Trib view denies the "doctrine" of Immanency. I addressed this somewhat earlier in the differences section, but I'll go into some more detail here. There is no "doctrine" of Immanency. The doctrine we Christians have is the doctrine of Eschatology, or some might call them End Times events or many simply refer to it as the doctrine of the 2nd Coming, and primarily it is the doctrine that Jesus will Return again at some point in the future. But there has been a lot of debate over many of the finer details. As far as Immanency is concerned, there is only the Pre-Trib *theory* of Immanency, which is a subset of the doctrine of Eschatology, though some denominations such as Calvary Chapel and the Assemblies of God, have sadly elevated this theory to the status of doctrine. And as I have demonstrated throughout this book, Immanency, the way Pre-Tribbers explain it, isn't logical and isn't Biblical. The fact is, doctrines are the truths of the Bible that we all can agree on that relate to our salvation and our understanding of the Faith. How we believe the Rapture will happen and the timing, etc. have absolutely no bearing on our salvation and whether Jesus will forgive us of our sins and make us "sons of God." The only way the doctrine of eschatology is important for our salvation is if Post-Tribbers are right and the Apostasy happens because of the false doctrine of the Pre-Trib movement.

But just to make it clear, I do not think teachers like Hank Hanegraaff and Chuck Missler and maybe even Tim LaHaye are going to go to hell because of their faulty logic on this topic. Unless, of course, these guys cling to their false beliefs just to make a buck, and not because they are truly and honestly mistaken.

I hope you can spot by now that this argument is based the idea that there are no signs. But once the blocks are knocked out of that idea, and people see that there are several signs that point to the Day of the Lord (which includes both the Rapture and the 2nd Coming), this point holds no validity.

Requires Church to be on Earth During Daniel's 70th Week

This argument is that the Church shouldn't be here for Daniel's 70th week. But nowhere in the Bible does it say that the church will not be here for that time period. In fact, the Church will be here for Daniel's 70th Week. Daniel never says that they won't.

Elsewhere Daniel uses the term "saints," a term synonymous with the church throughout the entire NT. Some argue that since the word "church" isn't mentioned by Daniel then it isn't there, but the OT doesn't use the word "church" anyway!

This is actually what's referred to as an argument from silence. Because many Pre-Trib teachers are being paid money to teach this lie (especially if they are part of denominations that insist on the Pre-Trib theory as doctrinal truth), they will use this tactic because otherwise it would mean they would be kicked out of their churches.

The line of reasoning Pre-Trib teachers use is: *The Daniel passage referenced here doesn't mention the church, so obviously that means we're not here*. But this is not a valid method of argument. Just because something isn't mentioned does not mean it isn't there. The Han dynasty was never mentioned in the Bible, but during the height of the Roman empire it too was at its height in China. Daniel is talking specifically about what is going to happen to his people, the Jews. So there is no point in mentioning the Church here. Furthermore, the church didn't exist during Daniel's time, so how would he know what to call believers in the God of Israel other than "saints?"

Who Will Populate the Millennium?

Another questions raised by the videos that were sent to me was the question of who will populate the millennium. If you want more on this see the chapter on the Millennium. We've already covered it there. It is the survivors that are mentioned all throughout the Prophets. It cannot refer to glorified saints for several reasons, the main ones being that these survivors are mentioned by Isaiah to die long after the age of 100, and that they will have children, two things that definitely do not describe glorified saints.

How can the Bride Come With Him?

Another question that was raised by the videos given to me is, How can the Bride come with Him? Easily, we're raptured up to meet Him in the air. Then as He descends, we come with Him back to the earth.

Who Are The Sheep And The Goats?

Here's a very strange question that one of the videos I watched raised was, *"who are the sheep and the goats?"* as if this was in some way important to a Pre-Trib doctrinal stance. Again this is using a parable as if it were a prophecy. We all agree that this parable is prophetic in nature, though it might not be literal. But for the sake of argument, I already addressed that question earlier in this book. The sheep are the followers of Christ. The Goats are the members of the flock that were not faithful. Remember, both Goats and Sheep are part of the same flock. It's not like Jesus is comparing the sheep and the wolves.

Church Experiences God's Wrath

Some Pre-Trib teachers accuse Post-Trib people of teaching that the Church experiences God's wrath. This is not true. The Post-Trib position never says that the Church experiences God's wrath. The Tribulation is nowhere called the wrath of God. In fact it clearly demonstrates that it is Satan's wrath. And we are told that God will protect us "through" not "from" it.

How Can Virgins Buy Oil In Matthew 25 without the Mark of the Beast?

This was another really strange question that was raised by one of the videos that was sent to me. How can the virgins buy oil in Matthew 25 without the Mark of the Beast? Easy, by using their credit card! I'm being sarcastic.

Again here a Pre-Trib teacher is trying to use a Parable as if it were a Prophecy. It is in fact a Parable. The Virgins don't really exist. They were a literary element Jesus used to convey the ultimate truth: If you are not following Him when He returns, you will not be allowed into the Kingdom. Anyway, maybe the virgins went down the block to the Christian who always traded them the oil through the black market, and that Christian oil merchant had been raptured so there was no oil to buy! Do you see how silly this type of debate becomes? I would like to point out without mentioning any names that the teacher on the video had a doctorate from a very prestigious Christian university who asked this question. This is such a ridiculous argument I can't even believe someone with a doctorate would make such a meaningless objection.

Contradiction with Daniel 9:27 – Israel and the Church Are Mutually Exclusive

Another objection raised was that there is a mutually exclusive distinction between the church and Israel. And Daniel 9:27 supposedly shows this. All Daniel 9:27 shows is that a covenant will made with "many." This very well could mean that the Antichrist will mediate between two opposing parties (the "many" referred to here), and then the Antichrist will break that treaty himself.

As to the idea that Israel and the Church are mutually exclusive. I wouldn't necessarily use the phrase "mutually exclusive." Israelites who follow Christ will be in the Rapture, those who don't but Repent when they recognize Him will be survivors into the Millennium, who will finally inherit God's promise to Abraham. This is the context of the Joel passage, "all who call on the name of the Lord will be saved." These people will marry and have children and take control of the physical promise to Abraham, and they will be governed by those who were transfigured in the Rapture. Those who refuse to repent will spend eternity in hell.

Some Additional Answers

In addition to the videos that were sent to me, there were several articles that I was asked by my Pre-Trib friends to read. One raised many of the same questions that I have already dealt with, but there were a few that should probably be included here just to make sure that they are addressed.

Is pretribulation rapture theology a new Church doctrine? Many Pre-Trib writers site Ephram, and I dealt with that at the beginning of this book.

Is the pretribulation rapture secret?
I was actually surprised that several Pre-Trib writers have come to realize that it is not a secret. And I agree with them. So you see even among Pre-Tribs there is disagreement.

What about the fact that Believers taken to Father's House John 14:3 vs. Believers come with Jesus to Earth Mat 24:30?

Again *we see* the use of Parable as if it were literal. Jesus did say I go to prepare a place for you, but often times, a "place" is a position of service, not just a literal home. Jesus is using the imagery of His Father's house, as a way of saying everyone can be included in the King*dom if* they will follow Jesus.

Another way of looking at this is that the place that Jesus went to prepare was for us after we die, until He returns. Or one could see it as Jesus preparing something that will descend with Him when He returns.

1 Co 15:51 says that the rapture is a mystery, but in Zechariah 12:10 the 2nd Coming is foretold.

The mystery that 1 Corinthians is talking about is a mystery for people who do no*t* know. So Paul is educating them to the mystery. The Corinthians are not Jews, and they do not know the Jewish prophesies. So Paul is revealing a mystery to them which the*y* did not know the answer to.

Christians taken first 1Th 4:13-18, 3, Mat 13:28-30 vs. Wicked are taken first Mat 25:1-13; Rev 3:8-10; Rev 4:1.

This is an interesting one, and is truly confusing, but not so much as to make a case for the Pre-Trib theory in light of all of the overwhelming evidence against it. It also says in Revelation that the Wicked are brought to Armageddon. So is Jesus contradicting Himself? Of course not. In light of all the other evidence, I believe that this must be referring to the sequence of events that are important to the listener.

To the believer, God in Revelation is showing us what will happen to the faithful first. But in this passage, God is pointing out to the unbelievers who were listening to Jesus preach, that the wicked will be dealt with. It's entirely possible that it is listed in order of priority, not sequence, as was a popular ancient technique.

I believe that Jesus has many angels to gather us all. So we are gathered and possibly at the same time the wicked are gathered to Armageddon. I addressed this some in the chapter on Armageddon. I am willing to admit that some passages are confusing, and we need to puzzle them through, but we also have to look at the whole, and not build our arguments up on enigmas. We can't use the enigma to lend support to our core theories. The best we can do sometimes is just to point that the enigma exists and offer a possible explanation.

It is one thing to have solid scriptural support for a doctrine (of which the Pre-Trib fantasy has none) and then to try to address some of the more confusing passages that seem to be, or are somehow related. It is an entirely different thing to build an entire case off of enigmatic passages, and then present a doctrine that flies in the face of other scripture, church history, tradition and common sense.

He comes to present the Church to Himself 2 Co 11:2 vs. He comes with His Church for judgment and to set up his Kingdom Rev 19:6-9, Zec 14:3-4; Jud 1:14-15; Rev 19:11-21

Another thing that some of the Pre-Trib writers use as a proof is this apparent contradiction. But there is nothing that says these can't happen at the same time. Again 2 events for 1 Event.

Casts Satan out of heaven to earth Rev 12 vs. Binds Satan for a thousand years Rev 20

Some Pre-Trib writers see a great distinction between these two events mentioned in Revelation 12 and Revelation 20. However, I believe that Satan being cast out of heaven refers to something in the past that happened before Jesus came the first time.

Isaiah quotes God when he describes how far Lucifer fell. And later Jesus also says that He say Satan thrown from Heaven, so obviously this event in Revelation 12 is a past tense event that is completing the entire picture John is showing.

The simplest answer to explain the mention of this in Revelation 12 is that John felt it was important to show that Satan was the root cause of all of the problems.

Another possible explanation is that Satan is trying to ascend to heaven again in Revelation 12. The Bible tells us that his chief flaw was thinking that he wanted to ascend to the place of the most High. We see this same idea in the depiction of the Tower of Babel. Satan has always wanted to sit on God's throne. The question is has this happened several times, or just once or did it happen once and will happen again, or is this passage in Revelation Satan's last attempt to ascend into Heaven.

The Bible just isn't clear. From Job we get the impression that Satan can access Heaven when all of the angels are summoned, but that doesn't mean that he always has access to heaven.

It is always dangerous to read into the text what isn't there. We have to read what it really says, not what we want it to say.

Occurs in the twinkling of an eye 1Co 15:52 vs. Comes to earth to do battle at specific locations Isa 63:1-3, Rev 16:16, Zec 12:9-10

Here is another set of proof texts that I examined in various Pre-Trib articles. They are trying to demonstrate that there is an important distinction between the fact that the Rapture happens in the twinkling of an eye, but apparently the 2nd Coming takes some time. But the distinction here is not valid.

This is an example of taking a verse completely out of context. 1 Cor. 15:52 specifically says that we are changed in the twinkling of an eye. There is nothing there that is disharmonious with the line of reasoning that we are raptured and changed (glorified) in the twinkling of an eye, we meet Christ in the air and then we descend to do battle.

Jesus descends with a shout. 1Th 4:16 8 vs. No shout mentioned Rev 19:11-21

This is a misuse of Scripture as well, because Pre-Trib people do not believe that Jesus descends at all in a Pre-Trib Rapture scenario. They believe that we are secretly raptured and that Jesus doesn't descend.

However, I would like to point out that according to the Thessalonians passage, Jesus descends with the trumpet call of God and with the shout of the angel. With the 7th Trumpet in Revelation 11, there is a proclamation shouted by the angel and the trumpet call. So again, here is another example of how Pre-Trib teachers misuse Scripture.

Jesus comes as a thief in the night 1Th 24:43 vs. Jesus comes at the end of 7 years of tribulation Dan 9:24-27, 12:11-12; Rev 11:2, 12:6,14, 13:5

This passage in Thessalonians specifically says that Jesus only comes as a thief in the night to those who are not prepared. "But you are children of the light and of the day..." in other words, those of us who are watching the signs will be expecting Him, and will not be caught off guard. Furthermore, the passages listed only bolster the Post-Trib stance that Jesus does indeed come back at the end of a 7 year period. I would argue that the first 3.5 years are the buildup and the latter 3.5 are the actual Tribulation. But again these passages actually harmonize quite well with a Post-Trib view, far better in fact than they do with a Pre-Trib view.

Appendix - 16 Scriptural Proofs of a Pre-Trib Rapture – Yeah Right!

As I was preparing the final edit on my book, I was sent an article* that provided sixteen scriptural proofs that the rapture is Pre-Trib. My reader wanted to know if there was any validity in this article and these proofs. Sadly, almost all 16 of these so called proofs are misused and incorrect. I am including it here as a way for you to understand how I examine an article to see if it actually lines up with Scripture, and logical analysis.

Proof #1: Revelation 19:11-21 doesn't mention a resurrection. – The rapture is a resurrection of those "in Christ" (1 Thess. 4:13-18). Isn't it a little bit odd that in Rev. 19:11-21, which is the clearest picture of the second coming of Christ, there is no mention of a resurrection? The rapture will be the biggest event since the resurrection of Jesus where hundreds of millions of Christians will be resurrected and translated, yet there isn't any mention here. Don't you think it deserves at least one verse? The rapture isn't mentioned because it doesn't happen at the second coming.

Doesn't have to, from Revelation 13 until 19, it is a description of all of the events that happen in a short span of time. So in response to there not being a "single verse," we have 7 whole chapters that describe in very vivid detail the events surrounding Jesus' return.

Proof #2: Zechariah 14:1-15 doesn't mention a resurrection. - This is an Old Testament picture of Jesus returning to earth at the second coming. Again, no mention of a resurrection.

This passage is dealing with Christ's rescue of Israel. Why would He mention the Resurrection in this passage when it's the resurrected saints that had just been raptured that are coming to the rescue with Jesus? These Israeli's that are being saved are not going to be glorified. They miss the Rapture and have to survive to repopulate the Millennium.

Proof #3: Two different pictures are painted. - In the Old Testament, there were two different pictures painted of the Messiah—one suffering (Isa. 53:2-10, Ps. 22:6-8, 11-18) and one reigning as King (Ps. 2:6-12, Zech. 14:9,16). As we look back on these scriptures, we see they predicted two separate comings of the Messiah—the 1st coming as a suffering Messiah and the 2nd coming (still future) as a reigning King.

In the New Testament, we have another picture added. Again, we have two pictures painted which don't look the same. These two different descriptions of Jesus' coming point to two separate events we call "the rapture" and "the second coming."

This is a literal quote from the article that I read, and sadly it is not a proof of anything. It is merely an observance of something that is pure speculation. The author hasn't made a point here. He is merely speculating about something that isn't true. He is using a technique where he presents an argument that there is no Scriptural support for, and then argues from the silence of Scripture to support it. The OT does indeed show two separate comings of the Messiah, not 3. And the New Testament shows only 2 comings of the

Messiah not 3, so if anything, the author defeats his own argument by using this line of reasoning.

Proof #4: The Known Day and the Unknown Day. - Concerning the return of Jesus, the Bible presents a day we can't know and a day we can know. Matthew 25:13 says Jesus will return at an unknown time, while Revelation 12:6 says the Jews will have to wait 1,260 days for the Lord to return. The 1,260 days begins when the Antichrist stands in the Temple and declares himself to be God (Matt. 24:15-21, 2 Thess. 2:4) This event will take place at the mid-point of the seven year Tribulation (Dan 9:27). The Antichrist has authority to rule for 42 months, which is 1,260 days (Rev. 13:4) and will be destroyed by Jesus at His second coming (Rev. 19:20, 2 Thess. 2:8). The known and unknown days must happen at different times, meaning they are two separate events.

First of all, Matthew 25:13 does not say Jesus will return at an unknown time. He says “Keep watch. For you do not know the day or the hour of my return… only the Father knows….” That phrase was very likely a specific reference to festival of Rosh Hashanah, “the day which no man knows the day or the hour.” So it is very possible that Jesus was giving a very detailed time frame. It is also possible that Jesus was merely saying that it is not set in stone yet, and you do not know when it will happen. Secondly, Jesus said “you” don’t know when He’ll return. So we have to ask who was He talking to?

When we go to the passage that starts this long discourse where this parable (yes it was in the context of a parable again, but Pre-Tribbers don’t seem to understand the difference), we see that Jesus was in the Temple preaching and talking with His disciples. Now how can the Holy Spirit instruct Paul to tell us in Thessalonians that we will be alert to the signs, and how can Jesus tell us to look for certain signs in Matthew 24, and then tell us that we won't know when He's coming?!?

Again when we read this verse in context, we see that Jesus is giving a parable, and "you do not know when I will return," is the moral of the parable. He's telling us to live in a state of preparation. We see when we read chapter 25 in context with chapter 24 that this parable is the capstone of the warnings that He gives to the disciples. He tells them, elsewhere that even He doesn't know the exact day or hour when He is going to be sent back, but He does know that there will be certain predictable signs that lead up to His return, and that the disciples are to watch diligently for those signs. In verse 29 of chapter 24 we get the very phrase in the Latin Vulgate that gives us the "Post Tribulationem" view. This passage that Pre-Tribbers always bring out really just defeats their argument when read in context of the preceding chapter.

Secondly, "only the Father knows," implies that at that very moment, only the Father knew. It does not mean that after Jesus ascended that He did not get word of when He would return from the Father. And we have the Revelation of Jesus being revealed after the Ascension. So apparently God wanted more details of the end of time given to His disciples.

I'm not arguing that we can mathematically figure out exactly when Jesus will return, or that He is going to return on Rosh Hashanah, or anything like that. But I do believe that once we see the Antichrist in that temple, making treaties with the Jews, etc. it will help us hone our clocks in on a closer time frame.

Proof #5: A door open in heaven (Revelation 4:1). - The door in heaven is opened to let John into heaven. We believe John's call into heaven is prophetic of the Church being caught up at the rapture (see proof #6). In Revelation 19:11, heaven is opened again, this time to let the armies which are already in heaven out. This is the Church, which has been raptured at a previous time, following Jesus out of heaven at the second coming.

Proof #6: "Come up here." (Revelation 4:1).
A voice called for the apostle John to "Come up here," and immediately he was in heaven. This could be a prophetic reference to the rapture of the Church. The words "Come up here" are spoken to the two witnesses who are killed in the middle of the Tribulation, who are resurrected and ascend into heaven (Rev. 11:12). Therefore, the phrase "Come up here" could mean the Church is raptured in Rev. 4:1. The word "Church" is mentioned 22 times in Rev. 1-3, but is not mentioned again until Rev. 22:17.

I'll address points 5 and 6 together because they are both based on the same faulty interpretation of the *text. Some* believe John's call into heaven is prophetic, however i*t is not*. John was called into heaven in a singular sense and there is no scriptural or textual support for this faulty logic. We dealt elsewhere with the fact that "saints," a term synonymous with the church throughout Scripture is used over and over again in Revelation. Also, when the two witnesses are resurrected, and ascend that could be a sign to all wavering Christians to stand firm because their resurrection is nigh at hand.

Proof #7: The 24 elders have their crowns. - After John is called up into heaven, he sees the 24 elders with their crowns (Rev. 4:4-10). We know that Christians will receive their rewards (crowns) at the rapture (2 Tim. 4:8, 1 Pet. 5:4). We will be repaid at the resurrection of the righteous (Luke 14:14). The elders couldn't receive their crowns unless the resurrection (rapture) has taken place.

There is no textual clarity about who or what the 24 elders are. They might be some type of angelic being. There is nothing in this passage that stipulates that these 24 elders are human. In fact, we know that humans are represented by 12 thrones, one for each of the 12 tribes of Israel. So perhaps these 24 thrones are for high level angels. We just can't be sure about this, so we shouldn't build our doctrine off of speculation. In all fairness, if you examine the article on it's website, the author of the article doesn't agree with this stance, as he copied these points from another website. I'm happy to see we agree on something. Furthermore, we might not get our crowns exactly at the point of the Rapture, we might get them at the point of death when we stand before Jesus. This is a very debatable point and open to a great deal of speculation.

Proof #8 Holy ones are already with Jesus in heaven (Zech. 14:5, Rev. 19:14). - The armies in heaven, clothed in fine linen, follow Jesus out of heaven at His second coming (Rev. 19:14, Zech. 14:5, Col. 3:4). These are not angels because Rev. 19:8 tells us the fine linen is the righteousness of the saints. In order to come out of heaven we first have to go in, indicating a previous rapture.

Even Post Trib people believe by 19:14 the Rapture has happened. This is no proof of a Pre-Trib rapture. We all believe that when we die we go to be with Christ. When He returns, whether with a Pre-Trib, Post-Trib, Mid-Trib, Amillennial, or even Post Millennial return, we all believe that He will bring the departed souls of believers with Him, so this passage is not enough to build a Pre-Trib doctrine.

Proof #9: Kept from the hour of testing (Rev. 3:10). - Revelation 3:10 says we will be kept out of the hour of testing which will come upon the whole earth (the Tribulation). Some have wrongly believed "keep" means to keep through, or protect through the Tribulation. Suppose you approach a high voltage area with a sign that says, "Keep Out." Does that mean you can enter and be protected? No, it means you are forbidden from entering the area. But this verse also says He will keep us from the hour of testing. It is not just the testing, but the time period. If a student is excused from a test, he still may have to sit in the class while others take the test. But if he is excused from the hour of testing, he can go home. The Church will be called home before the hour of testing.

First of all, this verse specifically states that He will only keep the particular church He is talking to from the hour of testing. We see that another church, which is just as good, will go through severe persecution. Secondly, the author needs to study his Greek, because it does mean “through,” here. It certainly does not mean “out of,” though it could be translated as “out from.” Finally, using an English command phrase “keep out” to explain a

Greek blessing "kept through" is not at all the same thing. They are like comparing apples to oranges.

The word in English "keep" in addition to meaning "stay," or "hold" also meant "a fortress," or "to be contained," and it's use and philology in the phrase "keep out" is very different from the derivation of the phrase "keep through" in the Greek.

Finally, the church being called home is not valid. Our home is here with Christ in the Millennium. Heaven is a waiting place for us to wait, while we're dead, until we are called home, to be with Him here. This is clearly demonstrated by the martyred saints (who couldn't even be there in a Pre-Trib scenario, because they would have to wait until the end of the Millennium to be glorified) in Revelation 6, who long for the day when they get to return and see their murders avenged.

Proof #10: Angels don't resurrect people when they gather them for judgment. - When the angels are sent forth to gather the elect at the second coming (Matt. 24:29-31), some have wrongly interpreted this as the rapture. There is one huge problem with this interpretation. If we are resurrected at this time, why would we need angels to gather us? In the resurrection, we will be like the angels (Matt. 22:30), able to travel in the air at will. Obviously, these people who are gathered are not resurrected, therefore it can't be the rapture. No one would claim the wicked are raptured at this time, yet Matthew 13:39-41, 49 says the angels will not only gather the elect, but also the wicked. This gathering is not a resurrection.

Nowhere (even in Matthew 22:30) does it say that we will be able to "travel in the air at will." Maybe we will be able to, but it doesn't tell us that, and we go to the Bible looking for Truth, not to justify our preconceived beliefs.

Furthermore, we are not changed until we are with Christ. So even if we can travel in the air after our glorification, until the angels get us to Him we will need a ride to get there. The fact that this happens in the twinkling of an eye isn't lost here either, it just means that angels are incredibly fast, which makes sense when they are beings that dwell in another dimension and on a different time scale. But this entire argument is based on speculation and not on any hard textual support.

Proof #11: Both wicked and righteous both can't be taken first. - First Thessalonians 4:13-17 says the righteous are taken and the wicked are left behind. Matthew 13:30, 49 says the wicked are taken first and righteous are left behind. This points to two separate events, the rapture and the second coming.

Why not? Doesn't Jesus have enough angels to send them out to be taking us both at the same time? But again, Matthew 13 is a reference to a parable and the moral is about being taken to destruction. 1 Thess. 4 is talking about actual factual events that Jesus revealed to the apostles. And again, all of the first century church, the 2nd century church, the 3rd century church, and the 4th century church were completely Post-Trib. Then from the 4th century until the 1800's the church was either Amillennial or Post-Trib, and then came the Pre-Tribbers.

Perhaps, in a point of concession from the 6th century on there might have been some Pre-Tribbers, but that Pre-Trib doctrine was more about the murder and death of the entire church, and not about a raptured church as we understand it commonly today. So anyway you look at it, why would all of these early Christians see these passages being about 1 Rapture and 1 Resurrection happening on 1 day?

Proof #12: Jesus returns from the wedding. - When Jesus returns to earth at the second coming, He will return from a wedding (Luke 12:36). At the rapture, Jesus is married to His bride, the Church. After the wedding, He will return to earth.

Jesus uses the phrase “as though you were waiting for your master to return from a wedding feast,” which shows us that He is comparing how we are supposed to wait, with what He wants to find us doing when He returns. This does not say that He is at a literal wedding feast yet. We see elsewhere that the wedding feast is held in Jerusalem. Then He follows that up by saying, “so you can welcome Him…” This clearly shows that Jesus will be staying when He arrives. And then He talks about eating with the servants. So we see that this is an illustration not an actual literal rendering of what is going to happen. We have to read what the text actually says, in context, we can’t just grab verses to support our pet theories.

Proof #13: Jesus will receive us to Himself, not us to receive Him (John 14:2-3). - Jesus said He would prepare a place for the Church in heaven, then He would come again to receive us to Himself. Why would Jesus prepare a place for us in heaven and then not take us there? At the rapture, He will come to receive us to Himself, "that where I am (heaven), there you may be also." If the rapture occurred at the same time as the second coming, we would go up to the clouds and then immediately come back to earth. That would contradict John 14:2-3.

Jesus said this knowing full well that there would be over 2,000 years of people dying who are Christians. Of course He prepared a place for us to wait all that time, and Revelation demonstrates quite clearly in several passages about what it's like up there before He returns. At the time of the Rapture, we will receive Him when He returns. The passage cited in Luke 12:36 demonstrates that for Pre-Tribbers who are used to using parables out of context. But literally, 1 Thessalonians 4 and 5 demonstrate our greeting him as well as 1 Cor 15. And no there is no contradiction with John 14:2-3 when they are not talking about the same thing.

Proof #14: The one who restrains is taken out of the way. - In 2 Thess. 2:6-7, Paul says "the one who restrains will be taken out of the way" before the Antichrist can be revealed. We believe this refers to the rapture because the Church is clearly the biggest obstacle to the Antichrist becoming a world ruler.

The author believes that the restrainer is the church, but with no textual proof, only speculation. There literally is not enough information to jump to that conclusion. Every other doctrine that we cling to as Christians has countless solid, point blank Biblical passages to support it. But the Pre-Trib fantasy has absolutely nothing to support it, and yet they cling to it persistently.

Proof #15: The separation of the sheep and goats (Matt. 25:31-46). - If the rapture occurred at the second coming, why would the sheep and the goats need to be separated immediately after the second coming? A rapture at the second coming would have already separated the sheep and the goats. With a Pre-

Tribulation rapture, the people saved after the rapture will need to be separated after the second coming.

We see over and over in Scripture that even after Jesus returns, such as during the wedding feast, that people are trying to get into the feast. Who are these people? They are the ones that did not get raptured. He said many will come up to Him in that day. Come up from where? They came (i.e. traveled) to get to the feast, because they didn't make the rapture. They are separated out because they were the believers who were believers in name only. The goats are also animals that are part of the flock. Elsewhere Jesus used the example of wolves being an animal that might be encountered. But sheep and goats are all part of the same flock. Some are good and some are bad. Jesus will separate them with the Rapture, but the goats will still come around trying to get in, and He will say, "depart from me I never knew you." And furthermore, in a Pre-Trib rapture scenario, there is no explanation for survivors into the Millennium, but this parable is pointing to survivors. Check the chapter on the Millennium for more information.

Proof #16: Who will populate the Millennium? - If the rapture occurs at the second coming and the wicked are cast into hell at that time, who will be left to populate the millennium? Only people in their natural (non-resurrected) bodies will be able to have children (Matt. 22:30). With a Pre-Tribulation rapture, the people saved after the rapture who are alive at the second coming will populate the earth during the Millennium.

I disagree. As I just mentioned it is in fact the other way around. If there is a Pre-Trib rapture and the Tribulation period is so severe that no one can survive, then there would be no survivors. There is no textual support that all people are cast into hell at the Rapture. In fact Revelation 19 shows that only the False Prophet and the Beast are cast into Hell at Jesus' return. Everyone else has to wait until Revelation 20:15, which takes place after the Millennium.

**16 proofs are from Cornerstone Church garden city Kansas website **(I do not think proof 7 is valid since I do not believe the 24 elders are the Church) http://www.fellowshiponline.org/bib.html*

I agree with the author about his disbelief in proof 7 above. But then he goes on with the Seven Supernatural Translation events. You can check them out at his page. I will describe them here briefly.

His first three supernatural events that he points as evidence for a rapture are Enoch, Elijah and Jesus' own resurrection and ascension. I agree on all of these things. We will be raptured. The question is when?

The next four events he uses to point to a proof that we will be raptured Pre-Trib are the rapture of the church, the resurrection and ascension of the two witnesses, the resurrection of the saints at the end of the Great tribulation and the final resurrection and judgment after the thousand year reign. The problem with using this as evidence for a Pre-Trib rapture is the timing of all of these things are debatable, and Post Trib people believe all of these things too, and believe they point to the fact that we will be Resurrected and Raptured at the same time.

The author finishes up with a section entitled: Some highlights of the book of Revelation are – He gives several interesting portions of Revelation, but makes no compelling arguments for a Pre-Trib theory.

He ends with: The seven Church ages – He uses each of the 7 churches in Revelation as “ages” of the church. However, we know that these churches were real physical churches, and not ages at all. This whole theory is interesting, but there is no real historical or scriptural support or validity to it at all. The problem with many Bible teachers is that they are willing to spread tradition and speculation, but not Truth. Tradition is not our final authority, Scripture is.

Both of the author’s concluding studies were interesting, but they do little to sway me in any way towards a Pre-Trib viewpoint. But thank you, reader, for submitting them to me anyway.

** Proof quotes are taken from the article: “Proofs for a Pretribulation Rapture.” This Article can be found in its entirety at www.thepropheticyears.com written by Don Koenig.*

Special Thanks:

I want to thank my cousin Tim Ford for pointing out the truth of the Pre-Trib fantasy all those years ago. I'd like to thank my wife Trevor for being such a good research assistant in this book. I'd also like to thank L.A. Marzulli for taking time out of his busy schedule to clear up a couple points I had questions on. And also Steve Quayle for his support and inspiration. I'd like to thank the many pastors over the years that I have been able to debate and discuss these issues with, most notably Len Allen and Dr. Bob Eckler. And finally, I'd like to thank my writing partner on another project, Greg Kemp, for discussing some of the parallels of this project with that one, and for encouraging me throughout it all. God bless you all.

ABOUT THE AUTHOR

Willy Minnix is a pastor, musician, graphic artist and author of several books covering topics such as music theory, theology and fiction. And also has released several CDs. This book has two companion CDs entitled "Tribulation Songs," of music written during difficult times in our history, and inspired to help carry us through any hard time to come. information about the show can be found at www.wunt.org, and you can learn more about Willy at www.willyminnix.com.

More information about Willy's books and other materials can be found at www.willyminnix.com

Get the companion CDs and more from Water Moccasin Publications!

Tribulation Songs Volume 1 and 2

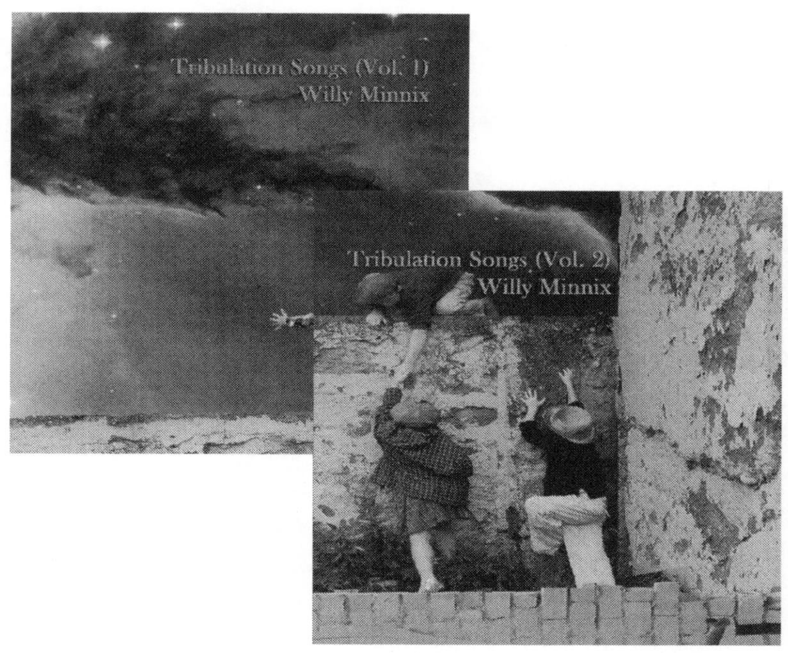

Including Songs:

I Feel Like Traveling On, I'm A Soldier In The Army of the Lord, I Shall Not Be Moved, We're Marching To Zion, Stand By Me, Samson and Delilah, Will There Be Any Stars in My Crown?, In My Time of Dying, and many more…

CreateSpace eStore: https://www.createspace.com/2131384

Mandolin Dead Man's Tuning
Volume 1: Basics

How to play mandolin in open D tuning, also called Dead Man's Tuning or DDAD tuning.

This is the first book in a series that teaches how to play mandolin in alternate tunings. It is perfect for beginners or advanced players who want to learn a different style of playing.

Topics covered are picking patterns, chords and basic theory, finger style and string technique. Original artwork and diagrams are well done and make the topics easy to understand. Also included are photographs of handmade mandolin's by renowned mandolin builder Larry Hopkins.

The included tablature contains both the standard sheet music as well as tablature in DDAD tuning and ADAD tuning for several of the songs. Many of the songs are duets designed for teachers and students, original songs, folk tunes, Irish melodies and traditional blues, jazz and bluegrass tunes arranged for both Dead Man's Tuning and ADAD tuning. Several of the songs are recorded on Mr. Minnix's CD "Mandolin Studies," which is also available.

This is one of the only books available on the subject of alternate tunings for mandolin.

CreateSpace eStore:
https://www.createspace.com/3786876

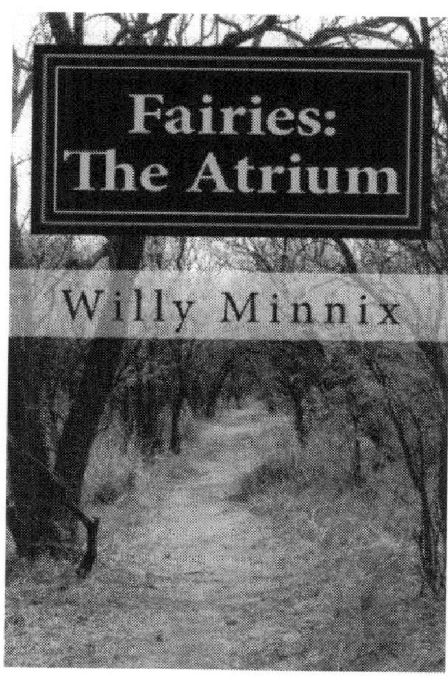

Fairies: The Atrium

A short stories and poems that were first published in the Christian Sci-Fi Journal.

Included are the short stories "Fairies: The Atrium" and "I Went Down To The Crossroads" which first appeared in the CSFJ in 2004.

CreateSpace eStore:
https://www.createspace.com/3816996

Mandolin Studies

This is a collection of songs mainly written for the mandolin, with a few written as mandolin duets.

This is the first companion CD to the book series: Mandolin Dead Man's Tuning.

Songs included are: Corbyn's Song, Trevor's Green Eyes, Dana's Tune, Black Jack Davey, Aborted, and several more songs for the mandolin…

CreateSpace eStore:
https://www.createspace.com/2027103

Go Tell It On The Mountain (Expanded Edition)

70 minutes, 20 tracks

Willy Minnix's original 2009 Christmas album updated with several extra cuts that were given away during Christmas 2011.

Songs include several favorite Christmas carols, and a several originals including "Merry Christmas Girl," "Santa Didn't Give Me What I Wanted," and "It's Christmas."

CreateSpace eStore: https://www.createspace.com/2097862

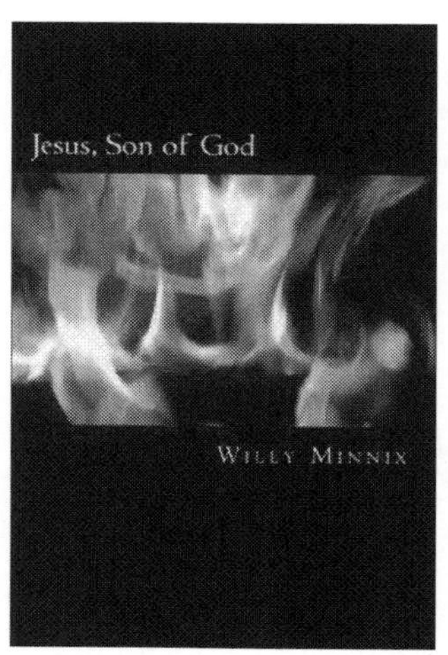

Jesus Son of God

Willy Minnix, author, musician and pastor delivers a collection of sermons, essays and thoughts about the life of Jesus of Nazareth. Topics covered in this book include the Divinity and Humanity of Christ, Christ our Savior, the Judgment of Christ, Christ's Forgiveness, the Body of Christ, Christ our Coming King and several other topics related to Jesus Christ. Each topic is discussed with Biblical clarity. This book was written to answer some of the most common questions that every day people have about the Christian faith. For those who want to know Jesus more, join in as Willy explores what the Bible teaches about the life and person of Jesus, Son of God.

CreateSpace eStore: https://www.createspae.com/3918679

Made in the USA
Charleston, SC
06 November 2013